Pan Breakthrough Books open the door to successful self-education. The series provides essential knowledge using the most modern self-study techniques.

Expert authors have produced clear explanatory texts on business subjects to meet the particular needs of people at work and of those studying for relevant examinations.

A highly effective learning pattern, enabling readers to measure progress step-by-step, has been devised for Breakthrough Books by the National Extension College, Britain's leading specialists in home study.

Geoffrey Knott is head of the Accountancy Division at Norwich City College of Further and Higher Education. On the examiners' panels of the Association of Certified Accountants and Association of Accounting Technicians he has been closely connected with the Business and Technician Education Council, notably as a member of the B2 Finance Board. He acts as a consultant management accountant to businesses in East Anglia.

Geoffrey Knott is the author of Practical Cost and Management Accounting, *also published in the Pan Breakthrough series.*

Pan Breakthrough Books

Other books in the series

Background to Business
The Business of Communicating:
  Improving Communication Skills
The Business of Data Processing
Computers Mean Business:
  An Introduction to Computers in Business
The Economics of Business
Effective Advertising and PR
English in Business
Introduction to Personnel Management
Keep Account:
  A Guide to Profitable Book-keeping
Making Numbers Work:
  An Introduction to Business Numeracy
Management: A Fresh Approach
Marketing: A Fresh Approach
Practical Accounts 1
Practical Accounts 2
Practical Business Law
Practical Company Law
Practical Cost and Management Accounting
Supervision: A Fresh Approach
Understanding Company Accounts
Understanding Industrial Relations
Understanding Office Practice
Using Statistics in Business 1
Using Statistics in Business 2
What Do You Mean 'Communication'?:
  An Introduction to Communication in Business

Pan Breakthrough Books

Understanding Financial Management

Geoffrey Knott

A Pan Original
Pan Books London and Sydney

First published 1985 by Pan Books Ltd,
Cavaye Place, London SW10 9PG
9 8 7 6 5 4 3 2 1

ISBN 0 330 28592 0

Photoset by Parker Typesetting Service, Leicester
Printed and bound in Great Britain by
Cox & Wyman Ltd, Reading

If you wish to study the subject matter of this book in more depth, write to the National Extension College, 18 Brooklands Avenue, Cambridge CB2 2HN, for a free copy of the Breakthrough Business Courses leaflet. This gives details of the extra exercises and professional postal tuition which are available.

Contents

Figures

Introduction

Financial management has developed as a separate area of study in recent years for three main reasons:

- Recognition by businesses and public bodies, large and small, of the importance of continuous assessment of their need for finance; an awareness of the sources of finance; and to ensure the optimum use of resources provided by that finance.
- The increasing number of specialist finance managers appointed by large companies and public bodies.
- Continuing development and application of analytical techniques in financial decision-making.

Consequently, financial management is a separate subject in the examinations of all the major professional accountancy bodies, and features in most university, polytechnic and college degree and management courses concerned with finance.

This self-learning book is therefore aimed both at the needs of students of finance, and also at practising managers – whether financial or non-financial – who require an easy-to-read and up-to-date text on financial management.

The book is structured so as to present a logical sequencing of material, and each chapter contains activities, self-check and review questions aimed at dissuading the reader from adopting a passive role. Readers will obviously benefit if they cover up answers before attempting questions.

Activities within sections of each chapter are used either as interim test questions, or to prepare the reader for a following topic by getting him to complete an exercise by reference to his own experience or to previous material in the book.

Self-check questions appear at the end of most sections to test understanding of the content of the preceding section.

Review questions cover concepts and techniques in the preceding chapter, either to reinforce self-check questions, or to integrate material in that and previous chapters.

Finally, I gratefully acknowledge the encouragement and assistance given to me by Pan Books Ltd, John Meed of the National Extension College, Cambridge, and Graham Mott of Newcastle-upon-Tyne Polytechnic. Also the patience and encouragement of my wife Dorothy and my family, without whose support I could not have completed this book.

Part 1
Introducing financial management

1 The business objective and financial management

The business objective

When individuals or organisations elect to use their expertise, time and money in a particular way, they have an objective in mind. The objective governs the decisions to be made.

For example, the management of a football team newly promoted to the first division would have the *long-term* objective of becoming top of that division. Improved spectator facilities and planned development of junior players would help in achieving this objective. In the *short-term*, however, the main objective would be to survive in the first division. Improved training and the immediate purchase of experienced players would help here.

Activity

Andrew Wilson has decided to leave his relatively safe job with a large insurance company to set up on his own as an insurance broker. He will operate from home, and will therefore need only a small amount of 'start-up' money to purchase office equipment.

What do you think will be Andrew's main objective in becoming self-employed?

If we ignore the value that he would probably place upon being independent of employers, Andrew would obviously hope to be better off financially than he was with his previous employer. He would expect to receive a net income, after paying his business expenses, of more than the total of his previous salary plus the interest that he would have earned on the capital invested in office equipment.

The figures for his first year's operations might be as follows:

	£	£
Net earnings from broking business		20,000
less Previous salary	16,000	
Interest on capital invested in office equipment	200	16,200
Net surplus for the year		£ 3,800

Note that Andrew has exchanged a relatively 'safe' income of £16,200 for a more *risky* business income of £20,000. Competition, or a downturn in business, might well reduce his future business income below its present level, and he will then have to decide whether the probability of his future business income being more than £20,000 is greater than the risk of it being less than £16,200. Andrew's attitude to risk will be the deciding factor in the continuance or otherwise of his business.

Activity

Andrew's brother John, who is the production manager for an electronics firm at a salary of £15,000 per year, has also become restless. Particularly so since his recent large win on the football pools. He is considering starting his own business in the manufacture of electronic educational aids.

Premises for the venture could be rented but an amount of £100,000 would be required to invest in machinery and other equipment. John estimates that, in the first year, there is a 50% chance of net earnings being as low as £20,000, but a 50% chance of them being as high as £35,000.

Prepare some figures to show how John might fare, at worst, at best, and on the average, during his first year in business.

John's expected average earnings are (50% × £20,000) + (50% × £35,000) = £10,000 + 17,500 = £27,500

	£		
	At worst	*Average*	*At best*
Expected net earnings after providing for all expenses, including the future replacement of his machinery and equipment	£20,000	£27,500	£35,000
less Management salary in previous job	15,000	15,000	15,000
Net earnings	£ 5,000	£12,500	£20,000
Capital invested – machinery, etc.	£100,000	£100,000	£100,000
Percentage rate of return on capital invested	5%	12.5%	20%

Although John will make a profit at each level of activity, he must be convinced that the risk he is taking, of giving up a salary of £15,000 plus the return he could expect from an equivalent investment, is worth it. If the comparison is not favourable, after examining his current and future forecasts, he ought not take the risk.

From this last example, we see that a lonely, unrelated figure of *profit* is an inadequate business objective. Profit must, first, be related to the *capital invested* to ascertain the yield on that investment, then the yield compared with that obtainable from an investment of equivalent *risk*. Ultimately, the objective should be to maximise the wealth of the business owner consistent with the risks involved.

If John Wilson went ahead with his electronics venture, he would probably reach a point at which further growth in business was beyond his financial capacity. He would invite other people to join him in shared ownership of the business by forming a *limited company*; the term 'limited' meaning that the liability of each shareholder for the debts of the company is limited to the amount of money they have subscribed or agreed to subscribe to the business. These shareholders would not necessarily help in the day-to-day running of the company – they appoint *directors* to do that; but they do expect to receive a share of the profits each year in the form of *dividends*.

Shareholders' expectations do not stop at dividends, however; for they also anticipate that the value of their shares will grow as that part of the profit retained in the business is put to work, together with additional funds *borrowed* from other people. If these dividend and growth expectations are not realised, the market value of their shares will diminish, for prospective investors in the company will not pay a high price for inadequate returns.

The main aim of company managements is, therefore, to maximise profit on capital invested, whilst keeping risk at an acceptable level. Success in doing this will *maximise shareholders' wealth – reflected in the market price of their shares.*

There are, however, certain constraints upon the objective of maximum profit, and because of these perhaps the word 'optimise' is more appropriate. For example, government legislation which curbs the power of monopolies tends to keep prices, and thus profits, lower than they might otherwise be.

Activity

List other factors that you consider act as constraints upon maximisation of profit.

Your list should include:

- government policy in the form of price controls and taxation;
- the necessity to spend resources to curb environmental damage;
- health and safety regulations within the manufacturing plant, and also applying to the product;
- the recognition by firms of their social responsibilities in support of cultural and sporting activities;
- adequate provision for employees' welfare in the form of pensions, etc.;
- growing political pressure for more employee participation in both management and profit;

- the possibility that company managements (being distant from shareholders) may settle for 'satisfactory' rather than 'maximum' profit. For example, they may prefer to play safe and ignore risky but apparently highly profitable projects, to protect their jobs.

How can the profit maximisation objective be applied to nationalised industries in the United Kingdom? Some were losing money when the state took them over, and their position is little changed today. These include the National Coal Board and British Rail. Others have had fluctuating fortunes over the years.

Some people argue that, as consumers of scarce capital resources, nationalised industries should compete for them in the marketplace, and if unable to utilise them profitably, should abandon or reduce their operations as any other business would. However, this ignores social responsibilities. For example, the wholesale closure of all unprofitable coal mines would lead to great personal hardship in the areas affected, especially where there is little alternative employment.

One way of dealing with this problem is to subsidise services which lose money, where there are sound social reasons for doing so. There is no reason, however, why the viable railway routes and coal mines, as well as whole nationalised industries, should not have profit targets.

Self-check

1 State which of the following is the main objective of a business:

a increase its market share;
b maximise its sales;
c produce the greatest possible range of products;
d maximise the wealth of its owners – in the long term;
e to survive.

2 What do you consider to be the main objective of the committee who run your local swiming pool?

1 **d** maximise the wealth of its owners – in the long term.

2 To provide the community with the most efficient swimming recreational service, at lowest cost.

The role of financial management

Any enterprise, whether run by one person or many, having a profit objective or not, needs money to acquire resources to operate. Resources include the skills and expertise of people, raw materials and land, each of which is limited by ownership and supply, and therefore commands a price. By this definition money for investment is also a resource – being limited in supply and certainly commanding a price.

Money for investment is referred to as *finance*, and it is available only because it has been withheld from consumption. Finance may have been accumulated and contributed by the owners of an enterprise, or it may be borrowed from outsiders. Whatever its source, the responsibility for its acquisition, allocation and conservation is largely the province of financial management. Figure 1 shows the business planning and control cycle of a limited company, drawn to highlight the part played

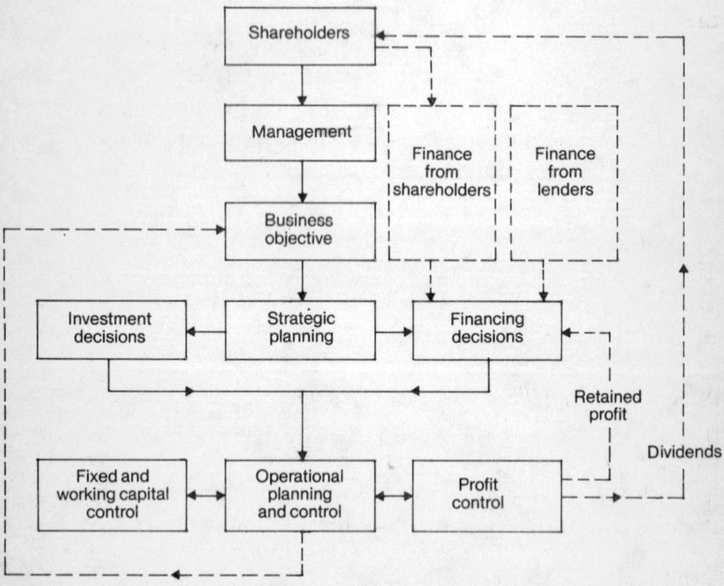

Figure 1. Financial management in the business planning and control cycle

by financial management to achieve the business objective of optimising the wealth of its shareholders.

Strategic planning concerns decisions about what product or service is to be supplied, and to what group of customers. The resources required to achieve these plans will involve further decisions regarding *investment* and *financing*; followed by an efficient monitoring process to ensure that the acquired resources are being used as planned.

The role of financial management therefore embraces:

- *Investment decisions* (allocating finance).
- *Financing decisions* (acquiring finance).
- *Controlling resources* (conserving finance).

Self-check

The following items are on the agenda of a meeting of the management committee of a sports club. Indicate which of them will be of particular interest to the financial manager, stating in each case whether the decision to be made is concerned with financing (F), investment (I), or resource control (C).

1 A proposed increase in subscriptions.
2 Building an additional squash court.
3 Suspend a member of thc club.
4 Provide a lock for the door of the equipment store.
5 Apply to the Sports Council for a grant.
6 Purchase a minivan to transport teams to events.
7 Write letters to members who are in arrears with their subscriptions.
8 Choose the players to represent the club in a darts match.
9 Decide the date of the next meeting.

1 F – to provide additional finance.
2 I – will require the allocation of long-term funds.
3 None
4 C – to safeguard resources.
5 F – to provide additional finance.

6 I – to allocate finance to the purchase of an asset.
7 C – to control resources.

Investment decisions

To many the word *investment* suggests matters worlds apart from their daily lives. Stocks and shares, take-over bids, the *Financial Times* index – the stuff from which only the lives of people who are 'something in the City' are made! If we look more closely at the ways in which we dispose of our incomes, however, we find we are all investors to varying degrees.

Most people take out some form of insurance policy to cover risks to life or property. The premiums we pay are then invested by insurance companies in government and industrial securities to ensure that the fund out of which they will ultimately have to pay claims is maintained. Indirectly, therefore, most of us are investors in stocks and shares through our insurance policies.

> *Activity*
>
> List other investment decisions which might be made by the average family.

Some of the following will probably be in your list:

1 Savings in the National Savings Bank, building societies, and Trustee Savings Bank.
2 Savings invested in the shares of limited companies.
3 Unit trust investments.
4 Contributions to a pension fund.
5 Purchase of a dwelling house and land.
6 Purchase of antiques, precious metals, jewels, works of art and rare postage stamps.

Note that investments can be made in one of two ways; either by:

- entrusting money into someone else's management; or by
- purchasing assets that we manage ourselves.

Insurance policies and items **1** to **4** above are in the first category, items **5** and **6** in the second.

Whichever way we choose to invest, we expect the original sum invested to be recovered after a period of time, together with an additional sum, in the form of interest, rent or profit, to compensate for the risk and waiting involved. The element of risk in losing our original investment, or in receiving high or low incomes from our investment, will govern whether we put our money into, say, relatively risky shares or into the 'safe' National Savings Bank. Individuals with limited resources will, therefore, appraise alternative investments very carefully, with the aim of maximising their potential wealth, whilst keeping risk at the level acceptable to them. Higher risk will only be traded for higher returns.

Business firms behave in much the same way. Whether considering expanding or replacing production facilities, the purchase of another business or investment in the shares of other concerns, the trade-off between risk and rate of return is paramount in the decision-making process, and calls for the application of the most sophisticated investment appraisal techniques.

Financing decisions

Baden Alan, leader of a Norwich venture scout group, was anxious to know whether it would be possible to take twenty of his young charges to the Austrian Alps next year. Most of the boys' parents could afford to pay only half of the anticipated cost of £400 each.

His young assistant Clive, who worked in an accountant's office, offered to help Baden by drawing up a cash forecast for the next twelve months. The statement appeared as follows:

	£	£
Cash held at present		2,000
Expected receipts:		
Parents' subscriptions and donations	500	
Parents' and friends bingo receipts	7,000	
Parents' and boys fundraising	3,000	
County council grant for new hut	7,500	
Three-year loan from bank for van	7,000	
Sale of old minivan	2,000	27,000
		29,000
Expected payments:		
New scout hut	10,000	
Replacement minivan	7,000	
Bank loan repayment (minivan)	2,500	
Running expenses – minivan	2,000	
Travelling expenses	500	22,000
Forecast cash available		7,000
less Austrian trip subsidy 20×£200		4,000
Forecast ending cash balance		£ 3,000

Baden was greatly cheered by this information. It looked as though his trip could go ahead. However, Clive cautioned him. 'Although the grant and loan assist our plan,' he explained, 'the eventual availability of cash depends mainly upon our making the bingo and fundraising successful.'

'Never fear,' assured Baden, 'now we know clearly what our financial position is likely to be, we can concentrate efforts on achieving the forecast cash target.'

From the above we see that financing concerns the acquisition of money necessary to help achieve objectives, and that the approach to financing decisions is, in essence, the same for everyone. Individuals, scout groups and limited companies must:

- assess how much finance they need for long- and short-term purposes;
- have knowledge of, and make efficient choices from, the various sources of finance available.

Activity

From the venture scout cash forecast given above, can you summarise the two main sources of finance, and then divide each of them into two further subgroups?

Internal sources: (a) arising from the efforts and resources of parents and boys; (b) sale of existing surplus assets.
External sources: (a) loan from the bank; (b) grant from the county council.

To sum up: we finance activities by using either our own money or someone else's. The shareholders of a limited company will either agree to a restrained dividend policy which provides for the reinvestment of profit, or they will subscribe further cash themselves.

Funds from *external* sources come essentially from new shareholders, lenders and government grants.

Self-check

Indicate which of the following statements describes the essentials of financing decisions.

1 Ensuring that the accounts present a true and fair financial view.
2 Assessing the profitability of an investment.
3 Assessing how much money is required, and the sources from which it can be obtained.
4 Comparing the financing arrangements of different companies.

3 Assessing how much money is required, etc.

Effective control of resources

Having set his sights firmly on the Austrian Alps, venture scout leader Baden will be highly motivated to achieve the financial targets set for the coming year. He will ensure that investment in the new hut, together with helpful parents and scouts, will yield the expected cash surplus from bingo and other efforts.

Running expenses on the new minivan will be tightly controlled; it will be kept in good condition to maintain its second-hand value.

The hut and the vehicle are both relatively long-lasting (fixed) assets, but other resources, such as stores, amounts receivable from subscriptions (debtors) and cash, warrant the same attention. Slack control of stores can cost a fortune. Failure to collect subscriptions will upset cash flow projections, as will excessive expenses – perhaps affected by unforeseen inflation.

These control problems apply no less to business organisations, any differences being ones of scale and environment. It is not enough to acquire finance and convert it into the resources necessary to carry out investment plans. Control is a continuing process.

For example, effective control of resources by a manufacturing company would include:

- Checks to discover whether the forecast benefits of past investment decisions have actually materialised.
- Assessing whether continuing investment projects should be phased out and replaced by more profitable new ones.
- Maintaining debtors, stocks, cash and creditors at their most efficient levels, including provision for inflation.
- Ensuring that foreign currency dealings are protected by available market operations, and overseas investments managed efficiently.

Self-check

Explain whether you agree with the following statement by a business manager:

'As long as investment appraisal is carried out efficiently, and finance obtained at cheapest cost, we should attain our objective of maximising profit.'

Sound investment and financing decisions are certainly prerequisites to attaining long-term objectives, but this is never the end of the story.

Invested resources must live up to their promise or give way to more profitable use. In addition, good housekeeping should be practised regarding stock, debtors and cash.

Review

1 It is sometimes claimed that the main objective of a business is to increase its total sales; the more sales – the more profit! Do you agree?

2 State which of the following are the main functions of financial management, and briefly explain the nature of each.

a Issuing shares.
b Financing decisions.
c Compiling cost statements.
d Keeping a record of shareholders.
e Producing the annual accounts.
f Paying dividends.
g Controlling the resources of the organisation.
h Internal auditing.
i Investment decisions.

1 Higher sales do not necessarily result in higher profit; if for example, excessive costs exceed selling prices. Again, if additional investment is necessary to increase sales, then the *additional profit* should represent an adequate return on the *additional investment*, bearing in mind any additional risk attaching to the extra sales.

2 i *Investment decisions* – are concerned with the efficient allocation of finance.
b *Financing decisions* – relate to the acquisition of finance required to support planned investment.
g *Controlling the resources* of the organisation – including monitoring investments to ensure that they continue to be as profitable as planned; and making sure that short-term assets such as cash, debtors and stock are effectively controlled.

2 Financial analysis

The need for financial analysis

In Chapter 1 you saw how investment and financing decisions are vital elements of planning to achieve the objectives of an organisation. Following implementation of these decisions, there is a continuous monitoring process to ensure that resources are used effectively.

Monitoring requires information. The financial manager will rely, to a large extent, on the periodic financial reports and statements produced by the accounting system.

> *Activity*
>
> If a company's sales are £2 million more than planned, is this necessarily a good trading result?

Not necessarily; for if the additional sales cost £2 million to produce, no profit will result. Further, even if there is a margin of profit, it might not be sufficient to justify the additional investment in machinery, buildings and stocks of materials needed to support the increase in sales. The profit, as a percentage of capital invested, has to be acceptable.

There must be at least two related figures to yield meaningful information, with the result presented as a ratio, index or percentage as appropriate. Profit, as a percentage of sales, tells far more than separate profit and sales figures.

What range of information is required and can be deduced from a study of financial statements? Given that the three main functions of financial management concern investing, financing and controlling resources, we ought to ask questions to discover whether these functions are being effectively carried out. Four main questions may be asked, shown in figure 2 linked with their respective function.

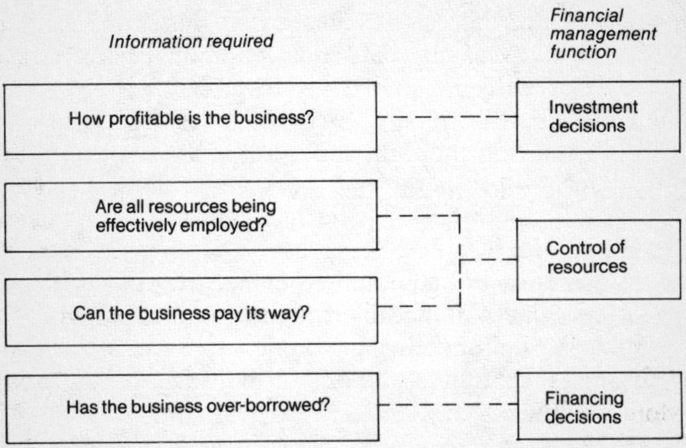

Figure 2. Information needed for financial management

We now search out interrelated figures in the financial statements, which, when combined and presented as ratios or indices, help most to answer these questions.

The financial information available to interested people *outside* a business (e.g. bankers, stockbrokers and investment analysts) is very sparse. Limited companies are compelled by the Companies Acts to publish a profit and loss account and a balance sheet once every year, and disclosure requirements are specified in the Acts. Most companies do no more than comply with the law, but this does not prevent the extraction of some very useful information from these statements. Indeed, since the passing of the Companies Act 1981, most of the ratios discussed in this chapter can be gleaned from published figures.

Introducing Pike and Newton

Ten years ago Colin Pike gained a university degree in computer engineering. Then, with financial assistance from his family and factory accommodation provided by his local authority, he set up in business manufacturing microcomputers and other computer equipment. His success was phenomenal, and continued expansion pushed his total sales to their current year's figure of £2 million. The finance for this expansion came mainly from reinvested profit, some additional help from his family and a recently negotiated bank overdraft.

Colin's friend at university, Richard Newton, had started up a similar business at the same time, but in another part of the country. He also prospered but, because he did not have the advantage of family backing, he had borrowed very heavily during the last year.

Both businesses are now limited companies, but not *public limited companies* (plc), because they are not authorised to seek *public* subscription for their shares.

Their most recent profit and loss accounts and balance sheets are shown below:

Trading and profit and loss accounts for the year to 31 December 19XX

	Pike Electronics	*Newton Computers*
	£000s	£000s
Sales	2,000	2,000
Cost of sales	1,400	1,500
Gross profit	600	500
less:		
Administration expenses	80	60
Selling and distribution expenses	130	115
Directors' fees and salaries	40	30
Interest on overdrafts and loans	6	45
	256	250
Net trading profit	344	250
Corporation tax	172	125
Shareholders' profit	172	125
Dividend paid	10	5
Profit for the year retained	162	120

Balance sheets at 31 December 19XX

	Pike Electronics £000s	Newton Computers £000s
Fixed assets (at cost)	1,000	1,150
less Depreciation	450	500
	550	650
Current assets:		
Stock	600	350
Debtors	400	250
Bank	—	50
	1,000	650
less:		
Current liabilities:		
Trade creditors	250	150
Tax payable	250	250
Bank overdraft	50	—
	550	400
Working capital	450	250
Total assets	£1,000	£ 900
Shareholders' capital and reserves:		
Called-up share capital	500	100
Profit and loss account	500	500
	1,000	600
Creditors falling due after more than one year		
15% loan (repayable in 10 years)	—	300
	£1,000	£ 900

How profitable is the business?

Return on owners' capital

People who deposit money in a building society or savings bank account look for relative safety and ease of withdrawal, and therefore expect to receive only a modest interest rate. On the other hand, owners of business enterprises expect a higher return on their investments because there is a greater risk that they will lose their money. In a limited company this return can be measured by expressing profit, after corporation tax, as a percentage of shareholders' capital.

Activity

Calculate the shareholders' rates of return from the accounts of Pike and Newton.

Pike: 172÷1,000=17.2%; Newton: 125÷600=20.8%.

Newton is yielding a higher return on shareholders' investment than Pike, but three very important comments are pertinent here:

1 Although Newton has borrowed more and has paid more interest on those borrowings, this has been beneficial. The borrowed money has earned more than the net interest (after tax) paid, and the surplus benefits shareholders without any apparent sacrifice on their part.

2 Balance sheet values may be based upon original cost, and profit may not take account of the cost of replacing assets at ever increasing prices. It is now standard accounting practice for some companies to show separate inflation-adjusted statements, but because this is not universal, published figures must be read with some caution.

3 If Pike and Newton were public limited companies, and their shares were quoted on the Stock Exchange, that quotation would normally represent the true market value of the shares. Theoretically, this should not differ from balance sheet values, but for the reason stated in note 2 above, and others to be discussed in the chapter on valuation of shares, it probably will.

Return on management's capital employed

To compare how *managers* have performed against planned activity, or with another company of similar size and operations, we have to take a view different to that of shareholders for four reasons:

- Taxation liability is not necessarily a direct proportion of profit. Among various adjustments made in the computation of tax, for example, are allowances for investment in industrial machinery and plant. *Profit before tax* is therefore a more stable comparative.

- Capital employed includes not only shareholders' funds but also money borrowed. This could include bank overdrafts that are constantly renewed and therefore a permanent feature of the way the business is financed.
- Interest paid on loans is not an expense of operating; it arises because of the way a business is *financed*, and should therefore be added back to profit before tax, to smooth out differences in financing arrangements.
- Some capital may be invested *outside* the business in long-term investments not connected with its main activity. Interest or dividends received from these investments should not count as *operating* profit, and the capital so invested should be deducted from the total capital employed.

After adjusting for the four aspects noted above, the ratio of management's return on capital employed is calculated as:

$$\frac{\text{profit before tax, interest and investment income}}{\text{total assets}} \times 100\%.$$

Activity

Calculate the return on management's capital for Pike and Newton. Note that neither company has capital invested outside their business. Also, assume that Pike's overdraft will be constantly renewed long-term borrowing.

Pike	Newton
$\frac{344+6}{1{,}000+50} \times 100 = 33.3\%$	$\frac{250+45}{600+300} \times 100 = 32.8\%$

Note that Pike has performed slightly better than Newton. This is contrary to the shareholders' ratio which showed Newton coming out on top. The reasons for this can be seen by breaking down this ratio into its components as explained below.

Profit to sales; sales to capital employed

Net profit equals sales less cost of sales. It follows that if capital invested in a business is expected to produce a certain level of profit, this can be accomplished only if that capital generates an associated level of sales, for without sales there would be no profit.

By maximising the ratios of profit to sales and sales to capital invested, the ratio of profit to capital invested will be maximised. This can be expressed as follows:

$$\frac{\text{profit}}{\text{capital employed}} = \frac{\text{profit}}{\text{sales}} \times \frac{\text{sales}}{\text{capital employed}}$$

Note that sales cancel out on the right-hand side of the equation.

> *Activity*
>
> Calculate the *net profit to sales* and *sales to capital employed* ratios for Pike and Newton, showing them in the form of the equation given above to prove them correct.
>
> Hint: the profit and capital employed figures should be those already used in calculation of the return on management's capital employed ratio.

Pike

$$\frac{350}{1{,}050} = \frac{350}{2{,}000} \times \frac{2{,}000}{1{,}050}$$

$$33.3\% = \underline{17.5\%} \times \underline{1.905}$$

Newton

$$\frac{295}{900} = \frac{295}{2{,}000} \times \frac{2{,}000}{900}$$

$$32.8\% = \underline{14.75\%} \times \underline{2.222}$$

The two companies make interesting comparison. Pike has earned a higher profit on each £1 of sales than Newton, but the latter has generated a greater number of £s sales for each £1 of capital invested. Even though their profit to capital employed is almost the same, strengths and weaknesses are more tellingly revealed by breaking the primary ratio discussed in the previous section into its two subsidiary components.

Cost to sales ratios

By digging a little more deeply, and calculating the ratio of each expense head in the profit and loss account to sales, further insight is given into the composition of the profit ratios already discussed.

Activity

Calculate each cost in the profit and loss accounts of Pike and Newton as a percentage of sales. What do the ratios tell you of the operating performances of each company, and how do they compare? Reminder: leave interest out of your calculations.

	Pike		*Newton*	
	£000s	%	£000s	%
Sales	2,000	100	2,000	100
Cost of sales	1,400	70	1,500	75
Gross profit	600	30	500	25
Expenses:				
Administration	80	4.0	60	3.0
Selling	130	6.5	115	5.8
Directors' fees, etc.	40	2.0	30	1.5
Total expenses	250	12.5	205	10.3
Net profit	350	17.5	295	14.7

Comments

- Although the total sales are the same for each company, Newton has the higher production cost of sales, and consequently a lower gross profit than Pike. This might be because:
  (a) each of the companies sells a different mix of products, some with higher production costs than others, or higher selling prices, resulting in different margins of profit;
  (b) Pike is more efficient in production, leading to lower unit costs, or pays less for its materials and services;
  (c) Newton has not increased its prices in line with costs;
  (d) stock has been valued or counted incorrectly.

- The position between the two companies is reversed when expense ratios are compared. Pike is less efficient here and loses some of the advantage gained in production and/or selling.

Self-check

1 The profit to sales and profit to capital employed ratios of the Acme Company are 12% and 18% respectively. What is the sales to capital employed ratio?

2 Which of the following statements is **(a)** correct or **(b)** incorrect in connection with the calculation of the return on management's capital employed?

i dividends paid to shareholders are deducted from profit;
ii taxation is added back to profit;
iii capital invested outside the business, not connected with main activities, is disregarded;
iv interest paid on loans is added back in arriving at profit;
v management salaries are added back in calculating profit;
vi long-term borrowed capital is ignored;
vii dividends received on investments *outside* the business are included in profit.

3 The Acme Company reports a gross profit to sales ratio lower than expected. What could be the reasons for this?

1 Let z=the sales to capital employed ratio. Then 0.12×z=0.18; therefore z=1.5.

2 **(i)** incorrect; **(ii)** correct; **(iii)** correct; **(iv)** correct; **(v)** incorrect; **(vi)** incorrect; **(vii)** incorrect.

3 **a** A different mix of sales than planned.
b Selling prices not raised in line with costs.
c Incorrect stock valuation.
d Inefficient buying, or production, leading to higher costs.

Are all resources being effectively employed?

You saw in the last section that the sales to capital employed ratio measures the effectiveness of *total* asset usage. As total assets include fixed assets and working capital, a further analysis of each of these groups related to sales can help to pinpoint why the overall ratio is better or worse than expected.

Activity

What are the sales to fixed assets and working capital ratios of Pike and Newton? Reminder: Pike's overdraft is treated as a long-term loan and not a current liability.

What do the ratios tell you?

	Pike	*Newton*
$\frac{\text{sales}}{\text{fixed assets}}$	$\frac{2{,}000}{550}=3.64$	$\frac{2{,}000}{650}=3.08$
$\frac{\text{sales}}{\text{working capital}}$	$\frac{2{,}000}{500}=4.00$	$\frac{2{,}000}{250}=8.00$

Because Pike has a lower amount invested in fixed assets, that company has the better sales to fixed asset ratio. A further breakdown into types of fixed assets might be more revealing.

However, excessive working capital investment by Pike gives Newton the better overall asset turnover ratio.

Self-check

1 A quarter of the value of buildings and machinery shown in a balance sheet relates to progress payments on a new factory that has not yet started to produce. What effect will this have on the sales to capital employed ratio?

2 Why is it useful to break down the sales to capital employed ratio into asset categories?

1 This would reduce the sales turnover ratio because of a higher than normal asset ratio. The deterioration would be corrected when the new plant 'comes on stream'.

2 A sales to capital employed measurement may hide deficiencies that would be revealed by examining the relationship between sales and each asset category. Some assets may have performed well, others badly.

Can the business pay its way?

If you are unable to meet your current commitments either out of cash resources or by borrowing, you are *technically* insolvent. You could possibly pay your debts by selling some possessions or property, but even this drastic action may not be enough. Your total liabilities would then exceed your total assets, and you would be *legally* insolvent.

This need for cash (or liquidity), applies no less to a business, and its 'liquidity' ratios can give some indication of its capacity to pay current debts. The ratios are concerned with current assets and current liabilities, the term 'current' implying that the value will be received or paid within one year.

Current ratio

This is calculated by dividing total current assets by total current liabilities. It has been referred to as the '2 to 1' ratio because banks tend to look favourably, as regards credit, upon firms who maintain the ratio at that level.

Pike and Newton show the following current ratios:

	Pike	*Newton*
$\frac{\text{current assets}}{\text{current liabilities}}$	$\frac{1{,}000}{500} = 2{:}1$	$\frac{650}{400} = 1.63{:}1$

Activity

Do you think that, as Pike has the higher ratio, it is more liquid than its competitor?

It would be if both stock and debtors could be converted into cash *within the same time*. It is likely, however, that Pike is holding too much stock, and that a proportion of its debtors are delaying payment of their debts. For these reasons the current ratio may not be a very sound indicator of liquidity.

'Quick' or 'acid test' ratio

A much better measure of solvency, this ratio relates current assets (less stock) to current liabilities. Stock is left out of the reckoning because it is not quickly turned into cash; although this is not so in retailing businesses.

In general one would look for a 1 : 1 ratio to show that cash or near cash matches debts payable.

Activity

Calculate Pike's and Newton's acid test ratios.

	Pike	*Newton*
$\frac{\text{current assets (less stock)}}{\text{current liabilities}}$	$\frac{400}{500} = 0.8:1$	$\frac{300}{400} = 0.75:1$

Rather surprisingly, both companies seem to be at risk in this respect. Things may not be as black as they look, however, for tax payable may not be due for some months, by which time cash will have accumulated from operations to meet the bill. If tax is payable immediately then both companies have liquidity problems, and may have to resort to further temporary borrowing.

Stock turnover

Stock has a considerable influence upon the effective use of resources and liquidity ratios, which we have already considered; but it can be examined even more closely.

Cost of sales in a period, divided by the cost of stock normally held, reveals the *velocity* or *turnover* of stock moving through the business. It is normally expressed as an index, e.g. '10 times'. An alternative calculation of (cost of stock÷cost of sales)×365 shows how many days' sales the stock held represents. The lower the stock relative to sales, the less capital is tied up, as long as stock is maintained at a level that does not cause hold-ups in production or selling. A high index or number of days' stock held might be caused by the inclusion of obsolete or slow-moving items, or simply overproduction or bad buying.

Too high an investment in stock will therefore not only result in the deterioration of profit to capital employed, but may also be a prime cause of liquidity problems.

Activity

Calculate the stock ratios of Pike and Newton in terms of both turnover and time.

	Pike	*Newton*
Turnover:	$\frac{1,400}{600}$ =2.3times	$\frac{1,500}{350}$ =4.29 times
Time:	$\frac{600}{1,400}$ ×365=156 days	$\frac{350}{1,500}$ ×365=85 days

Newton is patently managing its stocks more efficiently than Pike.

Stock can be further analysed, particularly in manufacturing firms, into raw materials, work in progress, and finished goods. By relating each of these categories to cost of sales, one could discover whether raw materials was being overstocked, whether there are bottlenecks in production or whether there is a decreased demand for the finished product.

Average debt collection period

As with stock, an excessive investment in debtors will lower the return on capital employed, and may also contribute towards the liquidity problems of a business.

The length of time currently being taken by customers to pay their debts can be calculated as: (debtors÷credit sales for the period)×365. Note that the denominator is credit sales, as debtors cannot be associated with cash sales.

Activity

Calculate the average collection period for the Pike and Newton companies, and suggest reasons for any difference between them.

Pike: (400÷2,000)×365=73 days;
Newton: (290÷2,000)×365=46 days.

Here again, Newton appears to be managing its assets better than Pike. If, say, 55 days is the normal period allowed to customers to pay their debts, then Pike has some explaining to do. His credit control or debt collection procedures could be at fault.

Conversely, although Newton appears to be efficient, his overzealous collection of debts *within* the normal credit period may be causing him some loss of customers.

Average creditors' payment period

Businesses are normally expected to allow their customers time to pay their debts. Conversely, they expect the same treatment from their suppliers of raw materials and services. The average credit period allowed by suppliers is calculated as: (creditors÷purchases for the period)×365.

In our illustrative example a separate purchases figure is not given, but as the cost of sales includes materials and services, it can be used to make a comparison between our two companies.

Activity

What are Pike's and Newton's average creditors' payment periods?

Pike: (250÷1,400)×365=65 days;
Newton: (150÷1,500)×365=36 days.

Pike again shows up badly, and presuming that the normal credit period is 36 days, it rather looks as though it is delaying payment to suppliers to help overcome its cash problem.

Self-check

1 Why is the current ratio sometimes referred to as the '2 to 1' ratio?
2 The acid test ratio is a better measure of liquidity than the current ratio. Do you think this is always the case?
3 The following figures relate to an electrical appliance wholesaler. The stock at the beginning and at the end of the year were the same.

	£		£
Sales	1,500	*Current assets*:	
Cost of sales	1,000	Stock	125
Gross profit	500	Debtors	250
		Cash	225
		Current liabilities:	
		Trade creditors	200

Calculate the current and acid test ratios, stock turnover, average debt collection period and average creditors' payment period. Comment briefly on the firm's liquidity position. What have stock and debtors to do with liquidity?

1 Banks in particular have traditionally favoured a 2 : 1 ratio. They consider that gives them adequate security against default in repayment of debts owing to them.
2 In the case of a retailer, where stock is turned into cash within a relatively short time after purchase of goods, the current ratio is probably as effective as the acid test in measuring liquidity.

3 Current ratio: 600 : 200=3 : 1
Acid test ratio: 475 : 200=2.4 : 1.
Stock turnover: 1000÷125=8 times.
Average debt collection period: (250÷1,500)×365=61 days.
Average creditors' payment period: (200÷1,000)×365=73 days.
The firm is extremely liquid, probably too much so; in which case it is not controlling its resources effectively.

4 Over-investment in stock and debtors will divert cash that is needed to pay suppliers; cash which will otherwise have to be borrowed from the bank.

Has the business overborrowed?

In the last section we used ratios to measure a firm's ability to meet *short-term* obligations. It is equally important to know that a business is not overburdened with *long-term* debt. Such borrowing does eventually become a short-term repayment or replacement problem, and meantime there is the short-term commitment to pay annual interest on the loan.

The advantage of long-term borrowing is that business owners are able to expand without having to contribute additional funds themselves. They resort to borrowing only if they expect that the profit generated from its use will add to their wealth after the loan interest has been paid.

Long-term debt to net assets

The reliance of a firm on long-term borrowed capital can be measured by relating long-term debt to total assets less current liabilities. The following are the borrowing (or gearing), ratios of Pike and Newton:

		Pike		*Newton*
long-term debt/net assets		50:1,050		300:900
	or	1:21	or	1:3

This shows that £1 in every £3 of Newton's net assets is financed by long-term borrowing. Pike's borrowing is negligible. Newton is heavily dependent upon borrowing, and if the ten-year loan was repayable at an early date, it could be in financial trouble.

Total debt to total assets

A more comprehensive ratio that shows a firm's dependence upon borrowed money includes *all* current liabilities as debts. This measurement is particularly significant to suppliers who are highly sensitive to risk when granting credit. For our two companies, the relevant ratios are:

	Pike	*Newton*
total debt/total assets	550:1,550 or 1:2.82	700:1,300 or 1:1.86

When these figures are compared with the long-term debt ratios, suppliers will see that, although Newton has a higher proportion of long-term debt, Pike is relying upon debt finance far more than was previously revealed. This is confirmed by comparing the two companies' average creditors' payment periods.

Interest cover

The chance of not being able to repay a long-term loan is a relatively *long-term* risk. The *short-term* risk relates to interest payments. To measure the interest paying capacity of a business we calculate how many times interest payable is covered by pre-tax, pre-interest profit.

> *Activity*
>
> Calculate how many times Pike's and Newton's loan interest payable are covered by profit.

	Pike	*Newton*
$\frac{\text{pre-tax, pre-interest profit}}{\text{interest paid}}$	$\frac{350}{6}$ =58 times	$\frac{295}{45}$ =6.5 times

Pike appears to have plenty of reserve borrowing capacity. Interest cover is generally expected to be at least five times, and Newton has little margin over this. Generally, the more stable and growing profits are, the lower this ratio could be.

Self-check

1 What are the twin risks of overborrowing?

2 Which of the following measures a firm's reliance upon long-term borrowing, and which interest cover?

a Interest paid divided into profit before tax and interest.
b Total assets divided by total debt.
c Fixed assets divided by total liabilities.
d Long-term debt related to net asset value.
e Interest paid divided into after-tax profit.

1 The twin risks of overborrowing are: the *short-term* risk of not being able to pay interest due; the *long-term* risk of not being able to repay the loan.

2 d Long-term debt related to net assets value.
a Interest paid divided into profit before tax and interest.

Limitations of ratio analysis

Ratios can be useful indicators of adverse or encouraging business trends, but they are only *starting-points* in the quest for information. They do not tell *what* is going right or wrong; they merely invite further questions.

In particular, the following points must be noted when analysing financial statements by using ratios:

- One year's figures are insufficient; *trends* are gleaned from a comparison of at least five years.
- When comparing with other firms, ensure that the bases upon which the ratios have been calculated are the same. For instance, asset valuation bases might differ.
- Valid comparisons can only be made with firms of the same size and activity.
- The bases used to calculate ratios should be consistent.
- The ratios discussed in this chapter are not exhaustive. Further useful ratios will be met in later chapters.
- Note that ratios do not stand in isolation – they are interrelated. For example, poor profitability will affect liquidity.
- Ratios relate to a particular point in time. Seasonal factors

can distort them, and these should be known.

- Figures can be 'window-dressed'; that is, made to look better than they really are. For example, loans can be repaid temporarily, and then renegotiated after the production of the financial statements.

Review

Listed below are various financial ratios of JP Tools, an average-sized company in its industry, calculated from last year's accounts. The industry average is also shown for comparison.

	JP Tools	*Industry average*
Profit to shareholders' capital	17%	15%
Profit to management's capital	29%	28%
Profit to sales	16%	14%
Sales to capital employed	1.8×	2.0×
Sales to fixed assets	4.0×	4.0×
Sales to working capital	5.0×	6.0×
Current ratio	1.8 : 1	2.0 : 1
Acid test ratio	0.9 : 1	1.2 : 1
Stock turnover	5.0×	6.0×
Average debt collection period	48 days	42 days
Average creditors' payment period	55 days	49 days
Long-term debt to net assets	1.0 : 3	1.0 : 4
Total debt to total assets	1.0 : 2	1.0 : 2.5
Interest cover	4.0×	6.0×

Note: × = times.

Specify the ratio(s) most applicable to each of the situations outlined below, and in each case comment upon how the comparison between JP Tools and the industry average affects the issue at stake. Assume that each of the circumstances is independent of the others.

1 JP Tools has requested its bank to lend it £50,000 for a two-year period.

2 A new supplier to JP Tools is considering what terms to apply to that company.

3 An investor requires to know whether JP Tools is a worthwhile investment.
4 Because of expansion, JP Tools is seeking substantial additional long-term capital.

1 Essentially, the bank would be concerned with the company's ability to service and repay a loan. *Liquidity* would be uppermost in their minds, and the current and acid test ratios, the average debt collection and creditors' payment periods would help their assessment. Present reliance upon *borrowed* capital is indicated by the total debt to total assets ratio; and because earnings are needed to generate liquidity, the bank would look for a reasonable profit to management's capital ratio.

All JP's liquidity ratios compare unfavourably with the industry average, although profitability is better. Relatively high investment in all assets points to a condition known as 'overtrading', and the bank will have to consider the loan application with caution.

2 Suppliers take a similar view to that of banks, but are particularly interested in the average creditors' payment period, and total debt to total assets ratios – both worse than the average in the case of JP Tools. They might be wise to insist upon a credit period of no longer than the industry average.

3 All ratios should interest a prospective investor, but particularly profit to investors' capital. In this respect, the *market values* of its shares might be a better denominator to use than the balance sheet figures, as the latter will probably represent historic cost values.

JP is bettering the industry average on shareholders' return, but future dividends may be at risk because of poor liquidity.

4 Long-term debt to net assets: total debt to total assets, and interest cover are the particular ratios of concern to prospective long-term lenders. Assets mortgaged to cover existing borrowing may leave little asset value as security for new loans. Interest cover is already low, so future profitability is crucial. Comparison with the average shows that JP is already borrowing excessively.

Part 2
Investment decisions

3 Investment appraisal

Financial management involves investment decisions, financing decisions and control of the resources resulting from those decisions. Part 2 of this book is devoted to investment decisions.

The importance of effective investment decisions

To satisfy the ever-expanding social and economic aspirations of its people, a nation must plan to increase its wealth. This can be achieved only if a substantial part of the national income is channelled into investment, rather than immediate consumption.

Swiftly changing technology in a highly competitive international trading environment also calls for a growing proportion of resources to be diverted into research and development of new, high-technology products.

Governments can influence such investment by providing financial assistance and by creating demand from the public sector; but industry must also play its part by seeking opportunities for investment, ensuring that scarce capital is directed into the most productive uses.

Within each firm, investment decisions are part of an overall strategic plan aimed at achieving the business objective. Care is essential in the appraisal of projects for two main reasons:

- Investment involves a complete commitment of scarce resources for a long period, a commitment that may be impossible or extremely difficult to reverse.
- An ever-increasing trend towards the creation of larger business units by amalgamation and nationalisation means that serious economic and social consequences can flow from bad investment decisions.

The nature of investment decisions

Next year's harvest is possible only if some of this year's crop is withheld from consumption to provide the seed for next year's crop.

The finance so essential to all businesses, to invest in buildings, plant, machinery and other assets, is available because they have either withheld profit from distribution as dividends to shareholders, or because they have access to someone else's savings.

Savings are the lifeblood of investment.

> *Activity*
>
> Mrs Burrows was a prudent lady who had always put by some of her income for a 'rainy day'. She kept her savings in an old stocking under the floorboards of her house, because she did not trust other people to look after her money. What would be your advice to her?

Apart from reminding her to check her stockings for holes, and warning her that there is a very real possibility that her money might be stolen, you would probably tell her that she could do much better by putting it into some kind of savings account. It would be safeguarded and she would still have easy access to it. In addition, she would be paid interest to reward her for deferring consumption of her savings, to compensate her for loss of value due to inflation to some extent, and for whatever risk of loss might be associated with the savings bank.

If Mrs Burrows followed this advice she would be *investing* her money. She would be 'locking up' her savings in anticipation of receiving future cash in the form of interest and the ultimate return of her original investment.

Mrs Burrows's example illustrates the essence of all investment, whether by individuals or by businesses. Let us suppose that she was expecting a 10% return on an investment of £1,000. If she was paid a *certain* £100 at the end of each year for five years, at the end of which time her £1,000 was returned, she would patently have earned a return of 10% per year – ignoring inflation and taxation.

Business investments also normally require an *initial* outlay of cash on such assets as buildings, machinery and raw materials; but thereafter the cash flows generated in each year by the project are part interest and part return of initial capital invested. The acceptability or otherwise of each project is not as easy to assess as Mrs Burrows's investment. Cash flows will probably be irregular and difficult to forecast because different projects are subject to varying degrees of risk.

A further problem is to determine the *required rate of return* on business investments. Mrs Burrows was happy to receive 10% because this was equal to the best alternative opportunity to invest her money at similar risk. Likewise, shareholders in, or lenders to, companies will expect returns on the money that they have invested commensurate with the risks involved. Shareholders will look for a higher return than lenders because, whilst the latter enjoy the safety of a fixed and contractually payable sum, shareholders can only receive dividends if there is any profit remaining after all prior claimants have been paid.

The expected yield rate on investments within a company must therefore satisfy the *cost of capital* requirements of the shareholders and lenders who provide the funds for that investment. We will be examining the question of cost of capital more closely in Chapter 14.

Types of business investment

Though each investment is unique, most of the many and varied industrial and commercial projects can be put into one of the following categories:

- replacement of existing assets;
- expansion of existing products or services;
- new products or services;
- research;
- social and welfare.

Replacement of plant and machinery, buildings and vehicles is probably the largest category. Given that the activity for which it is required is still profitable, worn-out machinery has to be replaced. The main problems to solve then are: when to replace, and with what? Whatever our decisions in this respect, they must ultimately rest on the premise that the benefits of replacement must exceed the costs.

Expanding existing products or services can simply mean the addition of more capacity to that already existing in a factory; but it may involve taking over another business, or opening up a new plant in Britain or overseas. Much more forecast information is required than in replacement decisions.

The development of new products in a changing and highly competitive market is vital to survival. Old products lose their head of steam eventually and a continuing product development programme is necessary to provide new products to replace the old, and so keep profit stable and growing.

The investment of money into research must be as objective as possible. Products may not be identifiable at this stage, but management should still endeavour to direct resources allocated to research into those areas that they consider offer most potential for development into new products.

Social and welfare projects cover sports facilities, restaurant and recreational facilities, pensions, medical provision, health and safety, security, and crèches for children of working mothers. The costs of such projects are known but the benefits hard to evaluate. Because of this, their costs are more likely to be recovered either by apportionment over revenue-earning projects, or by increasing the rate of return required by all projects.

Methods of appraisal

Accounting rate of return

In his first year in his computer business, Colin Pike relied upon a young, unqualified accountant to keep accounts and provide information for decision-making. However, growth in future years was anticipated to be so great that he engaged an experienced, qualified accountant as his financial manager.

One of the first areas examined by the new accountant, Jim Bowles, was investment appraisal. He discovered that investment decisions were made generally by forecasting the average annual profit after depreciation, over the life of each project, and then expressing that average figure as a percentage of the total capital invested in the project.

Determined to show that this 'accounting rate of return' approach could be totally misleading, Jim produced the following figures by way of illustration:

Project		*A*	*B*
		£	£
Capital invested, beginning of year 1		11,000	11,000
Profit before depreciation:	*Year*		
	1	1,000	6,000
	2	2,000	5,000
	3	3,000	3,000
	4	5,000	2,000
	5	6,000	1,000

'To keep the calculations simple, I will ignore taxation for the time being,' explained Jim to Colin.

He then produced the following calculations to show the accounting rate of return for each of the projects **A** and **B**.

Project	*A*	*B*
	£	£
Total profit over 5 years	17,000	17,000
less Depreciation (total over 5 years)	11,000	11,000
	6,000	6,000
Average profit per year	1,200	1,200
Accounting rate of return:		
(1,200÷11,000)×100	10.9%	10.9%

'As both projects yield a rate considerably below our minimum required rate of return of 15%, they would be rejected if we used this method of appraisal,' Jim said. 'But are they as equal as they appear?' he queried.

'Certainly not,' replied Colin. '**B**'s cash flows are the exact reverse of **A**'s. Cash received early in the life of a project is more attractive because it can be reinvested sooner to earn more profit, or to reduce the cost of our overdraft.'

'That's right,' said Jim. 'The accounting rate of return approach is unreliable for three main reasons:

- it ignores the timing of cash flows;
- averaging profit assumes equal profit each year;
- late cash flows are treated as equal to early cash flows, which ignores the weakness that late cash flows are far more difficult to predict, and can therefore be subject to a high degree of inaccuracy.'

Self-check

1 Calculate the accounting rate of return for an investment of £5,000 which yields profit before depreciation as follows: year 1, £1,000; year 2, £2,000; year 3, £5,000.

2 Would your rate of return be different if the timing of the profits was reversed?

3 What is the major drawback of using the accounting rate of return as an investment appraisal criterion?

1

	£
Total profit	8,000
less Depreciation	5,000
Net profit	3,000
Average profit	1,000
Accounting rate of return:	
(1,000÷5,000)×100=	20%

2 No, it would be the same, because *total* profit is the same.

3 It ignores the *timing* of cash flows.

Payback

'Plainly, the accounting rate of return is unsatisfactory for more than one year's assessment,' continued Colin. 'Our approach must take early cash flows into account if only because our present rate of expansion is demanding more and more cash.'

Jim agreed. 'What you are suggesting is that we should look for early payback of capital invested in projects, and this is a criterion that many companies use – either on its own, or in conjunction with some other method.'

> *Activity*
>
> Calculate how long it would be before each of the projects **A** and **B**, illustrated in the first section, recovered their capital investment.

A: 4 years (profits for the first four years=£11,000).
B: 2 years (profits for the first two years=£11,000).

'As **B** has the shorter payback period it would be preferred to **A**, but it would only be acceptable itself if it met some previously agreed payback standard of say two years.'

'The method is simple,' continued Jim,' but its biggest weakness is that it ignores profitability. Cash flows after capital is recovered are completely ignored. Let me illustrate this point by introducing another project, **C**, which has the same capital investment of £11,000 and the following cash flows:

Year 1	*2*	*3*	*4*	*5*
£5,000	£6,000	£2,000	£1,000	nil

'Note that **C** has the same payback period as **B**, and would therefore be just as acceptable on that basis, but that its following cash flows are not as valuable as those of **B**. In addition, even the cash flows within the payback period are reversed – **B** being superior in this respect.'

Jim then summarised the defects of payback as follows:

- profitability is ignored, as cash flows after capital is recovered are not considered;
- the incidence of cash flows within the payback period are not taken into account;
- large capital investments are equated with small ones, if they have the same payback period.

'Payback may have some merit, however, in considering projects whose cash flows are extremely uncertain – though there are other ways of dealing with risk.

'In addition, it could be used as a timing device to "screen out" projects with extremely long paybacks, when it is known from experience that such long-life investments are rarely profitable.'

One pound is worth more now than in a year's time

'It is quite obvious to me now, Jim, that the *timing of cash flows* is at the very heart of investment decisions,' observed Colin.

'If we ignore the question of uncertainty in connection with cash flows for the time being, then you are quite right,' the accountant responded. 'Accounting rate of return ignores timing in cash flows completely, whilst payback only recognises the importance of timing up to the point when capital invested is recovered.

'We somehow have to incorporate the *time value* of money into our investment appraisal procedure.'

'If you were offered the alternative of being paid £1 now or £1 in one year's time, there is no doubt that you would opt for £1 now, because you would be able to invest that £1 to grow into a larger sum at the end of one year. At an interest rate of 10% your £1 would grow to £1.10.

'At the end of two years your £1 would grow to £1.21, and you would be equally indifferent between receiving £1 now and £1.21 in two years' time – assuming of course that 10% interest adequately satisfies your feelings about the risks of waiting. This can be illustrated:

	£
Invested now	1.00
10% interest end year 1	.10
Sum at end of year 1	1.10
10% interest end year 2	.11
Compound sum at end of year 2	1.21

And this can be written as an equation:

$$A=P\times(1+i)\times(1+i)$$
or $A=P\,(1+i)^n$

Where A = the sum received at a future date
P = the amount invested now
i = the rate of interest expected
n = the number of years hence the sum is receivable

'You will probably recognise this as the *compound interest* equation, and also recall that it can be converted into a formula to ascertain the *present value* (P) of a known or forecast amount receivable in n years' time, expressed as:

$$P = A\div(1+i)^n$$

'Applying the compound interest formula to the figures used above we have:

$$A=1\,(1+.10)\times(1+.10)$$
$$A=1\,(1+.10)^2$$
$$A=1.21.$$

'Or, applying the present value equation:

$$1=1.21\div(1.10)^2.$$

'Using the last equation, an equivalent *present value* can be calculated for any sum receivable in the future, assuming an appropriate rate of compound interest.'

Jim paused, then asked Colin to calculate, to three places of decimals, the present values of individual £1s receivable at the end of one, two and three years, at 10% compound interest.

Activity

Calculate Colin's answers.

One year	*Two years*	*Three years*
$P=\frac{1}{(1.10)}=.909$	$P=\frac{1}{(1.10)^2}=.826$	$P=\frac{1}{(1.10)^3}=.751$

'Very good,' complimented Jim.' Now see if you can prove that £0.751 received now is the equivalent of £1 in three years' time, at 10% compound interest, by successively adding interest to the original sum.'

Activity

Complete this assignment for Colin.

	£
Invested now	.751
10% interest end year 1	.0751
Sum at end of year 1	.8261
10% interest end year 2	.08261
Sum at end year 2	.90871
10% interest end year 3	.090871
Sum at end year 3	.999581*

*Not quite £1 because £0.751 is approximate.

Jim then explained that tables are available giving the present values of £1 at the end of successive years at progressive rates of interest (see Appendix A), and they can be a very useful aid in the evaluation of investment projects.

Discounted cash flow – net present value

Jim Bowles continued: 'By reference to the last activity you can deduce that, at a 10% rate of return, £1,000 receivable in three years' time, will repay an initial investment of £751, as well as paying compound interest on the investment during those three years, i.e. £1,000×.751 (present value factor at 10% for 3 years) =£751.

'It is more likely, however, that the £751 investment would generate an irregular pattern of cash flows over the three years, and that the present value of those cash flows would be more or less than £751. The initial capital invested would be over or under recovered. The following illustrates this point:

	Cash flow	*Present value factor @ 10%*	*Present value*
	£	£	£
Beginning year 1	– 751	1.000	– 751
End year 1	+ 400	.909	+ 364
End year 2	+ 350	.826	+ 289
End year 3	+ 300	.751	+ 225
Net present value (NPV)			£+ 127

'Because the forecast cash flows from this investment yield a *surplus* net present value (NPV), it would be accepted. Conversely, if the net present value shows a *deficit*, the project would not go ahead.

'Another way of showing this is to treat the initial sum invested as a loan which is gradually recovered over the life of the project, after accounting for interest *on the outstanding balance* of the loan each year – rather like a mortgage loan on a house. The following figures illustrate this treatment:

	Cash flow	*Interest @ 10% on outstanding balance*	*Repayment of capital*	*Investment balance outstanding*
	A	*B*	*A–B*	
	£	£	£	£
Beginning year 1				– 751
End year 1	+ 400	– 75	+ 325	– 426
End year 2	+ 350	– 43	+ 307	– 119
End year 3	+ 300	– 12	+ 288	+ 169

'The above table reveals a surplus at the end of three years of £169, which has a present value of £127 at 10% (£169×.751), the same as the NPV in the previous table.'

'Can I just check that I have understood you correctly?' interrupted Colin. 'Let me interpret the last two sets of figures.

'If the cash flows generated by an investment during its life recover the original capital, plus interest at the required rate of return on the outstanding capital at the commencement of each year, then the project is acceptable.'

'That's right,' agreed the accountant. 'In a nutshell – an investment which yields an NPV of zero or greater is acceptable, whereas one that results in a negative NPV should be rejected.'

Self-check

Using a required rate of return of 15%, determine whether projects **A** and **B**, illustrated in the section on the accounting rate of return, are acceptable or not.

	DCF factor @ 15%	*Cash flow A*	*Present value – A*	*Cash flow B*	*Present value – B*
Year 0	1.000	– 11,000	– 11,000	– 11,000	– 11,000
Year 1	.870	+ 1,000	+ 870	+ 6,000	+ 5,220
Year 2	.756	+ 2,000	+ 1,512	+ 5,000	+ 3,780
Year 3	.658	+ 3,000	+ 1,974	+ 3,000	+ 1,974
Year 4	.572	+ 5,000	+ 2,860	+ 2,000	+ 1,144
Year 5	.497	+ 6,000	+ 2,982	+ 1,000	+ 497
Net present values			– 802		+ 1,615

Note: year 0 is the beginning of year 1.

A has a *negative* NPV and is not acceptable; *B* has a *positive* NPV and is acceptable.

Discounted cash flow – yield rate

Colin resumed the discussion: 'You have convinced me that our accounting rate of return approach could lead to wrong decisions, Jim, but I would feel lost not knowing what the rate of return on a project is. A positive NPV is fine but it cannot compare directly with financial market rates of return.'

'That's fair,' Jim said, 'but a yield rate can, in fact, be calculated. You will appreciate that a project with a *positive* NPV must be yielding a rate that is higher than the minimum rate of return, whereas a *negative* NPV means that the yield is less than the required rate. At zero NPV all the capital invested in a project has been recovered, and interest has been paid on the outstanding capital at the beginning of each year of the project's life.

'In order to "home in" on that yield rate it is necessary to try a first discounting rate and then, according to whether the NPV is above or below zero, choose a higher or lower rate, which hopefully will result in the NPV being the "other side" of zero. It really is a question of trial and error.

'The following example illustrates the approach:

	Cash flow	First trial factor @ 12%	PV	Second trial factor @ 9%	PV
	£		£		£
Year 0	– 100	1.000	– 100	1.000	– 100
1	+ 60	.893	+ 53.58	.917	+ 55.02
2	+ 55	.797	+ 43.84	.842	+ 46.31
Net present values			– 2.58		+ 1.33

'The yield rate of these cash flows is somewhere between 9% and 12%, and can be found by interpolation. This simply means that we add an arithmetic proportion of the difference between the two trial rates to the lower rate, according to how much the NPV of the latter is from zero, as shown below:

$$9\% + \left(\frac{1.33}{1.33+2.58} \times 3\%\right) = 10\% \text{ (approx.)}.$$

'In this example, the investment would be approved as long as the required rate of return is less than or equal to 10%. The DCF yield rate method compares that rate with the required rate. If the yield rate is higher than the required rate, the project is acceptable, if it is less, the project should be rejected.'

Activity

1 Draw a graph of the net present values of the above project at progressively increasing rates of interest, commencing with 1%. Plot NPVs on the vertical and rates of interest on the horizontal axes.

2 Does your graph confirm the yield rate calculated in the previous illustration?

1

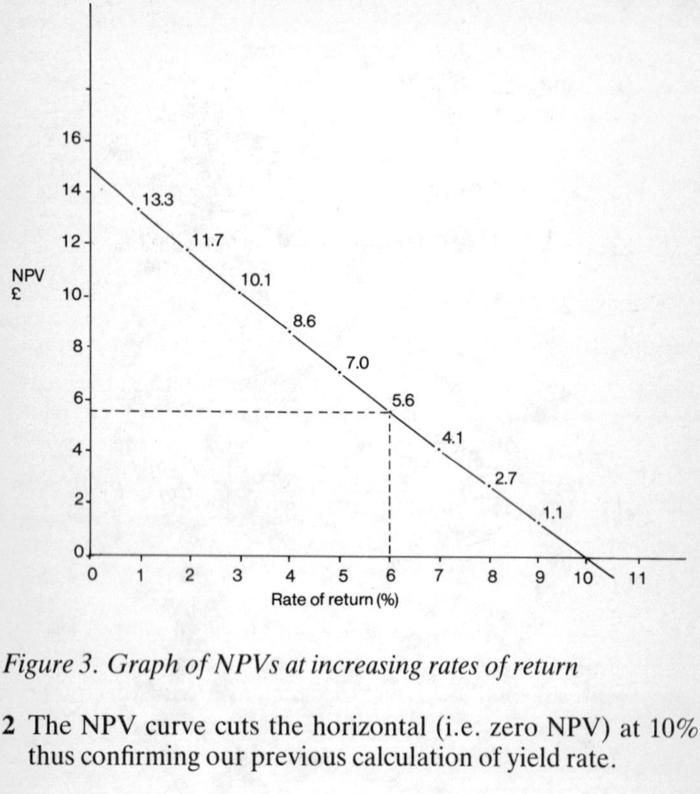

Figure 3. Graph of NPVs at increasing rates of return

2 The NPV curve cuts the horizontal (i.e. zero NPV) at 10%, thus confirming our previous calculation of yield rate.

Self-check

1 Calculate the yield rates of projects *A* and *B* used in the previous self-check question.

2 Explain whether you think the yield rate method will result in the same accept or reject decision as NPV.

Note: (a) Use year 0 for the beginning of year 1 in all future assignments in this book. (b) Put a minus sign immediately before *negative* cash flows; other cash flows will be treated as positive.

1 Yield rate – project *A*:

Year	*Cash flow* £	*PV @ 15% DCF rates**	*2nd trial DCF factors @ 10% rates*	*PV @ 10% DCF rates*
0	– 11,000	– 11,000	1.000	– 11,000
1	1,000	.870	.909	909
2	2,000	1,512	.826	1,652
3	3,000	1,974	.751	2,253
4	5,000	2,860	.683	3,415
5	6,000	2,982	.621	3,726
NPV		– 802	*NPV*	955

*See page 56 for present values at 15%.

By interpolation: $10\% + \left(\frac{955}{802+955} \times 5\%\right) = 12.7\%$.

Yield rate – project *B*:

Year	*Cash flow* £	*PV @ 15% DCF rates**	*2nd trial DCF factors @ 28% rates*	*PV @ 28% DCF rates*
0	– 11,000	– 11,000	1.000	– 11,000
1	6,000	5,220	.781	4,686
2	5,000	3,780	.610	3,050
3	3,000	1,974	.477	1,431
4	2,000	1,144	.373	746
5	1,000	497	.291	291
		1,615		– 796

*See page 56 for present values at 15%.

By interpolation: $15\% + \left(\frac{1{,}615}{1{,}615+796} \times 13\%\right) = 23.7\%$.

2 If *A* and *B* are considered separately, the yield rate method results in the same decisions as NPV. That is, *A* is not acceptable because its yield rate of 12.7% is below the required rate of return of 15%; whereas *B* would be approved because its rate of 23.7% is well above the required rate.

The yield rate can normally only be determined by trial and error, but a short-cut approach can be used when cash flows each year are assumed to be the same (i.e. an annuity). The present value of an annuity of £1 for increasing annual periods at various rates of interest can be found in Appendix B; the annuity factors simply being the totals of the factors to be found in each column in Appendix A. The present value of an annuity is the annual sum receivable multiplied by the appropriate annuity factor.

You will recall that the yield rate equates the cash flows of a project to zero. In the case of an annuity, if we divide the capital outlay of the project by the annual sum, we arrive at the annuity factor. Then referring to Appendix B, if we look along the row relating to the life of the project to find the annuity factor just calculated, the yield rate will be the column in which that factor can be found.

For example, if capital outlay is £3,791 and cash inflows £1,000 for each of five years, the annuity factor is £3,791÷£1,000=3.791. Looking along the five year row, the factor nearest to 3.791 is in the 10% discount column. This is the yield rate.

What do we mean by cash flow?

Forecasts of market size, market share, selling prices, cost of capital and operating costs involve skilled and painstaking work before final figures emerge. The arithmetic of DCF is simple but if the underlying figures and assumptions are suspect, the relative sophistication of discounting will be wasted.

When compiling proposed investment cash flows three principles apply:

- Include *incremental* cash flows only; that is, those that will occur because the project goes ahead. Accordingly, costs such as rent and rates, which are already incurred, will not be included in individual projects. This would not be so, of course, if a new building were to be rented specifically for a new project.
- Include *any cash flow changes* caused by the investment

decision. For example, a warehouse that might be used for a proposed project could alternatively be let. The rent forgone is an opportunity cost treated as a cash outflow resulting from the investment decision.

- Do not confuse profit with cash. In particular, depreciation is normally deducted as a cost in profit measurement each year. In investment terms, depreciation should not be treated as an *annual* cash flow, because it relates to assets normally purchased and paid for at the commencement of a project.

The relationship between cash flow and profit measurement requires a closer examination. The statement below shows the orthodox calculation of profit attributable to a proposed investment, following by some notes regarding its compilation.

		Year		
	1	*2*	*3*	*4*
	£	£	£	£
Sales	10,000	8,000	8,000	6,000
Variable costs	5,000	4,000	4,000	3,000
Fixed costs	2,500	2,500	2,500	2,500
Net profit	2,500	1,500	1,500	500

Notes:

1 Included in fixed costs each year are amounts for:
  a *depreciation* of £1,500 for a new machine to be bought especially for the project at a total cost of £6,000;
  b hire of machine specifically for the project – £500;
  c *an allocation* of the establishment and administration costs which are already incurred £500.

2 Variable costs includes £600 wages payable to skilled workers who would be idle but still employed by the company if this project did not proceed.

3 Sales of £2,000 in year 1 will not be paid for by a customer until the end of year 2.

4 If the project did not go ahead, the space it would otherwise occupy could be let at an annual rental of £300.

5 If the new machine was bought, an old machine would be sold for £400.

6 The new machine would have a scrap value of £500 at the end of year 4.

Activity

Make a brief note of how each of the items listed above should be treated in your compilation of *investment* cash flows, bearing in mind the principles mentioned earlier in the section.

1 a *Depreciation* – exclude from annual cash outflows. Cost of the machine to be shown as purchased at the beginning of year 1.
b *Machine hire* – include as an incremental cash outflow.
c *Allocated administrative costs* – exclude as a cost; will be expended anyway.
2 *Skilled workers' wages* – exclude; will be paid to workers regardless of this project.
3 *Sales* – transfer £2,000 to year 2 cash inflow.
4 *Rent receivable* – *opportunity cost*; include as an outflow.
5 Sale of old machine – bring in as a cash inflow at the commencement of the project.
6 *Salvage value of new machine* – bring in as an inflow of cash at the end of the project's life.

Activity

Assuming a rate of return of 15%, and using the adjusted relevant cash flows in the above example, show by calculating the net present value, whether the new machine should be purchased.

	Year					
	0	*1*	*2*	*3*	*4*	*NPV*
Capital cost	{ – 6,000 400					
Sales		8,000	10,000	8,000	6,000	
Variable costs		– 4,400	– 3,400	– 3,400	– 2,400	
Machine hire		– 500	– 500	– 500	– 500	
Rent (opportunity cost)		– 300	– 300	– 300	– 300	
Machine salvage					500	
Net cash flow	– 5,600	2,800	5,800	3,800	3,300	
DCF factor @ 15%	1,000	.870	.756	.658	.572	
Present value	– 5,600	2,436	4,385	2,500	1,888	5,609

Notes:

1 Capital or revenue cash outflows at the start of the project are shown as 'year 0', since they are assumed to have occurred on 1 January in the first year.

2 Although it does not apply to this project, capital outflows occurring other than at the beginning should be included in the year in which they happen.

3 Revenue cash flows, in or out, are assumed to take place at the year end, to coincide with the discount rate factors which also relate to the year end. This is normally an acceptable approximation but, if shorter period discounting is more appropriate to certain types of investment decisions, tables of such rates can be obtained.

Self-check

State with reasons whether each of the following items should be included in the forecast cash flows of an investment proposal:

a Depreciation of the machine to be specially purchased for the project.

b Cost savings resulting from the implementation of the project.

c The salary of a supervisor who is currently employed by the firm, and who will continue to be so.

d An increase in the sales of other products, consequent upon going ahead with the new project.

e The book value of an existing machine which will be replaced by the new machine.

a No. Depreciation is merely an accounting method of spreading the prepaid cost of an asset over its estimated useful life.
b Yes. These are *incremental* cash flows – they happen because the project is accepted.
c No. This is a cost to which the firm is already committed, and it will not be affected by the project.
d Yes. These are *incremental* cash flows; but only include the *difference* between selling price and variable costs – *not* the full additional sales value.
e No. Unless the amount realised upon sale or trade-in of the old machine coincides with book value.

Working capital

The resources used by an investment, particularly in manufacturing businesses, include not only buildings, plant and machinery but also increases in working capital; extra stocks of raw materials and work in progress to support the manufacturing operations; additional stocks of finished goods and debtors to support the selling function. Cash will be expended in the early years of a project to build up these resources but, because it is working capital and not machinery that will be worn out by the end of the project life, most of it will be recovered – probably in the project's last year, save for loses normally associated with working capital, such as bad debts and stock spoilage or waste.

Self-check

Paul Schofield wants to lease a shop for three years to sell cassette tapes and discs. The shop rental is very low at £500 per annum payable in arrear, but he estimates he will have to purchase initial stock costing £10,000. Thereafter, he will replenish stock sold on a weekly basis.

He estimates the net cash flow from product sales – that is, cash sales less the direct cost of the goods sold – will be:

	£
Year 1	7,000
Year 2	8,000
Year 3	9,000

Assuming that he will recover 90% of his stock value by the end of year 3, and that other annual operating costs will be £3,000, should Paul open his shop? His required rate of return is 18%.

	Year				
	0	*1*	*2*	*3*	*NPV*
Stock outlay	– 10,000			9,000	
Shop rental		– 500	– 500	– 500	
Other running costs		– 3,000	– 3,000	– 3,000	
Net cash sales		7,000	8,000	9,000	
Net cash flow	– 10,000	3,500	4,500	14,500	
DCF factors @ 18%	1.000	.847	.718	.609	
Present value	– 10,000	2,965	3,231	8,831	5,027

The substantial surplus NPV indicates that Paul should proceed with his venture as long as he has no better alternative in mind.

Note particularly that his stock outlay is substantially recovered by the end of the venture.

The effect of taxation on cash flows

Inexorably, the Inland Revenue will take their slice from investment cash flows. It is true that, as individuals, we are entitled to certain personal allowances against income, but beyond that taxation will reduce our net cash flows. At the standard rate of income tax at first, then at progressively higher rates.

Limited companies pay corporation tax on their assessable profits at a standard rate, to be progressively reduced from 1984, with some relief for companies not reaching a certain level of profit.

Some relief is afforded to businesses, however, which though not allowed to deduct depreciation from profit, are allowed to deduct capital allowances against profit for new plant and machinery, industrial buildings, equipment and motor cars at the following rates (1983–84):

	Capital allowances on cost
Plant, machinery and equipment	100% in the year of purchase
Motorcars	25% per annum on reducing value
Industrial buildings	75% in the year of purchase then 4% per annum up to 100%

However, commencing 1984–85, the 100% allowance will be progressively reduced to 25% per annum. In line with other project cash flows, it is important that effect is given to taxation when it is actually paid. A one-year time-lag is normally associated with taxation payable on project cash flows. Conversely, capital allowances on project assets will *reduce* the taxation payable, and should be recorded as cash inflows, again time-lagged by one year after the relevant assets are paid for. This implies that any capital asset purchased *during* year 1 will affect tax paid in year 2.

Further, when assets which have previously attracted capital allowances are eventually sold for scrap or are traded in, tax is payable on the amount received.

As an example of the effect of taxation upon investments, the cash flows shown on page 63 are repeated below, with an assumed corporation tax rate of 50% applied to capital allowances, and net revenue cash flows.

	Year 0	*1*	*2*	*3*	*4*	*5*	*NPV*
Capital cost	−5,600				500		
Capital allowances			2,800			− 250	
Taxable net cash flows		2,800	5,800	3,800	2,800		
Corporation tax			−1,400	−2,900	−1,900	−1,400	
Net cash flow	−5,600	2,800	7,200	900	1,400	−1,650	
DCF factor @ 15%	1.000	.870	.756	.658	.572	.497	
Present values	−5,600	2,436	5,443	592	801	− 820	2,852

Even after adjustment for taxation this proposal still looks good, thanks largely to the early cash inflow from the capital allowance. A point to note from this example is the additional year 5 brought in to accommodate the negative cash flows arising from the tax payment time-lag. The assumption being that the company is in an overall taxpaying position in that year, and indeed in every year of the project's life.

If the company had not been paying tax on its overall activities at the start of the project, and perhaps for a year or two more, so that the otherwise taxable cash flows of this project are absorbed by losses elsewhere, corporation tax would not be shown as paid for those years. Likewise, the capital allowances would be carried forward until a year in which profits exist for them to be set off against.

Self-check

1 Explain whether the taxation effects of the following either (a) increase or (b) decrease the net present value of an investment.

(i) capital allowances;
(ii) cost savings;
(iii) incremental costs.

2 When compiling investment cash flows, adjustments for taxation allowances or deductions are made in the same year as the cash flows to which they relate. Is this statcment correct? Explain.

3 At the end of its useful life it is expected that an electric kiln can be sold for £5,000. Its cost now is £50,000. In the investment appraisal cash flows, would it be correct to show £45,000 as the net cost of the kiln in year 0?

4 If the company contemplating installing the kiln is expected to be in its current non-taxpaying position for the next four years, what affect would this have on your answer to question **3**?

1 (i) *Increase.* Capital allowances effectively reduce asset costs and therefore increase net present value.

(ii) *Increase.* 'Savings' implies that cash, which would otherwise flow out, does not do so. This is equivalent to an inflow.

(iii) *Decrease.* Costs result in cash outflows, and therefore reduce net present value.

2 The statement is not correct. These tax adjustments *are* calculated on the related cash flows, capital or revenue, but are accounted for as cash inflows or outflows in the period in which they affect payment of tax to the Inland Revenue.

3 It would not be correct. The original cost and the salvage value occur in different years, and should be dealt with accordingly. In addition, the cost of the kiln would attract tax capital allowances at say 52%, to be treated as a cash *inflow* of £26,000 in year 2. Likewise, its sales value of £5,000 would be taxed and treated as a cash *outflow* of £2,600 in the year following its sale.

4 The cash flow relating to the capital allowance of £26,000 would be delayed until year 5, and then take effect if the whole amount could be absorbed by the *assessable profit* for that year. Any unrelieved balance of capital allowances can be carried forward. The time value of the capital allowance is, of course, reduced by its delayed set-off against profit.

Investment appraisal and inflation

If businesses are to prosper they must manage inflation successfully. They must ensure that costs are controlled and that any unavoidable increases in costs of materials, labour and overheads are anticipated and reflected in selling price policy.

If the rate of inflation is expected to be zero for the foreseeable future, investors will expect rates of return on their investments solely related to the *risks* to which their money is exposed – risks both of operations and time. An investor may happily accept such a *real* rate of return of say 5% knowing that his £100 investment will grow to £105 in one year.

However, if the general level of prices is expected to increase by 10% in the coming year, the investor would look for a return of approximately 15% to maintain his purchasing power in real terms. The 15% he would receive is known as the 'money' or 'nominal' rate of interest. If the inflation forecast proved to be correct, the 'real' rate of return would be his risk-related 5%. If, on the other hand, the inflation rate was 12%, the investor's real rate of return would be only 15% – 12%=3%.

A more accurate *real* rate can be calculated by using the following formula:

$$r = ((1+m) \div (1+p)) - 1$$

where r = the real rate of return
m = the money rate of return
p = the rate of inflation

Substituting the figures in the previous paragraph we have:

$$r = ((1+.15) \div (1+.12)) - 1 = 2.7\%.$$

To find the money rate of interest when the real rate and the inflation rate are given, the above formula can be translated to:

$$1+m = (1+r)(1+p).$$

Thus if the real rate is 6% and inflation expected to be 8%, investors would look for a money rate of return of:

$$1+m = (1+.06)(1+.08)$$
and $$1+m = 1.14$$
$$m = .14 \text{ or } 14\%.$$

If business projects cannot satisfy investors' expected *money* rates of return, finance will not be forthcoming. It follows that investment cash flows must be stated in *money* terms, at the actual £s expected to flow during each period of a project's life, *because the required rate of return incorporates expectations of inflation over the same period.* We will then be matching inflation-adjusted cash flows with an inflation-priced rate of return.

Activity

Ultra Engineering plc wants to purchase a machine costing £80,000 to produce a component for the motorcar industry. *At present prices and costs* the annual cash inflows from this five-year venture are expected to be £20,000, and at the end of five years the machine could be sold for £5,000 at present prices. The company's target rate of return over this five-year period is 12%. Using only the information given, show by calculating its NPV whether the project should be accepted. Ignore taxation.

Year	*Machine*	*Annual cash flow*	*PV factors @ 12%*	*Present value*
	£	£	£	£
0	– 80,000		1.000	– 80,000
1–5		20,000	3.605*	72,100
5	5,000		.567	2,835
Net present value				– 5,065

*Total of the individual factors for the first five years.

On the basis of the information given the investment should not proceed because it yields a negative NPV.

However, we may not have been consistent in our appraisal if inflation is expected to continue at a compound rate of 5% per annum during the next five years. The target rate of 12% presumably takes inflation into account, and therefore the project cash flows ought also to be adjusted for inflation.

Activity

Reappraise the Ultra proposal taking into account a 5% compound rate of inflation on all cash flows.

Year	*Machine*	*Annual cash flows*	*Net cash flow*	*PV factors @ 12%*	*Present value*
	£	£	£	£	£
0	– 80,000		– 80,000	1.000	– 80,000
1		20,000×1.05= 21,000	21,000	.893	18,753
2		21,000×1.05= 22,050	22,050	.797	17,574
3		22,050×1.05= 23,153	23,153	.712	16,485
4		23,153×1.05= 24,310	24,310	.636	15,461
5	6,381*	24,310×1.05= 25,526	31,907	.567	18,091
Net present value					6,364

*5,000×$(1.05)^5$=£6,381.

Inflation does not affect all cash flows at the same rate. For example, capital allowances are delayed in their effect upon tax cash flows, but as they are related to a *fixed* number of £s, no adjustment for inflation is made when the allowances are eventually deducted from tax paid.

Selling prices that are fixed by long-term contract, real wages and costs of energy-related resources are all examples of cash flows that may deviate from the general movement in the level of prices during the life of a project.

The section on working capital indicated that additional stocks of materials might be occasioned by the acceptance of a new project. Such stocks will have to be replaced continually at inflated prices, but this can be taken care of in the forecast cash flow related to purchases. In the final year of a project, the rundown of these stocks will be shown as an inflation-adjusted cash inflow, and not at the prices paid at the commencement of the project.

Self-check

1 a Using the appropriate formula, calculate to three places of decimals the real rate of return on a security if the money rate is 19% and the rate of inflation 12%.

b Using the same formula, calculate the money rate required to satisfy a real rate of 4% with a rate of inflation of 10%.

2 'If a company's required rate of return is applied to investment cash flows compiled at today's prices, the resulting NPV will indicate whether or not to accept the proposal.' Is this statement correct? Explain.

1 a

Real rate of return= ((1+money rate)÷(1+inflation rate))−1=(1.19÷1.12)−1=6.3%.

b

1+money rate= (1+real rate) (1+inflation rate)
1+money rate= 1.04×1.10
money rate= 14.4%.

2 The statement is not correct, because the required rate of return includes an estimated weighted element for inflation. Likewise, the project cash flows should also be stated at actual *money* values, that is, adjusted for rising prices. All cash flows may not be adjusted by the same inflation factor.

Review

Pike Electronics were attempting to break into the video game market. Colin Pike designed a low-cost box and display, with associated electronics, and ten original video games can be purchased from a software house, at a cost of £50,000.

Machinery to manufacture the video boxes will cost £100,000 now, but at the end of five years will only fetch £5,000 at today's prices, on the second-hand market. Additional working capital of £20,000 will be required immediately, all recoverable at the end of year 5.

Factory space to manufacture the games can be created by giving up space devoted to manufacture of a component that would currently cost £1,000 a year more to purchase from an outside supplier. Machinery used in the making of this component would be sold for £10,000 immediately.

Rates, heating and lighting costs are presently paid on this part of the factory at £500 per annum.

Sales are forecast at 2,000 video games a year for five years, and each game would be sold for £80 in the first year. It is expected, however, that this price can be raised by £5 in each of the following four years, to recoup rising costs, despite increasing competition.

The variable manufacturing and selling cost of each video, at present prices of materials, labour and overheads, is £50. Additional supervisory cost of £2,000 per annum (at current cost) would be needed for the new project.

5% inflation is expected in each of the five years.

Pike will continue to be in a taxpaying position for the next six years,and he currently pays corporation tax of 50%on his assessable profits.

Machinery attracts 100% capital allowances, whilst the software purchases can be written off against profits for taxation purposes, in equal instalments over five years.

Pike requires a rate of return of 15%.

Required

Prepare net present value calculations to help Pike decide whether he should proceed with this project.

Working 1

	Year 0	1	2	3	4	5	6
	£	£	£	£	£	£	£
Machinery	– 90,000					6,381	
Software	– 50,000						
Capital allowances:							
Machinery			45,000				– 3,190
Software			5,000	5,000	5,000	5,000	5,000
Working capital	– 20,000					25,525	
Capital cash flows	–160,000	—	50,000	5,000	5,000	36,906	1,810

Working 2

	0	1	2	3	4	5	6
Sales		160,000	170,000	180,000	190,000	200,000	
Costs		108,150	113,558	119,235	125,197	131,457	
Pre-tax cash-flow		51,850	56,442	60,765	64,803	68,543	
less Corpn tax			25,925	28,221	30,382	32,401	34,272
Revenue cash flows		51,850	30,517	32,544	34,421	36,142	–34,272
Net cash flows	–160,000	51,850	80,517	37,544	39,421	73,048	–32,462
DCF factors @ 15%	1.000	.870	.756	.658	.572	.497	.432
Present values	–160,000	45,110	60,871	24,704	22,549	36,305	–14,024

Notes:

1. As the NPV is £15,515 the project should go ahead.
2. The sale value of the old machine, £10,000, reduces the cost of the new machine to £90,000.
3. Working capital recovered has been adjusted for inflation.
4. Cost in year 1 comprise variable £100,000; extra component cost £1,000; supervisory £2,000; plus 5% inflation added; thereafter costs are inflated by 5% in each year.

4 Limitations of discounted cash flow

NPV or yield rate – which should we use?

When we apply the *yield rate* method to discover whether an investment is worthwhile, we ascertain the rate of return that discounts the cash flows of a project to zero. If that rate is higher than the *required* rate of return the project is acceptable.

Using net present value, any project with a *positive* NPV after applying the *required* rate of return to the cash flows is deemed acceptable. It follows that, if NPV is positive, the yield rate must be more than the required rate of return to discount the cash flows to zero.

Figure 3 shows the relationship between NPV and yield rate. It shows that if the minimum rate is 6%, NPV is positive at £5.60. The curve on the graph is seen to cut the horizontal axis (zero NPV) at 10%, which is higher than the minimum required rate. Whichever method is used, an 'accept' decision is indicated.

Most investment decisions feature independent projects whose viability will be judged according to whether they can meet the required rate of return criteria. Both NPV and yield rate point to the same decision.

Mutually exclusive investments – with equal capital outlays

One way for a business to expand is to purchase the assets of a similar business. A decision to do this would, of course, be preceded by a rigorous investment appraisal procedure, and it is possible that the decision might lie between the choice of one of two alternative companies. The two alternatives would be *mutually exclusive*, in that the choice of one will exclude the other.

Similarly, whether to buy one machine or another, or build one type of factory or another, are also examples of mutually exclusive proposals.

Activity

A company is faced with the choice of one of two investment opportunities, *A* or *B*. The capital cost of each is £200 and their estimated cash inflows are:

	A	*B*
Year 1	40	200
2	240	60

Assuming a cost of capital of 7%, calculate **(a)** the NPV, and **(b)** the yield rate, of each project. Which project would you choose?

a NPV:

		A		*B*	
Year	*DCF factors @ 7%*	*Net cash flow*	*Present value*	*Net cash flow*	*Present value*
	£	£	£	£	£
0	1.000	– 200	– 200	– 200	– 200
1	.935	40	37	200	187
2	.873	240	210	60	52
Net present values			47		39

b Yield rate – A:

		Trial @ 15%		*Trial @ 22%*	
Year	*Net cash flow*	*Factor*	*PV*	*Factor*	*PV*
0	– 200	1.000	– 200	1.000	– 200
1	40	.870	35	.820	33
2	240	.756	181	.672	161
			16		– 6

By interpolation 15% + ((16 ÷ 22) × 7%) = 20%.

Yield Rate – B:

		Trial @ 20%		*Trial @ 28%*	
Year	*Net cash flow*	*Factor*	*PV*	*Factor*	*PV*
0	– 200	1.000	– 200	1.000	– 200
1	200	.833	167	.781	156
2	60	.694	42	.610	37
			9		– 7

By interpolation 20% + ((9÷16)×8%)=24.5%.

Comparison between the two methods:
Using NPV, the choice would be *A*. Using yield rate, the choice would be *B*.

How can we resolve this conflict in ranking? First, a diagram will help to show how the problem arises. In figure 4 the net present values of each of the proposals have been plotted at progressive rates of return.

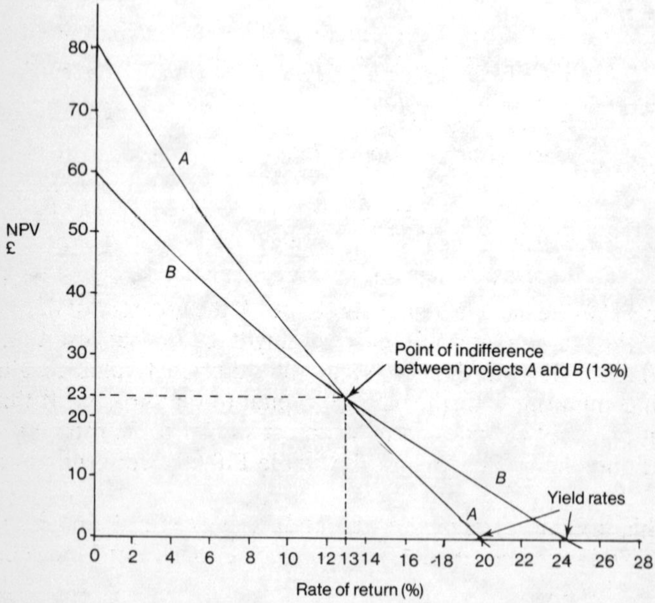

Figure 4. Mutually exclusive projects

Note how the slope of *A*'s curve is steeper than that of *B*. This more accelerated fall in value is because the *later* heavy cash flow of *A* is discounted more than the earlier cash flow of *B*. However, up to about 13% *A* remains superior to *B*, and if the required rate of return were below 13%, *A* would be chosen. For all rates beyond 13%, *B* comes out on top whether NPV or yield rate is used.

As the specified rate of return is 7%, and this is below 13%, *A* is the 'best buy', *because it adds more value to the business* after meeting the cost of capital.

Thus, the choice between mutually exclusive projects can best be made by using the NPV method because it will always result in choosing the alternative that adds the greater value to a business.

Mutually exclusive investments – with different capital outlays

The following figures compare the NPVs and yield rates for investment proposals *X* and *Y*. The two projects are mutually exclusive.

Project	*Asset cost*	*Cash flow per annum*	*Life*	*NPV @ 8%*	*Yield rate*
	£	£		£	%
X	5,000	1,200	10 yrs	3,052	20
Y	10,000	2,200	10 yrs	4,762	17

Again we have reversals of ranking between the two DCF approaches. *X* has the higher yield rate, *Y* the greater NPV.

In this case a normal reaction might be to suggest that, although *Y* has the higher NPV, the additional value results from committing a further £5,000 capital to that project. If this addition could be invested in a project similar to *X*, total NPV could then be greater than if the whole £10,000 were sunk into *Y*.

This argument might be acceptable, but only if finance is restricted for some reason. Without such a constraint *Y* must be chosen because:

- all the capital invested in that project is recovered;
- interest has been provided at the required rate of return;

- there is a net addition of £4,762 to the wealth of the company.

If there *is* another worthwhile investment requiring £5,000, then as long as that project satisfied the cost of capital of 8%, and the finance is available, it should proceed independently of *Y*.

The weakness of the yield rate approach, as regards mutually exclusive investments, is that it is only a *relative* measure of profitability. Whether the investment is £100 or £1 million the yield rate could be the same. Net present value, on the other hand, is an *absolute* measure of profitability.

Activity

From the above example it can be inferred that the £5,000 additional capital invested in *Y* has generated a cash flow of £2,200 – £1,200=£1,000 per annum for ten years.

a Calculate the NPV and yield rate of this *incremental* investment of £5,000.

b What does the result of your calculations imply?

a NPV:

(£1,000×6.710*)−£5,000=£6,710−£5,000=£1,710.

*This is the total of 10 years' discounting factors at 8%.

Yield rate:

@ 12% (£1,000×5.650)−£5,000=£650

@ 18% (£1,000×4.494)−£5,000=−£506

By interpolation 12%+(650÷[(650+506)×6%]=15% (approx.).

b The incremental £5,000 has yielded an NPV of £1,710 (this can be checked by reference to the original table) and a yield rate of 15%. The latter is better than the cut-off rate of 8%, and confirms that *Y* is superior to *X*, for it does everything that *X* can do, and also adds further value of £1,710 to the firm.

Given a choice between mutually exclusive investments, the NPV approach is safer to use than yield rate, but if knowledge of the latter is needed by management, it can be calculated on the incremental method demonstrated in the last activity.

Self-check

The Phew Cosmetic Co. has to decide which of two tube-filling machines it should purchase. The computed DCF data relevant to each is as follows:

Machine	*Capital cost*	*Net cash inflows Year 1*	*2*	*3*	*Yield rate*
	£	£	£	£	%
A	150,000	100,000	60,000	43,500	20
B	204,000	120,000	100,000	50,000	18

The managing director suggests that because machine *A* has the higher yield rate at lower capital cost, it should be preferred to *B*.

a Calculate the NPV of each proposal, assuming a cost of capital of 10%.
b Which of the machines would you choose based upon NPV?
c Which of the two DCF methods would you advise the managing director to use, and why?
d Is it possible to use yield rate to determine the better machine?
e If the cost of capital was 15% would your advice be different?

a Machine *A* £23,129; machine *B* £25,230.
b Machine *B*, as it has a higher NPV.
c NPV, because it reveals that machine *B* adds more value to the firm than machine *A*, after paying interest at the appropriate rate, and recovering its capital cost.
d Yes, by calculating the yield rate on the incremental cash flows. This would merely confirm the accept/reject decision already made by using NPV.
e Yes, the NPVs of *A* and *B* would be £10,983 and £8,900 respectively, making *A* the better 'buy' now. The arithmetic of compounding causes *B* to have a higher NPV at all rates up to approximately 12.5%, after that *A* is superior under both methods.

Projects having more than one yield rate

Most investments follow the pattern of an initial capital outlay followed by a series of cash inflows.

Very rarely, however, a project may have further *negative* cash flows during its life. For example, an open-cast mining operation requiring an expensive reinstatement of the land after the coal has been extracted could result in a negative cash flow in one year. In such cases it is possible for the project to have as many yield rates as there are changes in arithmetic signs during the cash flow series.

If yield rate is preferred by management, how is this problem to be overcome?

Activity

Using rates of return of 10% and 25% calculate the net present values of the following cash flows:

Year 0	*1*	*2*
£	£	£
– 1,000	2,350	– 1,375

	Year 0	*1*	2	*NPV*
	£	£	£	£
PV @ 10%	– 1,000	2,136	– 1,136	0
PV @ 25%	– 1,000	1,880	– 880	0

As you can see, two yield rates are possible here! Figure 5, which charts the NPVs of the cash flows at increasing rates of return, illustrates how this comes about.

Clearly there is no unique yield rate – there are two! However, NPV to the rescue! At required rates of return of between 10% and 25%, NPV is positive and therefore acceptable, outside these the project does not meet the required rate.

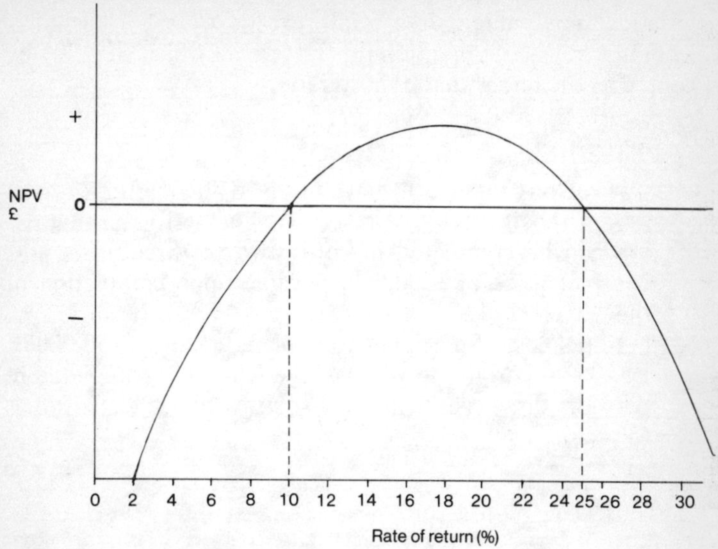

Figure 5. Multiple yield rates

Projects with unequal lives

Whatever the estimated lives of *independent* investment proposals, each one should be appraised upon its own merits, and accepted or rejected according to whether:

- it comes within the overall strategic plan of the company;
- it meets the minimum rate of return.

A problem of ranking projects according to profitability does, arise, however, when finance is restricted and capital has to be shared between competing projects. How this problem might be resolved is discussed later in this chapter.

But what of mutually exclusive projects with different lives? The achievement of the common objective by one of the alternatives before the other may present some advantage when the supply of finance is restricted, if the earlier released capital can yield some immediate benefit on another project.

If finance is freely available for all other projects, this benefit is illusory. The choice can then be made by opting for the one that adds most value to the firm – except when the customer specifies a date of completion for the project which can only be attained by the one with the shorter life.

Self-check

Corax Construction plc have received an enquiry for most urgent repair work to a reservoir. They estimate that the job can be completed in either two or three years at a contract price of £200,000, payable upon completion of the work.

Initial cost of machinery and plant would be £50,000 or £29,000 according to whether the work was completed in two or three years respectively; with other costs as follows:

Completion time	*Year* 1	2	3
	£	£	£
2 years	55,000	55,000	
3 years	40,000	40,000	40,000

The plant and machinery would have no residual value at the end of the contract.

Using a rate of return of 10%, but ignoring taxation, calculate which alternative is more attractive.

Year	*Net cash flows 2-year completion*	*3-year completion*	*DCF factors @ 10%*	*Present values Two years*	*Three years*
	£	£	£	£	£
0	– 50,000	– 29,000	1.000	– 50,000	– 29,000
1	– 55,000	– 40,000	.909	– 49,995	– 36,360
2	145,000	– 40,000	.826	119,770	– 33,040
3		160,000	.751		120,160
Net present values				19,775	21,760

The three-year completion date would be more profitable to Corax, but only marginally so. Earlier recovery of capital costs, less uncertainty and, possibly, taxation advantages might sway the company in favour of the shorter life project.

Note: the yield rates are approximately 24% and 22% respectively, which is the opposite of the NPV ranking. For reasons already discussed, however, this is not an acceptable method of appraising this mutually exclusive project.

How often should assets be replaced?

Next to buying a house, the largest capital expenditure for most people is the purchase of a car. Unlike houses, cars have short lives and have to be replaced frequently.

Activity

Given that you normally replace your car with a similar one, what are the major financial factors to take into account in deciding to replace your vehicle?

Your biggest problem is probably one of finance; but assuming that is readily available, you would intuitively feel that the optimum time to replace is when costs are at their lowest. The major financial factors to consider are:

- *initial cost* – as an annual cost this reduces the longer the vehicle is kept;
- *maintenance* – increases as the car ages and parts become worn;
- *trade-in value* – reduces with the age of the car (unless you keep it until it becomes an antique!)

Assume that you can buy a car for £5,000 and that its operating costs and trade-in values for four years, at present prices, are as follows:

Year	*Operating costs*	*Trade-in values*
	£	£
1	100	4,000
2	200	3,500
3	350	3,000
4	500	2,400

One method of solving the minimum cost problem is to schedule the costs and trade-in values of replacing the car annually, every two years, every three years and every four years. In our example, costs would have to be scheduled for twelve years (the lowest common multiple of 1, 2, 3 and 4) and comparison made between the *present values of the total costs* of 12 one-year, 6 two-year, 4 three-year and 3 four-year replacement cycles.

Adjustments would have to be made for inflation, and the cost of capital and taxation forecast for the twelve-year period – a rather unwieldy and daunting task.

A simpler alternative approach is not to adjust present costs and values for inflation, and to match this by discounting the cash flows for the four alternative life cycles, at a rate which also excludes inflation.

Assuming a 10% cost of capital (excluding inflation) for the next four years, and ignoring taxation for the sake of simplicity, the present values of costs associated with the different lives are shown below:

Year	*Cash flows*	*DCF factors @ 10%*	*Present values of different lives – years*			
			1	*2*	*3*	*4*
			£	£	£	£
0	– 5,000	1.000	– 5,000	– 5,000	– 5,000	– 5,000
1	– 100	.909	– 91	– 91	– 91	– 91
2	– 200	.826		– 165	– 165	– 165
3	– 350	.751			– 263	– 263
4	– 500	.683				– 342
Trade-in values:						
1	4,000	.909	3,636			
2	3,500	.826		2,891		
3	3,000	.751			2,253	
4	2,400	.683				1,639
Present value of net costs			– 1,455	– 2,365	– 3,266	– 4,222

Mistakenly, it might be thought that if we divide the present value of each optional life by the appropriate number of years we arrive at the average annual cost. This assumes, however, that the *present value* of equal amounts paid in each of, say, two years, is their sum.

At 10% the present value of £1 paid in each of two successive years is £1.736. Conversely, the *equivalent annual payment* for those two years is not £1.736÷2, but £1.736 divided by 1.736. The latter is the *annuity factor* at 10% for two years, and is simply the total of the present values of £1 paid in each of two successive years (see Appendix A). Annuity factors at other rates of interest can be found in Appendix B.

To find the *equivalent annual cost* for each alternative life, divide each present value by the annuity factor appropriate to the number of years as follows:

		Life-years		
	1	*2*	*3*	*4*
	£	£	£	£
Present value costs	– 1,455	– 2,365	– 3,266	– 4,222
Annuity factor @ 10%	.909	1.736	2.487	3.170
Equivalent annual cost	– 1,601	– 1,362	– 1,313	– 1,332

Cost is lowest at the end of three years, therefore replacement should take place every three years to keep costs to a minimum.

When to replace with different assets

If we are considering *when* to replace an asset with an *identical* asset, the equivalent annual cost approach discussed in the last section can be used. Replacement assets, however, are very often different from existing assets, both as regards costs and productivity. When these differences are substantial, the replacement decision must be based upon a comparison of replacement cost with the present value of *cost savings* plus *contribution* from additional sales.

In other cases the decision can be made, first, by ascertaining the *minimum equivalent annual cost* of continuing to operate the existing asset for one, two, three or more years; then comparing this with the *lowest* equivalent annual cost of the replacement machine.

For example, the figures below relate to an existing machine:

Year	*0*	*1*	*2*	*3*
	£	£	£	£
Sale value of machine	3,000	2,000	1,200	500
Operating costs		1,000	1,600	1,900

Activity

Assuming a cost of capital of 10% and ignoring taxation, calculate the equivalent annual costs of running the machine for a further one, two and three years.

Hint: treat the present sale value of the machine, £3,000, as an initial *cost* of continuing for *each* of the alternative periods. Otherwise, schedule the figures in exactly the same way as illustrated in the last section.

Year	*Cash flows*	*DCF factors @ 10%*	*Present values of continuing for 1*	*2*	*3*	*Years*
	£		£	£	£	
0	– 3,000	1.000	– 3,000	– 3,000	– 3,000	
1	– 1,000	.909	– 909	– 909	– 909	
2	– 1,600	.826		– 1,322	– 1,322	
3	– 1,900	.751			– 1,427	
Trade-in values:						
1	2,000	.909	1,818			
2	1,200	.826		991		
3	500	.751			376	
Present value of net costs			– 2,091	– 4,240	– 6,282	
Annuity factor @ 10%			.909	1.736	2.487	
Equivalent annual cost			– 2,300	– 2,442	– 2,526	

Having obtained this information, we compare it with the equivalent annual costs of the replacement machine.

For example, if the minimum annual cost of the new machine is £2,000 for a five-year life, the existing machine should be replaced immediately, as its lowest annual running cost is £2,300 at the end of the first year.

Self-check

Assume that the new machine has a five-year life, and that its minimum equivalent annual cost is £2,460 in year 4. When would you replace the existing machine?

At the end of two years, because the existing machine is less costly until then. After that, the replacement machine should be purchased for a four-year life.

Ranking projects when capital is rationed

Theoretically, a company ought to be able to finance all investment proposals promising a return higher than its cost of capital. This assumes that the providers of capital have full knowledge of the future prospects of the business, and that this is reflected in the costs of their finance, be they shareholders or lenders.

If the business 'smoke signals' indicate either a higher degree of uncertainty in future operations or that the business is already relying too heavily upon *borrowed* funds, the market should react and increase the cost of finance to that company. Even then the supply of funds should never 'dry up' as long as projects exist which yield higher returns than the cost of capital.

Capital rationing does exist, however, but it appears to be largely self-imposed by businesses for the following reasons:

a Owners of small businesses may rely solely upon retained profit for growth, either because they do not want to relinquish control or because they simply dislike borrowing.
b A policy regarding rate of growth may be related to what is considered to be management's ability to cope with growth.
c A company may defer going to the market for further funds until market conditions are more favourable.
d Companies may plan to keep assets under construction in a period down to a certain level, to prevent a lowering of the rate of return on assets *published in the annual accounts*.

Even though companies plan to restrict their growth for the reasons stated in **a**, **b** and **c** above, the costs of capital will ultimately reflect these policies, and rationing of funds is therefore regulated by the market. All projects yielding positive net present values at the market-adjusted cost of capital should proceed.

If rationing is market-imposed because of overgearing, it ought not to be a continuing restriction, because it will invariably be corrected by the injection of more equity finance into the capital structure of the business.

Priority in allocating capital will be given, first, to essential expenditure on research and development, and to comply with health and safety regulations, with the balance going to those projects which cannot be postponed (e.g. replacement) and finally those *which add most value to the business.*

This implies that those proposals that have the highest net present value per £1 invested should have priority.

The following table lists five proposed investments ranked in order of NPV to capital cost. A cost of capital of 8% is used.

Project	*Capital cost*	*Life yrs*	*Net cash flow per annum*	*NPV @ 8%*	*DCF yield rate*	*NPV/ capital*
	£		£	£	%	£
A	15,000	10	3,912	11,250	23	.75
B	22,000	10	5,608	15,630	22	.71
C	14,000	12	3,155	9,780	20	.70
D	13,000	8	3,741	8,500	23	.65
E	5,000	5	1,859	2,421	25	.48
	69,000					

If the amount of finance is restricted to £55,000 and each project is divisible – as with stocks and shares – the NPV to capital invested ranking will apply as follows:

Project	*Capital required*	*NPV*
	£	£
A	15,000	11,250
B	22,000	15,630
C	14,000	9,780
	51,000	36,660
add D 4/13ths of £8,500	4,000	2,615
	55,000	39,275

Note that ranking in order of yield rate, i.e. *E*, *A*, *D*, *B*, gives a lower NPV of £37,801. Thus when projects are *divisible* the optimum allocation of ration capital will always follow the NPV to capital invested ranking.

Most investment proposals in industry are *indivisible* and independent of one another, but still the search is for the highest value given the capital constraint. In these circumstances, different combinations of projects, including those with lower NPV ratings, may prove more valuable.

In our example, *A*, *B* and *C* use £51,000 with a total NPV of £36,660, but if we substitute *D* and *E* for *C*, £55,000 capital invested yields £37,801. That *D* and *E* have also got fast paybacks is also in their favour.

Should capital rationing extend for a period longer than one year, more complicated mathematical procedures, such as linear programming, can be applied to the solution of this wealth-maximisation problem.

Review

1 Appraisal data relevant to two mutually exclusive projects is given below:

Project	*Annual cash flow* £	*Capital cost* £	*Life* yrs	*NPV @ 8%* £	*Yield rate* %
A	100	502	10	169	15
B	144	780	10	186	13

a Which project would you choose and why?

b If a manager insisted that yield rate be used for appraisal purposes, how would you demonstrate its use?

2 A series of investment cash flows could yield more than one rate of return. When might this be so? How can such an investment be appraised?

3 The optimum replacement cycle for assets that are in continuous use by an organisation, and are replaced by similar assets, such as cars, can be calculated by:

a dividing the net present value of costs of each possible life by the appropriate number of years;

b choosing the life with lowest arithmetic average operating costs;

c dividing the net present value of costs of each possible life by the appropriate annuity factor;
d dividing the total net costs of each possible life by the appropriate number of years.

Which of **a**, **b**, **c** or **d** is correct?

4 In a single period of capital rationing, divisible projects can be ranked according to:
a the sizes of their net present values;
b their DCF yield rates;
c their ratios of NPV to capital invested.

Which of these will always result in the maximisation of value for the firm?

5 When investment proposals are indivisible, why cannot you use the approach indicated in your answer to question **4**?

1 a *B* would be chosen because it adds more value to the business after recovering its capital cost and paying 8% interest on the outstanding capital.

b The *incremental* capital invested in *B* of £278 generates an incremental cash flow per annum of £44. The yield rate can be calculated by dividing the capital cost by the annual cash flow, i.e. 278÷44=£6.32, and then looking along the ten-year row in Appendix B for the discount rate column that contains the nearest to that factor – in this case 9%.

2 Multiple yield rates can occur in a project that has *negative* cash flows later in its life. For example, if large costs are incurred in a year without offsetting revenues. In such a case the net present value method must be used.

3 c.

4 c.

5 Because projects cannot be broken down into fractions, the combinations of projects yielding the highest NPV within the capital constraint, will not necessarily coincide with the ranking of NPV to capital invested.

5 Dealing with risk in investment decisions

Introduction

Everest mountain climbers are said to take 'calculated risks'. They reduce the chance of failure by rigorous training. They use the best equipment, plan their expeditions to a fine degree, attempt only viable, if dangerous, routes on the mountain and climb only in acceptable weather conditions. When they have reduced risk to an acceptable level, they proceed with their venture.

Most of us prefer the lower slopes; the satisfaction is not so great, but neither is the risk.

Although the relationship between reward and risk was introduced in Chapters 1 and 2, when we considered investment appraisal in Chapter 3 we unrealistically assumed that future cash flows are known with certainty. Now this may be so with a fixed-interest government security, but it certainly will not be the case with a speculative goldmining operation. Investors should therefore consider not only the net present value of a project, but also the risk that its NPV could vary according to the economic conditions prevailing at the time of the operations. People who subject their capital to high risk will expect high rewards.

However, not everyone is prepared to take the same chances. Our *risk preferences* vary, and as investors we must judge that the likelihood of loss, set against the likelihood of gain, is an *acceptable* risk.

In this chapter we discuss how the rational investor, like the mountaineer, might take account of the uncertainties accompanying his decisions by:

- measuring and analysing the risk involved;

- reducing avoidable risk;
- matching unavoidable risk to his risk preferences.

Utility – the essence of risk

£1 to a starving man yields him more satisfaction than it would to a rich person. Conversely, the starving man has a lot more to lose if the £1 is not available to him.

> *Activity*
>
> Suppose you are offered two alternative opportunities to invest £5,000 for one year. Which of *A* or *B* below would you choose, assuming that you recover your £5,000 in each case?
>
> Alternative *A* would yield a *certain* net return of £3,000. Alternative *B* has a .5 probability of a net return of £2,000, and a .5 probability of a net return of £4,000.

Most people would choose alternative *A*, and if asked why, they would probably reply that they preferred the *certain* to the uncertain return. They would be implying that the half-chance of gaining £1,000 (i.e. £4,000 – £3,000) would not be sufficient to compensate them for the half-chance of losing £1,000 (i.e. £3,000 – £2,000). They would lose more satisfaction than they would gain.

This attitude can be understood more clearly by considering how much extra enjoyment you obtain from spending additional increments of £1,000. The first £1,000 spent upon the basic needs of food, shelter, clothing and warmth would give you tremendous satisfaction; but when these fundamental requirements have been met, each successive £1,000 yields less and less satisfaction.

In economic theory, satisfaction value is referred to as *utility*, and the concept can be illustrated by ascribing *assumed* utility values to increasing sums of money as follows:

Monetary value £	*Utility value*	*Marginal utility per incremental £1,000*
0	0	
1,000	10	10
2,000	19	9
3,000	27	8
4,000	33	6
5,000	38	5

Note:

a Each incremental £1,000 yields progressively less utility.

b Alternative *A* in our original investment opportunity has a utility value of 27.

c The weighted average utility of alternative *B* is (.5×19)+(.5×33)=26, showing that its lower utility is less attractive than the certain £3,000 of alternative *A*. Putting it differently, the possible gain of 6 units of utility (i.e. 33 – 27) is more than offset by a possible loss of 8 units (i.e. 27 – 19).

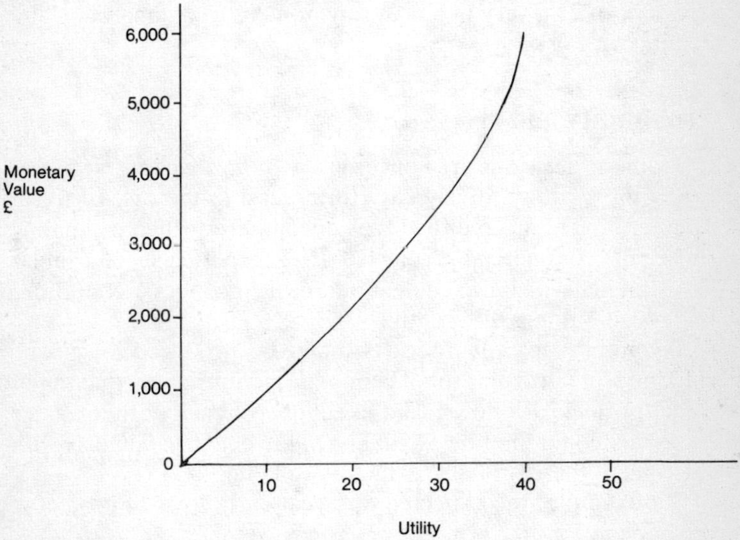

Figure 6. Utility function of a risk-averter

The utility and monetary values scheduled above are plotted in figure 6, revealing that utility increases at a diminishing rate as wealth increases, but decreases at an increasing rate as wealth is lost. It portrays the utility function of a risk-averse investor, but does not apply to all investors. Risk preferences vary between individuals, and so do their utility functions.

> *Activity*
>
> What would be the utility value of another investment, *C* which promises a .5 probability of £1,000, and a .5 chance of £5,000?

Utility value=(.5×10)+(.5×38)=24.

Notice how, as the expected money values of *A*, *B* and *C* grew wider apart, utility diminishes. From this we can infer that the risk of an investment is related to the dispersion of its possible outcomes.

Utility theory attempts to measure this risk, but however conceptually sound the connection between utility and risk, it does not offer a very practical way of measuring, analysing and dealing with risk.

Probability and risk

Investment decisions are concerned with *future* cash flows, and whilst these are relatively easy to forecast in the case of fixed-interest bonds, more difficulty is encountered when estimating those of commercial projects. Past experience of similar investments will be a guide, but future economic conditions might order things differently.

A number of cash forecasts might be produced, each one relating to a particular set of economic circumstances that might affect project cash flows. The likelihood of each of these states occurring could then be ascribed a value between 0 and 1, with the total of these probability factors equalling 1.

For example, the expected one-year cash flows of project *X* might be as follows:

Forecast economic state	*Forecast net cash flow*	*Probability of occurrence*		*Weighted value*
	1	2		3=1×2
	£			
Slump	1,000	.10		100
	2,000	.20		400
	5,000	.40		2,000
	8,000	.20		1,600
Boom	9,000	.10		900
		1.00	EMV	5,000

By multiplying the value of each estimate by its probability of occurrence and totalling the weighted figures (see column 3), we find the statistical midpoint known as expected monetary value (EMV), which can be compared with the EMVs of alternative investment proposals. In addition, the investor now has information regarding the likelihood of attaining different values, and also a picture of the variability of possible outcomes around the EMV. He is therefore far more aware of the risk of the project.

The dispersion of a limited number of discrete outcomes can be represented in graphical form as a *histogram*, and figure 7 is the histogram of the forecast cash flows of project *X*, showing the probability of their occurrence. Underneath it is a similar diagram representing the one-year cash flows of project *Y*, which are as follows:

Forecast cash flow	*Probability of occurrence*		*Weighted value*
£			£
3,000	.20		600
5,000	.60		3,000
7,000	.20		1,400
	1.00	EMV	5,000

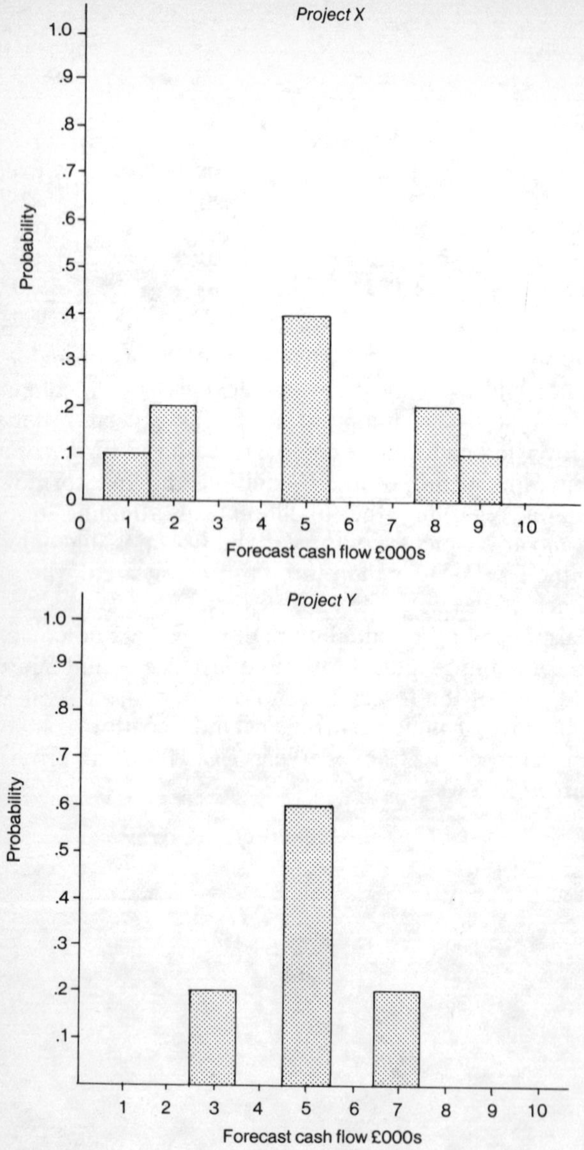

Figure 7. Histograms of project cash flows

Note that although the average expected cash flows of *X* and *Y* are both £5,000, those of *X* deviate from the EMV more widely than those of *Y*, making *X* the riskier of the two projects.

Measuring and analysing risk by using standard deviation

It would be rare for cash flows of investment projects to be limited to a few discrete outcomes as illustrated above. More likely the number would be unlimited and appear as the continuous bell-shapes shown in figure 8.

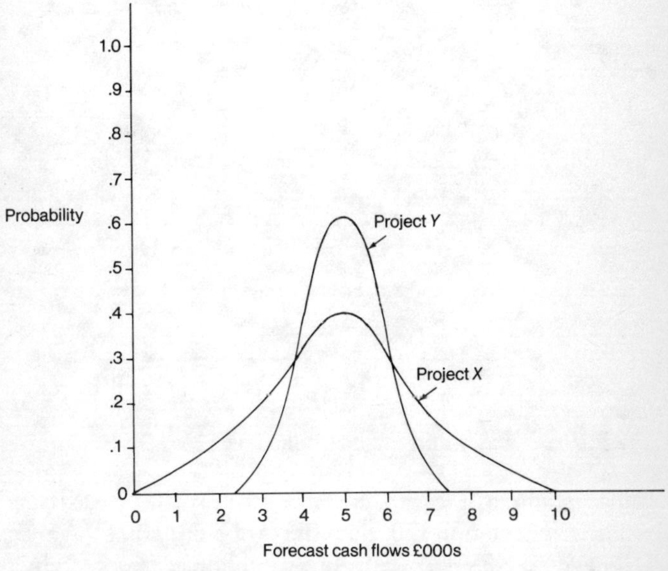

Figure 8. Probability distributions of cash flows

The symmetrical bell-shape of the continuous probability distribution is known as a *normal curve*. The flatter the curve – the wider the expected outcomes – the higher the risk. Conversely, the narrower the bell-shape, the lower the relative risk.

The useful natural property of the normal distribution is that there is a direct correlation between the statistical measure of dispersion, known as *standard deviation* (written ó) and the area under the curve. This relationship is illustrated in figure 9, which shows that the area between 1ó *each side* of the expected value, covers 68.26% of probable outcomes; 95% between 2ó, and 99.74% between 3ó. More detailed tables are available which give areas between the mean (i.e. the expected value) and any value to its left or right.

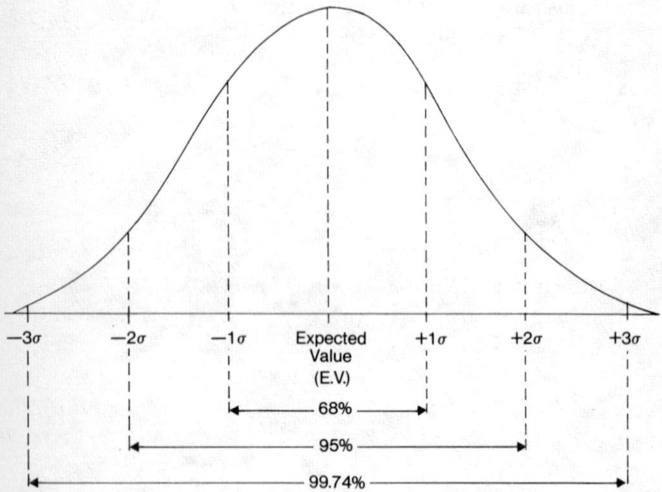

Figure 9. Probability and the normal curve

If, for example, the expected NPV of a project is £100 and the standard deviation £50, then the probability that the project would have an NPV less than zero would be represented by the area under the curve to the left of zero. In this instance, zero is two standard deviations from the expected value, i.e. (100−0)÷50=2ó.

Figure 9 shows you that, of the 50% of the total outcomes to the left of the mean, 47.5% covers 2ó, therefore there is a 50 – 47.5%=2.5% probability that the project will be less than zero.

Readers who have studied statistics will recognise the formula for calculating the standard deviation of a one-year probability distribution of cash flows as:

$$\sigma = \sqrt{\sum_{i=1}^{n} px_1 (x_1 - \bar{x})^2}$$

where px_1 = the probability of attaining value x_1
x_1 = each of the values in turn
$\bar{x}$ = the average expected value
n = the number of possible values

Derivations of this formula exist to extend the measurement of dispersion to multi-period cash flows, but there is no necessity to demonstrate the resultant calculation of standard deviation in this book. However, readers who are able to might like to calculate the standard deviations of the cash flows of projects *X* and *Y* given above.

The answers are 2,608 and 1,265 respectively.

Activity

1. Do the given standard deviations of *X* and *Y* confirm our previous knowledge of their comparable risks?
2. As regards the cash flows of *X*, what expected values lie between 1ό either side of the EMV?

1. Yes. *X* has the higher standard deviation, which confirms the dispersions portrayed by the two histograms. *X* is therefore the riskier project.
2. The lowest value is £5,000 – 2,608=£2,392; and the highest £5,000+2,608=£7,608. There is a 68% probability that the ultimate value will lie between these two figures.

Knowledge of standard deviation provides managers with information of the level of risk attending each proposed project; but it is equally important for them to know how this individual project risk correlates with the total risk already being undertaken on all present projects. This aspect is dealt with in detail in the last section of this chapter where we discuss the question of diversification.

When considering mutually exclusive projects that have the same expected value, the one with the lower standard deviation would be chosen. If the expected values differ, however, we have a problem. Without considering risk, the highest yielding project is the normal choice, but if total business risk is already high, a lower yielding investment with lower risk would be preferred. This choice can be aided by calculating the *coefficient of variation* of each project, which is simply the standard deviation divided by the expected value of the project.

For example, if project *A* has an expected value of £6,000, with a standard deviation of £3,000, and project *B* an expected value of £4,000 with a standard deviation of £1,000, the respective coefficients are:

$$\frac{\sigma}{EV} \ldots \quad \overset{A}{\frac{3{,}000}{6{,}000}} = .50 \qquad \overset{B}{\frac{1{,}000}{4{,}000}} = .25.$$

A has the higher standard deviation per £1 of expected value, even though the latter is more attractive than the expected value of *B*. If management are risk-averse they might well choose *B*, whose lower risk is signified by its lower coefficient of variation.

Self-check

1 Given the following probabilities and values of sales for the coming year, calculate the expected value of sales for that year.

Probability	*Sales value* £
.1	6,000
.2	10,000
.4	15,000
.2	18,000
.1	20,000

2 State which of the following measures standard deviation:

a expected value;
b dispersion of expected values around the mean value;
c present value;
d coefficient of variation.

3 If the expected net present value of a project is £8,000, with a standard deviation of £4,000, what is the probability that the NPV will be greater than £16,000?

1 £14,200.

2 **b.**

3 Number of ó that £16,000 is from the mean =(£16,000−£8,000)÷4,000=2ó. Figure 9 shows there to be 50 – 47.5% of values to the right of two standard deviations from the mean. Therefore, there is a 2.5% probability that NPV will be greater than £16,000.

Sensitivity analysis

Whilst the use of standard deviation to measure and analyse risk relates well to utility theory, three difficulties arise in its application to business investment projects:

- Estimating the probability distribution might be highly subjective.
- Probability distributions are likely to vary from year to year, and their dispersions would almost certainly widen with time because of increasing uncertainty.
- Business investment projects include many variables, e.g. sales prices, quantities, capital costs. Overall project risk is therefore a composite of the varying probability distributions attached to each variable.

Many sophisticated mathematical models, involving simulation and sampling techniques, have been developed to overcome these problems, and these are probably worthwhile when applied to projects involving a large commitment of resources. Most businesses look for a simpler approach to risk analysis however, and *sensitivity analysis* is one such approach.

The technique formalises a question that investors have always asked. If the values of any of the forecast variables change, what difference would each of these changes make to the forecast viability of the investment proposal? Each variable is examined in turn, all other variables being held constant, to ascertain how much that variable could change and still leave the project with a positive NPV or a yield rate higher than the acceptable rate of return.

Activity

A business investment with a capital outlay of £48,000 is expected to yield £8,500 annually for ten years. Applying a cost of capital of 10%, calculate whether the project is acceptable. Ignore taxation.

Present value of net cash flows – years 1 to 10:			
£8,500×6.145*			52,232
less Capital outlay – year 0			48,000
	NPV	=	£ 4,232

*Annuity factor – see Appendix B.

Because the project has a positive NPV it is acceptable.

Activity

By how much could the capital outlay in the above project change, before the project becomes unacceptable?

The capital outlay could increase by £4,232, at which point the NPV would be zero. Any further increase would be unacceptable unless accompanied by improvements in other cash flows.

Activity

Calculate how much the annual net cash inflow could reduce before the project fell below zero NPV.

Remember that all other variables remain unchanged.

Let X equal the lowest annual cash flow to produce a zero NPV; then:

$$X \times 6.145 = 48{,}000$$

$$X = \frac{48{,}000}{6.145}$$

$$X = £\ 7{,}811$$

To ascertain the minimum *life* needed to recover the capital outlay, calculate the annuity factor by dividing £48,000 by the annual cash flow of £8,500=5.647. Then look down the 10% column in the Appendix B annuity tables until you find the factor nearest to this figure. Scanning left along the row places the break-even life at about 8¾ years.

> *Activity*
>
> By how much could the rate of return increase before the project became unacceptable? Hint: the procedure here is similar to the life calculation, excepting that we know the life. We are therefore looking for the appropriate column in table B – rather than the row.

The annuity factor is 48,000÷8,500=5.647 (as above).

Looking along the ten year row in Appendix B, the nearest factor to 5.647 is in the 12% column, i.e. 5.6502. Therefore 12% is the maximum viable rate of return.

All the variables might then be summarised to reveal their comparitive sensitivity to change, as follows:

Variable	*Original value*	*Optimum value*	*Possible absolute change*	*% Possible change to original value*
Capital cost	£48,000	£52,232	+ £4,232	8.8
Annual cash flow	£ 8,500	£ 7,811	– £ 689	8.1
Life	10 yrs	8¾ yrs	– 1¼ yrs	12.5
Rate of return	10%	12%	+ 2%	20.0

The practicality of this analysis emerges from a comparison of maximum absolute or percentage changes with possible changes. If none of the variables are likely to change by as much as the values indicated, the project would be given a clean bill of health.

Capital cost would probably be a fixed contract price, and therefore not subject to any change. On the other hand, the annual cash flow is relatively sensitive. A possible reduction of 9% could put the whole project at risk. A further point is that the net annual cash flow is itself an amalgam of differently behaving variables, and a further breakdown into sales volume, selling price, variable cost and fixed cost could pinpoint a particularly sensitive area.

The major drawback to sensitivity analysis is that each variable is examined in isolation. It is quite possible for any of the elements of an investment decision to change, but also for combinations of them to change simultaneously. Indeed some variables are possibly interdependent. For example, if sales price increases, sales volume could diminish, depending upon the elasticity of product demand.

One can cope with these complications by using a desk-top calculator but the availability of relatively inexpensive and powerful microcomputers now makes the job of analysing multiple changes in variables comparitively easy. Even the smallest of firms can now afford the luxury of a computer to answer its 'what if?' questions – subject of course, to getting professional advice on suitable programmes.

In summary, sensitivity analysis can provide a practical aid to investment decision making by:

- highlighting the most sensitive variables before a decision is made, to enable action to deal with avoidable risk;
- identifying factors requiring close management control while the project is proceeding.

Self-check

Assume that, in the last activity, the annual cash flow of £8,500 was made up as follows:

		£
Sales 10,000 units at £2 per unit		£20,000
less Variable cost @ £1 per unit	10,000	
Fixed costs	1,500	11,500
Net annual cash flow		£ 8,500

Calculate the sensitivity, relative to zero NPV, of sales volume, selling price, variable cost and fixed cost. Hint: note from the last activity that a reduction of £689 in the annual cash flow is possible before the NPV of the project falls below zero.

Sales volume – can be reduced by the number of units valued at £1 contribution, with total value of £689, i.e. 689 – % change: 6.89

Sales price – can reduce to £2 minus (£689÷10,000) per unit=£1.9311 – % change: 3.4.

Variable cost – can increase to £1+(£689÷10,000) a unit=£1,0689 – % change: 6.9.

Fixed cost – can be increase by £689 – % change: 46.0.

Payback as a risk-screening device

Payback as a method of investment appraisal was discussed in Chapter 3, and you will recall its major weakness is that it ignores cash flows occurring after the capital break-even point.

Save where a firm is suffering acute cash liquidity problems, the use of a fixed, arbitrary payback period as the sole decision-making technique will almost always discriminate against profitability. To answer this justifiable objection a payback period calculate on *discounted* cash flows is sometimes used, but even this takes no account of (a) cash flows after the payback period, and (b) the range of probable outcomes of *payback* cash flows. The latter may themselves be risky, in which case both the payback and profitability criteria may not be satisfied.

If payback does not consider profitability then it is only being used to screen out *risky* projects, and might be effective in respect of:

- long-life projects; because the more delayed cash flows are, the riskier they become;
- swiftly changing areas of technology, where early obsolescence has to be protected against, e.g. in microelectronics and communications;
- investments in countries with an uncertain political future, e.g. those in which revolutionary or repressive groups are active;
- brand-new products, where future demand is completely uncertain.

In general application, when competing projects are equally profitable with similar risk characteristics, payback could be used as the final arbiter of acceptability.

Self-check

1 'Choosing investment projects on the basis of early payback, takes account of both risk and profitability.' True or false?

2 In which of the following circumstances might payback be used to screen out risky projects?

a highly profitable investments;
b projects to be carried out in countries with unstable political regimes;
c early product obsolescence;
d investments yielding an acceptable rate of return;
e new product proposals;
f long-life project;
g when capital investment is delayed.

1 False. Profitability begins after payback is achieved. However, payback could be used in assessing alternative projects that are equally profitable.

2 **b**, **c**, **e** and **f**.

Risk-adjusted discount rates

When you ask for a motor insurance quotation the insurance company will ask you to provide information on your age, health, accident record and details of the vehicle to be covered. Insurance premiums are adjusted to take account of possible risk, and assessment of risk is based on the information you supply. For example, a bad accident record will almost certainly cost you an additional premium.

The risk premium concept also applies to investors. If you have the choice of putting £100,000 into government securities or into a deep-sea treasure salvage operation, you would not dream of expecting the same return from each of these alternatives.

Government securities can be described as 'risk free', and they pay an appropriate rate of return. But for you to be attracted to the salvage operation, there would have to be a reasonable expectation that it would return a high premium over the risk-free rate.

Figure 10 shows the intuitive risk/rate-of-return relationship. Further arguments to support this relationship will be discussed at the end of this chapter and in Chapter 14. Investors generally can be said to be indifferent between the various risk/return combinations which lie on the line rising diagonally from the risk-free point on the vertical axis. The increasing risk premium compensates them for accepting more and more risk.

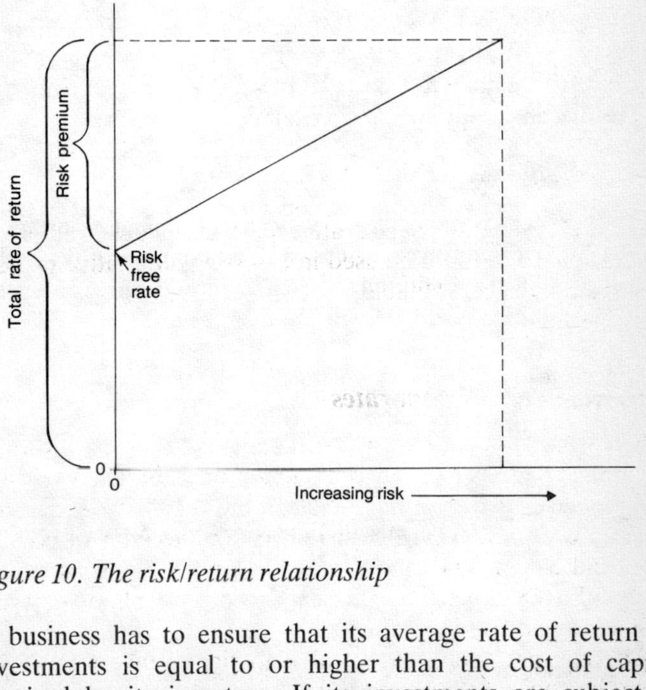

Figure 10. The risk/return relationship

A business has to ensure that its average rate of return on investments is equal to or higher than the cost of capital required by its investors. If its investments are subject to varying degrees of risks, its cost of capital reflects the investors' assessment of the *average* risk attached to the varied operations of the business. Higher-risk projects should therefore be discounted at rates exceeding the cost of capital, and lower-risk proposals at rates equal to or lower than the cost of capital. Differential risk rates are equally applicable to businesses that engage in only one type of activity, for their plans will include a spectrum of investment proposals from *low-risk* replacement of machinery to high-risk new product introduction.

The choice of rate will be influenced largely by the dispersion of possible cash flow outcomes. For example, a proposal with the promise of extremely high returns, but which might also result in a substantial loss, would be discounted at a rate including a high-risk premium. Projects whose outcomes are less likely to deviate from the expected average return would be discounted at a lower rate.

You will recall that when cash flows are discounted at higher rates, net present values are less. Thus, high-risk projects have to yield substantial cash flows to offset the higher discounting, *and* return an acceptable *positive* NPV.

Activity

A project is expected to yield a net annual cash flow of £2,000 for eight years, from an investment of £10,400. The firm's cost of capital is 10%. Should the project be accepted?

Present value of £2,000 for 8 yrs @ 10%:	£
£2,000×5.335	10,670
Less Capital outlay	10,400
Net present value	270

Accept the proposal because it yields a positive NPV of £270.

Activity

Assume that the same cash flows as in the previous activity, apply to two further proposals – *A* and *B*. The former is of above-average risk, and the latter below average. Using risk-adjusted rates of 15% and 8% respectively, assess whether either of these two investment proposals should proceed.

	£
A – PV of £2,000 for 8 years @ 15% . . . £2,000×4.487=	8,974
less Capital outlay	10,400
Net present value	(1,426)
B – PV of £2,000 for 8 yrs @ 8% . . . £2,000×5.747=	11,494
less Capital outlay	10,400
Net present value	1,094

Accept proposal *B*, but reject *A*. Note particularly that, had the company's cost of capital of 10% been applied to *A*, it would have been marginally acceptable. At the higher 'hurdle' rate of 15% its sensitivity to risk is exposed.

The risk-adjusted discounting method is similar to payback in one respect. It recognises the higher value of *early* cash flows by heavily discounting *later* cash flows. It is superior to payback however, in that it does take account of cash flows beyond the capital break-even point, and gives more weighting to cash flows within the payback period.

The problem of how to determine the cost of capital, and particularly the risk-adjusted rate, are dealt with in Chapter 15.

Self-check

Why would it be misleading to apply the average cost of capital as the discounting rate in a company whose investments are subject to varying degrees of risk?

Such a policy could lead to the acceptance of *high-risk* proposals which might not be viable if a higher, risk-adjusted, discounting rate were used. Conversely, acceptable *low-risk* projects could be rejected if an average rate were used.

Risk reduction

In an efficient organisation, the element of risk to be dealt with in the ways suggested in the previous sections of this chapter will be the *unavoidable* part after action has been taken to eliminate or reduce risk. Such action can be summarised under two broad heads:

- *administrative action* – when appraising, planning and controlling investment projects;
- *diversification action* – to ensure that total cash flows from all projects are not subject to excessive variations.

Administrative action Taking out insurance against the risks of accident due to fire, natural hazards, third-party claims, theft and burglary is perhaps the most obvious of management actions designed to minimise possible loss.

Another way of spreading risk is to arrange for particularly large-scale projects to be shared with one or more partners in a *joint-venture* or *consortium* agreement. Each partner contributes capital, takes part in the management and shares profits or losses.

At individual project level, uncertainty can be considerably smoothed out by taking some of the following actions:

- Putting adequate time and resources into forecasting.
- Maintaining checklists of expenditure, both capital and revenue, to ensure that nothing is overlooked.
- Completing contracts for supplies and with customers to ensure continuity and stability of terms of trade.
- Using 'hedging' operations to cover the risk of loss through changes in currency values and commodity prices. This is effected by buying *options* forward to buy or sell, at predetermined prices. In this way, for example, a manufacturer will know exactly how much he will have to pay for materials in the future and is able therefore, to quote selling prices with more certainty.
- Arranging for patent protection for new inventions and designs.
- Taking over sources of supply so that complete control can be maintained over them.
- Maintaining good industrial relations with employees through adequate communication and management participation.
- Ensuring that prescribed time-schedules for the completion of projects are being met. 'Schedule slippage' can seriously harm profitability, since delayed cash flows will reduce net present value.

- Frequent cash forecasting to ensure that adequate funds are available for each project.
- Continuous monitoring of projects to see that they are measuring up to expectations.

Diversification 'Don't put all your eggs into one basket' is sound general advice. Drop your basket and all your eggs are smashed!

It is the kind of advice that your friendly bank manager would offer if you asked him how you should invest your Aunt Agatha's legacy. Depending upon your present financial position and future needs, he would probably counsel you to hold your money in a number of investments, which together would form what is referred to as a *portfolio*. Some funds would go into low-risk, fixed interest, easily liquidated savings accounts or securities, to provide cash for emergencies. The remainder could go into high-income or capital growth securities according to need.

The attraction of sinking all of your funds into one security is that you *may* realise a high return on your investment; but there is also the danger that you may lose all of your money if the security is risky. Even investing in more than one security does not necessarily change this risk, however, if the several investments are in the same or a related industry, and their cash flows react in like manner to general changes in the economy. Such related investments are said to be *positively* correlated, as shown in figure 11(a), where changes in the cash flows of *B* are seen to be closely related to those of *A*. Clearly, no reduction in risk results from combining such investments.

When the cash flows of two investments behave in exactly opposite ways in the same economic climate – so that when the returns on one are rising they are falling on the other – correlation between them is said to be *negative*, and risk is reduced by their combination in a portfolio. Note how in figure 11(b) equivalent amounts invested in *A* and *D* result in compensating rising and falling cash flows over time, combining to yield the smoothed-out return C.

Most securities and business projects are nearer to positive than to negative correlation, though very rarely being perfectly

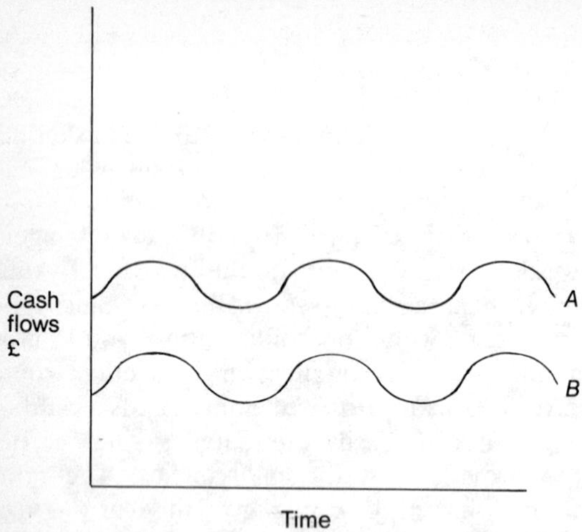

Figure 11a. Positively correlated investment cash flows

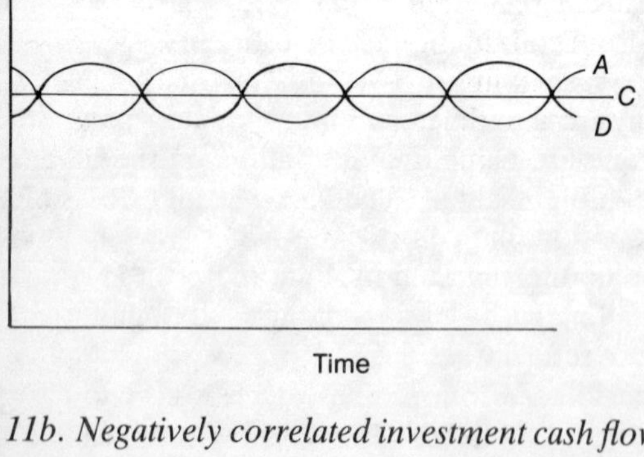

Figure 11b. Negatively correlated investment cash flows

positively correlated. There will therefore always be some benefit to risk in combining projects of unlike nature.

For example, if an investor has the opportunity to invest equal amounts in two securities *X* and *Y* with expected annual yields of 18% and 12%, and standard deviations of 16% and 10% respectively, the weighted average yield would be (.5×18%)+(.5×12%)=15%.

It might also be supposed that the standard deviation of the portfolio comprising *A* and *B* is the weighted average of the standard deviations of the two securities, i.e. (.5×16%)+(.5×10%)=13%. This would only be true, however, if the returns from the two securities vary in exactly the same way over time, i.e. are perfectly positively correlated. If they do not, it can be demonstrated mathematically that the portfolio standard deviation will be less than the weighted average of the deviations on the two securities.

This concept of risk reduction through diversification has encouraged financial researchers during the last thirty years to develop theories that have had a profound effect upon analysis related to investment in securities, and this work is having a growing influence upon decisions relating to investment in capital assets. The essence of this theory is discussed in the two following sections.

Selecting an optimal portfolio

Activity

Figure 12 depicts all the possible combinations (portfolios) of *risky* investments available to an investor, plotted according to their portfolio return and risk.

a At a risk level of 6% which portfolio would you choose?
b If you wished a return of 25% which portfolio would you choose?
c Explain your choices in **a** and **b** above.

a The one on the 'efficient frontier' yielding 15%.
b The one on the 'efficient frontier' with a risk level of 12%.
c Of all the portfolios with a risk of 6%, the one chosen yields

the highest return; of all the portfolios with a return of 25%, the one chosen has the least risk.

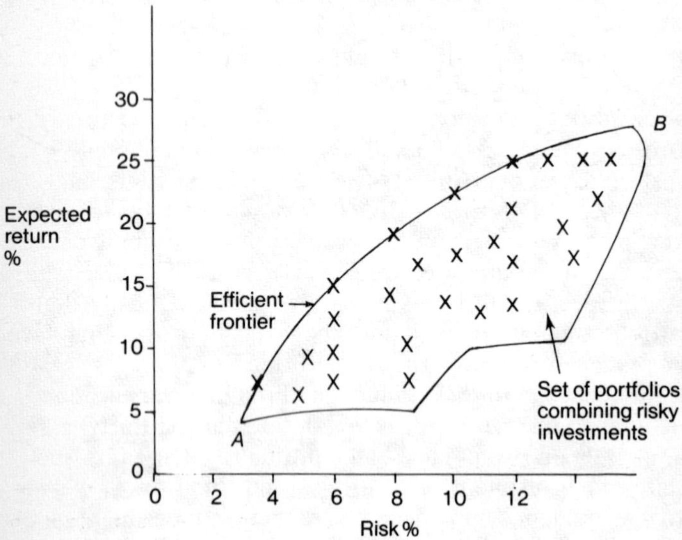

Figure 12. The efficient frontier

The curve *AB* in figure 12 is known as the 'efficient frontier' because all the portfolios lying along it are superior to all others within the set. They yield the highest returns at any desired level of risk, and the lowest risk at any desired level of return.

But which is the most efficient portfolio for an individual investor?

The answer can be illustrated by adding 'indifference curves' to the diagram depicting the opportunity set of portfolios – see figure 13.

Indifference curves are derived from figure 6, which depicts a risk-averse investor's utility function. Assuming that such a function can be determined, the indifference curves illustrate that increasing levels of risk have their prices in higher expected returns. The investor to whom the curves relate would be indifferent between any combinations of risk and return lying

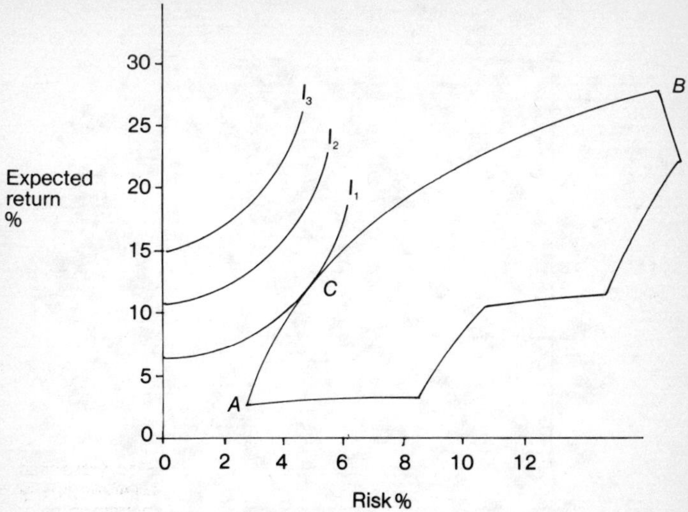

Figure 13. An investor's optimal portfolio

on each of the indifference curves. Figure 13 shows that the optimal risky portfolio for this investor is at point *C* where the lowest indifference curve touches the efficient frontier.

However, investors do not have to restrict themselves to risky investments. *Riskless* securities in the form of, say, government Treasury Bills can be added to their portfolios, and thus reduce total risk.

Figure 14 illustrates the effect of making a riskless security available to an investor.

A line drawn from the vertical axis at R_f (the risk-free rate of return) at a tangent to the set of risky portfolios at point *M*, now depicts a new efficient frontier R_fMQ, known as the *capital market line* (CML).

If we assume:

- that investors have exactly similar expectations regarding the risk and return of each security on the stock market, and
- that the stock market is efficient in that the market value of each security reflects all known information, and is the price that equates supply with the demand for that security,

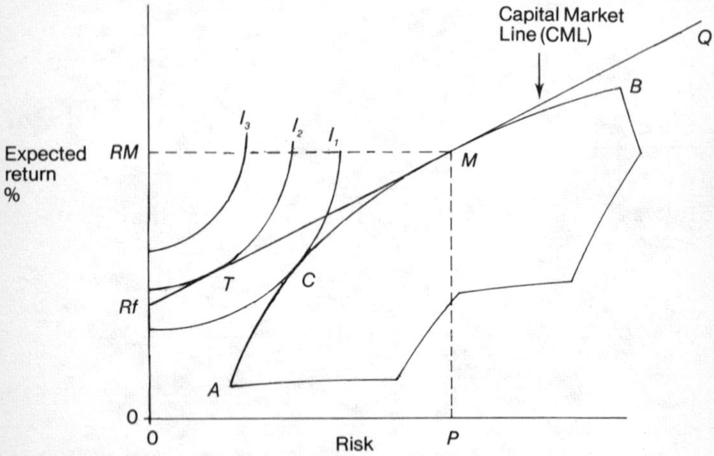

Figure 14. The capital market line

then the 'market portfolio' (*M*) must contain a proportion of every share, and is the only perfectly diversified risky portfolio.

Studies have shown, however, that even the market portfolio cannot completely eliminate risk. Undiversifiable (or systematic) risk still remains after all the risks peculiar to individual securities have been diversified away. This residual risk relates to the general economic and political outlook that affects all business activity. If the outlook changes, so does the expected return and value of the market portfolio. Figure 14 reveals that at its current level of systematic risk *P*, the market portfolio commands a risk premium of RM - R_f.

By combining the riskless security with the market portfolio in the proportion of R_fT: *TM* on the capital market line, our investor is able to reach a higher indifference curve at point *T*, and thereby realise the same return as before, i.e. *C*, but at lower risk.

Other investors with different risk preferences, whose indifference curves might be placed nearer to *M*, will invest proportionately more in the risky portfolio *M*, and consequently less in the riskless security. At *M*, investors will only hold the market portfolio.

If we assume, rather unrealistically, that investors can borrow at the same rate as they can lend, then where investors' indifference curves are at a tangent to the *CML* beyond *M*, they will *borrow* to boost their investment in the market portfolio.

Theoretically, investors should only hold portfolios on the capital market line, all others below it being less efficient as regards return and risk. The *CML* represents the return/risk relationship of various combinations of the risk-free security and the market portfolio, with risk being a linear function of the proportion invested in the market portfolio. For example, if *M* comprises 50% of the invested funds, and the standard deviation of *M* is 10%, the total portfolio risk is $.5 \times 10\% = 5\%$.

It is unlikely, however, that investors will hold the market portfolio, because of its sheer size; so how practical is the CML in helping them to choose an optimal portfolio?

The answer lies in the realisation that *the slope of the CML represents market risk only*, all other risk being diversified away. It follows therefore that because the *operational* risk of an individual security can be eliminated by combination with other securities in a well-diversified portfolio, investors will only be prepared to pay for the residual, systematic risk, which of course is market related.

Remember that the expected return and value of the market portfolio fluctuate with the underlying general economic and political trend. Likewise each security tends to move in sympathy with this 'market' risk, but not necessarily to the same degree as the market portfolio. A favourable outlook results in a general upward movement in share prices, and vice versa, but some prices will change proportionately more or less than the market portfolio.

Thus, just as the risk premium on a portfolio featured on the CML in figure 14 is a proportionate part of the premium on the market portfolio, so the risk premium on each security is a function of that security's sensitivity to changes in the required return on the market portfolio. This responsiveness to change can be derived statistically from past or forecast data, and is represented by a *beta* factor of more than, less than, or equal to 1; with 1 relating to the market portfolio.

Capital asset pricing model

The capital asset pricing model (CAPM) describes the equation for determining the expected return on a security (*RS*), given the current risk-free rate (i), knowledge of the expected return on the market portfolio (*RM*) (which is usually proxied by one of the market indices such as the Financial Times Actuaries' Index), and the beta (*B*) of the security as:

$RS = i + (RM - i)B.$

Here you see that the expected return includes the risk-free rate, plus a premium for risk calculated by applying the beta of the security to the risk premium on the market portfolio ($RM - i$).

For example, if a security *X*, has a beta of 1.1, the risk-free rate is 9%, and the expected return on the market portfolio is 15%, the expected return of *X* will be:

$$\begin{aligned} RS &= i + (RM - i)B \\ &= 9 + (15 - 9)1.1 \\ &= 15.6\%. \end{aligned}$$

If underlying economic influences then forced an increase in *RM* to 20%, the return on *X* should increase to $9 + (20 - 9)1.1 = 21.1\%$. This can be checked by adding to the previous return on *X* of 15.6%, 1.1 times the *increase* in the risk premium of the market portfolio, i.e. $15.6 + 1.1\,(11 - 6)$.

Thus, the return on a security with a beta greater than 1 increases or decreases more than proportionately to that of the market portfolio, and is said to be an 'aggressive' investment because of the greater variability (and therefore risk) of its returns. Conversely, a security with a beta of less than 1 is a 'defensive' investment because its return is not as volatile as that of the market portfolio, i.e. it is less risky.

We now possess a model that can be applied to the construction of an investor's portfolio, according to his specification of required return and risk.

When investments are combined into a portfolio, the expected return is a weighted average of the returns of all the separate securities. Likewise, the risk of the portfolio, *measured by its beta*, is simply a weighted average of the betas of the constituent securities.

If an investor is a risk-taker he will construct a portfolio with a beta greater than 1 (an aggressive portfolio), which should yield a return commensurate with that level of market risk. In so doing, he will assess the risk of an individual security according to the *marginal* effect it has on his diversified portfolio – and not according to its individual standard deviation.

Further discussion on the 'capital asset pricing model' can be found in Chapter 15 in the context of calculating the cost of a company's capital to apply to the appraisal of investments.

Self-check

1 When the returns on two investments move in sympathy in the same economic environment, are they (**a**) positively, or (**b**) negatively correlated?
2 'No risk reduction will result from combining two negatively correlated investments.' True or false?
3 Why will investors only pay for systematic risk?
4 What does the beta of a security measure?

1 Positively – as the cash flows rise and fall together.
2 False – as the returns behave in opposite fashion, there will be portfolio risk reduction.
3 Systematic risk is the residual risk after diversification has eliminated operating or unsystematic risk. Investors will therefore expect a return related solely to systematic risk, and will price securities accordingly.
4 The beta of a security measures the sensitivity of a security's returns to those of the market portfolio.

Review

1 Why would an investment *A*, with a certain return of £5,000, be more attractive to most people than *B* with a 50/50 chance of earning £8,000 and £2,000 respectively?

2 Show your calculation of the expected value of *B* in question **1**.

3 What does standard deviation measure?

4 If the returns from a project are normally distributed, with an expected value of £12,000 and a standard deviation of £6,000, what is the probability that the return from the project will be negative?

5 **a** What is the basic question posed by sensitivity?
b How can sensitivity analysis help in the appraisal of investments?

6 The forecast cash flows of a four-year investment proposal are as follows:

Year 0	1	2	3	4
(£7,000)	£4,000	£2,000	£1,000	£1,000

Calculate whether the project should be accepted under each of the following separate criteria:

i the cost of capital is 10%;
ii The required payback period is two years;
iii This is a low-risk project, warranting only a 7% discounting rate.

7 The following is a table of the % returns for three projects *X*, *Y* and *Z* for each of six years.

Project	*Percentage return on investment in year*					
	1	*2*	*3*	*4*	*5*	*6*
X	10	5	6	8	12	15
Y	8	4	4.8	6.4	9.6	12
Z	5	10	12	10	6	8

a Which pair combinations of *X*, *Y* and *Z* shows positive correlation? Explain.
b Which pair combinations of *X*, *Y* and *Z* show negative correlation? Explain.
c Which combinations will result in risk reduction?

8 If the risk-free rate is 10%, the return on the market portfolio 17%, and the beta of a security is .9, calculate the expected return on the security.

9 How would you calculate the expected return and risk of a diversified portfolio of securities?

1 Both promise an expected value of £5,000; but *B* has a lower utility value than *A*, because more satisfaction would be lost if £2,000 were realised, than would be gained from £8,000.

2 (.5×£8,000)+(.5×£2,000)=£5,000.

3 It is the statistical measure of dispersion of probable outcomes around their expected (mean) value.

4 (12,000−0)÷6,000=2σ=2.5% probability of a negative return.

5 a If the values of any of the forecast variables of a proposed investment change, what difference would each of the changes make to the viability of the project?

b i By highlighting sensitive areas for closer examination *before* the investment decision is made.

ii To spotlight the factors requiring closest management control during the project implementation stage.

6

i *Cost of capital 10%*		**ii** *Payback*	**iii** *Cost of capital 7%*	
Year 1	4,000×.909=3,636	3 years	Year 1	4,000×.935=3,740
2	2,000×.826=1,652		2	2,000×.873=1,746
3	1,000×.751= 751		3	1,000×.816= 816
4	1,000×.683= 683		4	1,000×.763= 763
	6,722			7,065
less Capital cost	7,000			7,000
NPV	(278)		NPV	65

i At 10% the project would be rejected because of its negative NPV.

ii The payback period exceeds the maximum of two, therefore reject.

iii At 7% the project would be accepted because it results in a positive NPV.

7 a *Positive correlation* – *X* and *Y*, because changes in the returns of *X* are accompanied by exactly proportionate changes in *Y*.

b *Negative correlation* – *X* and *Z*, and *Y* and *Z*, because when returns are high in *X* and *Y*, returns in *Z* are low; conversely, if returns are high for *Z*, they are low for *X* and *Y*.

c Those that have negative correlation, i.e. *X* and *Z*, and *Y* and *Z*.

8 $RS = i + (RM - i).9 = 10 + (17 - 10).9 = 16.3\%$.

9 The expected return of a portfolio is the weighted average of the returns of the separate securities; portfolio risk is also a weighted average – of the betas of the constituent securities.

6 Capital budgeting administration

Introduction

To achieve their objectives businesses must organise and administer their capital budgeting efficiently. The capital budgeting process, which embraces investment and financing decisions, is at the centre of strategic planning, as figure 1 in Chapter 1 revealed, and it is a continuous process.

Figure 15 portrays this continuity by showing that new investment proposals are born out of:

- resources put into new product development;
- further development or replacement of existing activities.

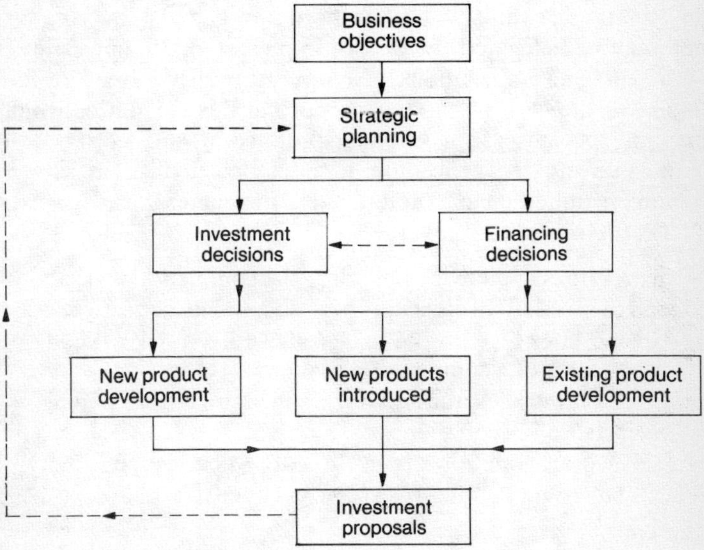

Figure 15. The flow of investment proposals

The administrative framework within which capital budgeting operates must cover four main areas to be effective:

- A clear statement as to who sanctions investment proposals, and guidelines regarding expected project profitability, and how to deal with risk.
- Standard checklists and documentation, to ease the recording and submission of proposal details.
- Accounting and administrative procedures controlling the acquisition, building, manufacture or installation of capital resources.
- The monitoring of the *results* of each project after implementation, referred to as a *post-audit*.

Investment guidelines and authorisation

The size of business and volume of investment decisions made will obviously determine the extent of the organisation for capital budgeting. The sole trader will make his own decisions; the small to medium-sized company will be largely administered by its board of directors; in the very large conglomerate or multinational company, a centralised capital budgeting committee may be delegated the task of implementing the investment and financing implications of corporate policy agreed by the board of directors. The staff supporting this committee would include specialists in marketing, production, finance, taxation and law, and the procedure to be followed to gain project approval embodied in a capital budgeting manual.

This manual would cover:

- Instructions and advice regarding the completion and submission of standard project approval documents.
- The methods of appraisal to be followed, e.g. NPV, yield rate or payback, or a combination of these.
- Target rates of return to be applied to different types of projects.
- Instructions about the application of project risk sensitivity.
- Guidance upon how to choose between mutually exclusive projects.

- Dispensation for project approval at plant level for proposals below a specified capital cost, say £5,000.

Self-check

Indicate which of the following would be included in the guidelines published by a company to assist its staff in the compilation of investment proposals:

1 An organisation chart.
2 Assessment of risk sensitivity.
3 Choosing between mutually exclusive projects.
4 The fixed assets register.
5 Target rates of return.
6 Instructions on how to complete proposal forms.
7 The profit and loss budget for next year.
8 Methods of appraisal.

2, **3**, **5**, **6** and **8**.

Preparing the investment proposal

Investments can be large or small, complicated or simple. For example, the purchase of an additional typewriter should not cause many appraisal problems. The amount of capital required is small, and the benefits to be derived from its use well known. On the other hand, business expansion requires a much deeper analysis of all the factors influencing the decision, and the standard checklists mentioned in the previous section would help here.

Activity

A confectionery manufacturer is considering the introduction of a new product. What information would be required to appraise the proposal?

Hint: the following headings will help you to compile your list: product details; assumptions; capital cost; revenue cash flows; taxation; method of appraisal; risk analysis.

Product details – description; extent of competition; whether new or replacement product; estimated life.

Assumptions – size, growth, and share of the market; home or export sales; expected inflation rate over the project life; selling price.

Capital cost – method of financing; cost of capital; buildings and supporting services; machinery and plant; moulds and tools; disposal values of new and existing machinery; additional working capital requirement and when recovered; government grants available; installation costs and time.

Revenue cash flows – sales cash inflows; loss of net revenue from existing products phased out or affected by sales of the new product; additional fixed costs.

Taxation – capital allowances on buildings, plant and machinery; is the company currently paying taxation on its profits?; are there any accumulated tax losses?; what tax rate to apply.

Method of appraisal – NPV, yield rate and payback.

Risk analysis – sensitivity analysis of each variable; perhaps the application of a risk-adjusted discount rate.

A much bigger problem than buying a typewriter, as you can see!

The amount of time and effort applied to project appraisal, even within a large firm, will vary. Straightforward machine replacement, save when alternatives have to be considered, will not cause much heart-searching. But commitment of a large capital sum to the expansion of existing productive capacity, or the purchase of another business, has to be given far more attention.

In the early stages, a very brief report outlining a proposal might be submitted, and if it is viewed favourably, the initiator would be requested to submit a formal project sanction document. This would be in a standard form, serially numbered for identification purposes, to outline the purpose and advantages of the proposed capital expenditure. The significant cash flows would be summarised, but supported by more detailed working papers.

In most cases, the cash flow figures submitted would be best estimates, but the effect of possible changes in any of the variables used in the sanction documents would assist the appraising body in their assessment of the risk of the proposal.

Figure 16 shows the information that might appear on a capital expenditure proposal summary form.

CAPITAL EXPENDITURE PROPOSAL

Submitted by : P. Nut — *No. NP. 4/84*
Department : New Product Development
Date : 1-2-84 — *Total capital required £195,000*
Description : Chocolate Minto

Justification:
Replacement for product 9/78
- see report at schedule 7

NPV @ 15%: +£7573
Yield rate: 16.7%
Payback Period: 3 Years

	Best estimate cash flows					
	Schedule				*Net Cash Flows*	
	1	2	3	4		
Year	*Fixed assets*	*Working capital*	*Operating cash flows*	*Taxation*	*Not discounted*	*Discounted*
0	−200,000 + 10,000	−5,000			−195,000	−195,000
1			+40,000	-	+ 40,000	+ 34,800
2			+40,000	+75,000	+115,000	+ 86,940
3			+50,000	−20,000	+ 30,000	+ 19,740
4			+80,000	−25,000	+ 55,000	+ 31,460
5			+70,000	−40,000	+ 30,000	+ 14,910
6			+60,000	−35,000	+ 25,000	+ 10,800
7	+ 15,000	+5,000	+40,000	−30,000	+ 30,000	+ 11,280
8				−22,500	− 22,500	− 7,357
Total					+107,500	+ 7,573

Affect on earnings per share (see schedule 5)

Year	1	2	3	4	5	6	7	8
	+.005	+.005	+.010	+.025	+.020	+.015	+.005	—

Risk sensitivity:
1 Rate of return
2 Product selling price
3 Variable cost – material
4 Taxation rate

} See schedule 6 attached

Figure 16. Capital expenditure proposal

Reference to schedules refers to the detailed workings needed to produce this summary. Note that the project appears to be only *marginally* profitable and that it is sensitive to risk in many areas. Note also the difference in incidence of *cash flows* compared with *earnings per share* – showing clearly that 'profit' is not substantially increased until year 3. Presumably this company will have developed alternative new product proposals, if 'chocolate minto' is not thought to show sufficient promise.

Once authorised, the project is included in the capital budget and a timetable drawn up for its implementation.

All investment proposals submitted for approval will be considered within the framework of:

- the organisation's agreed *long-term* policy expressed in its corporate plan;
- any limitations placed upon the availability of finance in the *short-term* budget;
- the forecast effect upon the profit and loss account; for even though proposals will meet long-term profitability criteria, relatively low *early* cash flows could have a distortive effect upon reported profit, and consequently upon dividends;
- their correlation with existing operations in terms of risk;
- priority proposals such as those concerned with health and safety, and replacement of facilities vital to the continuity of existing activities.

Continuing encouragement should be given to the initiation of investment proposals, whether the initiative lies with a new product development department or with individual production or marketing managers.

Self-check

Summarise what you would consider to be the main aspects covered in the appraisal of a heavy goods vehicle replacement proposal.

1 Capital cost.
2 Load capacity.
3 Trade-in values of vehicles.
4 Running costs per ton-mile.
5 Maintenance costs.
6 Taxation implications.
7 Estimated life.
8 Flexibility in use, e.g. articulated trailer capability.
9 Information on alternative replacement vehicles.

Monitoring the installation of project facilities

After its sanction, a copy of the capital expenditure proposal documentation will be passed to the accounting department, where appropriate records will be maintained to ensure that authorised capital expenditure is not exceeded. Orders will be placed, either internally or externally, for manufacture of equipment and plant, and expenditure on these will be checked against the approval documents, and charged into a capital work-in-progress account.

Periodic returns should be made to responsible management to indicate progress on each project and, if necessary, additional approval sought if expenditure is forecast to exceed the original approvals. One practical difficulty here is estimating the stage of completion reached on any project at any time, especially in connection with engineering projects. The task in relation to buildings is easier because reliance can be placed upon architects' progress certificates.

When all capital resources of a project are ready to become operational, an accounting transfer of total capital expenditure will be made from the capital work-in-progress account to the appropriate fixed asset accounts, and at the same time records will be opened relating to individual assets.

Post-audit of capital expenditure

Creative people such as artists and systems analysts tend to give little thought to their creations once they are completed and accepted. They prefer to move on to the next creative challenge. Spenders of business capital tend to adopt the same philosophy, so the learning process of comparing actual with expected project performance is lost. In justification of this attitude, it can be argued that initiators of ideas might be discouraged if they felt that the results of all their approved projects were to be closely scrutinised. The balance between discouragement and motivation is delicate.

It can be strongly argued that reviewing past decisions is part of the continuing role of good management. Periodic management accounting reports can supply a lot of the necessary information, especially where projects are wholly related to identifiable cost, profit or investment centres. Supplementary reports on sales quantities, material usage, labour hours worked, scrap and rectification costs will be especially useful at post-audit stage.

Where projects span more than one department, however, a special study will have to be set up, for unless post-audit is formalised, there is a good chance that review will not take place, especially in a large organisation.

Internal audit staff are probably best qualified to be allocated the role of post-auditors. They are normally independent of any particular department, and are a lot closer than anyone else in the organisation to all the procedural and operational aspects of particular projects. This presumes that they are truly *management* auditors, and not just 'tickers' of book-keeping entries.

Finally, it is important that post-audit, just like any other control system, is cost-effective. The benefits arising out of project review may sometimes only be capable of being assessed subjectively, but they should include:

- an improvement in the quality of future investment appraisal arising out of the use of better forecasting methods, assumptions and criteria;
- an improvement in management performance through better communication of the results of their past decisions;
- the taking of timely remedial or abortive action, should an early examination of project performance reveal that it is not living up to its promise; areas of sensitivity highlighted at the appraisal stage should be given priority in the monitoring process;
- the noting of *strengths* (to be encouraged and developed) and

weaknesses (to be corrected) in project appraisal and performance.

Self-check

Referring to the 'chocolate minto' proposal illustrated in figure 16; to what areas would you pay particular attention in a post-audit of this project?

Your list could include some of the following:

1 The four areas of sensitivity noted on the form.
2 Total market size, and the company share.
3 Capital cost and residual values.
4 Material, labour and overhead cost variances from standard.
5 The actual rate of inflation.

Review

1 Briefly describe the steps involved in the organisation and administration of capital budgeting.

2 Five of the following aspects comprise the framework within which a capital budgeting committee operates when considering investment proposals. Name the three that do not directly relate to this framework;

a Capital rationing.
b Industrial relations.
c Recognition of investment priorities.
d The long-term corporate plan.
e The budgetary control system.
f The effect of each project on the profit and loss account.
g The rate of inflation.
h Correlation of each project with the portfolio of existing projects.

3 'Project proposals will only include the most probable cash flow forecasts.' Is this statement true or false? Why?

4 Briefly describe the benefits to be derived from a formalised post-audit of investment projects.

1 a Sanctioning procedure and guidelines communicated, perhaps through the medium of a capital budgeting manual.

b Project proposals prepared and submitted on standard documentation.

c Monitoring the installation of project facilities.

d Post-audit.

2 b Industrial relations.

e The budgetary control system.

g The rate of inflation.

3 False. Alternative forecasts based upon different assumptions would point up the sensitive variables, to provide more informed decision-making information.

4 a Improved quality of future investment appraisal.

b Improved management performance.

c Early warning provided of projects not living up to their promise.

d Strengths and weaknesses in investment appraisal are brought to the surface.

Part 3
Financial planning

7 Establishing the need for finance

Introduction

Imagine that you have to move to another part of the country to take up a new job. For many reasons, and certainly financially, this could be traumatic. You may not receive your first salary for a month, and until then you and your family have to be fed and sheltered. Hopefully you will have some savings for such an emergency, or you might obtain a loan from friends, family or your new employer, to tide you over the lean period.

However, your problems are only just beginning; whilst you have solved your *short-term* problem of financing daily living expenses, much larger sums of money will be needed to finance purchase of a house, furniture and perhaps a car.

The car could perhaps be bought on hire purchase, or by arranging a personal two- or three-year loan through your bank; and a *long-term* housing loan could be arranged with a building society or a bank on the mortgage of your new home.

Your need for financial assistance arises mainly because you lack *immediate* access to sufficient money of your own. True, your new job will provide salary cash flows, out of which you can repay the instalments on your loans – but in the *future*, not immediately. It is this *non-synchronisation* of cash receipts and payments, especially where cash outflows are large if infrequent, that creates the demand for finance – for both private and business purposes. Investment and financing decisions are inextricably linked; investment committing funds to the early acquisition of buildings, machinery and working capital, that cannot possibly generate cash inflows in the short term to repay the total amount invested.

In Part 3 we examine how business finance needs may be assessed, then matched with sources of finance; and how a decision on the optimum mix of own and borrowed funds might be made.

In this chapter we look at the four main influences on the types and sources of finance ultimately chosen. These are:

- the *type of organisation* requiring the finance;
- the *purpose* for which the finance is required;
- for *how long* the finance is required;
- *how much* finance is required.

Business organisations requiring finance

Businesses are as varied in their sizes as they are in their activities, but there is some relationship between size and the type of activity carried on – certainly in the case of small businesses.

> *Activity*
>
> From your personal experience, or by flipping through the Yellow Pages, what types of business do you find are generally operated by one person?

Your list might include plumbers, builders, electricians, dentists, doctors, insurance brokers, shopkeepers, farmers, hairdressers, taxi-drivers and photographers.

Most of these occupations involve *personal service* provided within a limited geographical area. This does does not imply that they are only ever one-person operated. However, the sole business owners survive partly because of the lack of growth opportunity in a restricted locality, partly because they value their independence and partly because they are proud of their personal skills.

Where the type of business provides opportunities for growth, however, sole ownership restricts the availability of finance, partly because the resources of individuals is limited and partly because this has an affect upon the amount that lenders are willing to provide.

The sole ownership constraints can be lifted to some extent by forming partnerships, but again, growth is restricted by available resources, and the legal limits on the size of partnerships (twenty, or fifty in the professions).

Not surprisingly, these limitations, and the fact that each partner is *personally* liable for all the debts of the firm, led to the concept of *limited liability* and the legalising of limited companies.

Company shareholders' liability is limited to the amount that they have agreed to pay for their shares. This enables large amounts of capital to be channelled into a business from a large group of savers, some of whom may hold only a few shares. Indeed, shareholders are able to reduce their personal risk by investing in a number of diverse companies.

Thus, the limited company, particularly the public limited company (plc), which can make a direct invitation to the public to subscribe for its shares, is an admirable vehicle for growth, as it is able to access a wide range of sources of finance.

Purpose for which finance is required

We have seen that the need for finance in business arises mainly because cash receipts lag behind cash payments.

> *Activity*
>
> For what purposes would Colin Pike have needed finance when he first started his electronics business?

For fixed assets – including premises, plant, machinery, tools and presses, vehicles and patent fees.

For working capital – to pay wages, purchase materials for stock and production, rent of premises if not owned, production and marketing expenses and services; before receipts from customers self-financed these items. An additional cash buffer might also be required to cover any temporary shortage of funds.

After their initial acquisition, and given that the business continues its existing activities, these assets have to be continually replaced out of earnings to maintain operations at the same level. They therefore represent a *permanent* financial requirement. You will recall from Chapter 2 that Colin was fortunate to be able to call on his family for these *long-term* resources. No doubt he formed a limited company from the start with himself and his family as shareholders.

Activity

Although permanent assets should be permanently financed, can you think of any circumstances that would call for *temporary* medium- or short-term finance?

1 Short life investment projects would attract medium-term finance.
2 Short-term *bridging* finance, during a period of temporary cash shortfall, perhaps caused by *seasonal* fluctuations in income, delayed payments by customers, or a period of high inflation before selling prices have time to be adjusted upwards.

After the successful establishment of a business, expansion will hopefully follow, either by way of expanding sales of existing products, by venturing into new ones or both. More fixed and working capital will be needed, and inevitably the growth point will be reached when the amount required exceeds the resources of the existing shareholders and the willingness of lenders. The only way forward might be to acquire limited company status (plc) and float a *public* issue of shares.

Further stages of growth might not only be achieved by expansion of existing and new activities but by acquiring other businesses as going concerns. Here, the need for further finance can be obviated by issuing shares in the acquiring business to the owners of the purchased concerns, but only if this is agreed. If a share exchange is not agreed, additional finance must be found to pay off shareholders whose company is taken over.

In summary, a business has to finance:

- a layer of *permanent* fixed and working assets; and
- fluctuating *temporary* cash requirements.

Permanent assets should be provided out of long-term (over ten years) or medium-term (three to ten years) sources of finance to ensure continuing use of these assets. Fluctuating requirements can be met out of short-term sources to reduce the costs of borrowing and provide flexibility in financing arrangements.

Self-check

1 For what purposes would a ladies' hairdresser require finance when she first commences business?
2 Why do farmers sometimes resort to short-term business borrowing?

1 She will need premises and no doubt these will require decorating and to be tastefully furnished, equipment such as hairdryers, and special chairs. Stocks of materials, and an amount to cover operating expenses should her customers be granted credit.
2 There is a lengthy period between sowing time and receiving payment for harvested crops, during which time wages, operating and living costs have to be paid. Short-term bridging finance is required to cover this period.

How much finance is required?

Finance is the lifeblood of a business. The financial manager must, therefore, ensure that finance is available when required. This involves short- and long-term cash forecasting, completed by reference to the overall investment, production and marketing plans of the business.

At the business start-up stage, a careful assessment is made of the *initial* cost of fixed assets and stocks, and the further amount to cover operating costs before receipts from the first sales start to flow in.

A short-term forecast would help to assess the initial requirement for finance.

Activity

Ken Sharp has set up as a wholesaler supplying the retail baking trade. He has rented a local authority trading estate warehouse at £100 a month, and estimates that he will need permanent stocks of at least £10,000 value. A van, two forklift trucks, and storage racks and pallets will cost him a further £30,000, and his operating expenses are estimated at £2,000 per month.

Ken expects that sales in each of the first two months will be £6,000, rising to £12,000 per month thereafter. He sells to the trade at cost plus 50%, and allows his customers two months' credit. His trade suppliers allow him one month to pay, but all other expenses will be paid in the month in which they are incurred.

Required

a Prepare a cash forecast covering each of the first six months of Ken's business.

b What is the maximum amount of finance needed in this first six months?

a

Month		*1*	*2*	*3*	*4*	*5*	*6*
Receipts	*A*	—	—	6,000	6,000	12,000	12,000
Payments:							
Stocks – initial			10,000				
– replacement			4,000	4,000	8,000	8,000	8,000
Equipment		30,000					
Operating expenses		2,000	2,000	2,000	2,000	2,000	2,000
Rent		100	100	100	100	100	100
	B	32,100	16,100	6,100	10,100	10,100	10,100
Surplus/(deficit)	*A–B*	(32,100)	(16,100)	(100)	(4,100)	1,900	1,900
Opening balance		—	(32,100)	(48,200)	(48,300)	(52,400)	(50,500)
Closing balance		(32,100)	(48,200)	(48,300)	(52,400)	(50,500)	(48,600)

b Total capital required: £52,400 – see month 4. Note that the total capital required is not just the £40,000 to cover equipment and initial stocks, but also a further £12,400 for operating expenses, rent and supplies. This is due to the delay in receiving payment from customers. The position would, of course, be worsened by the interest payable on any loan negotiated with the bank. Indeed, if Ken has been wildly optimistic regarding sales or costs, or receipts from customers, the capital requirement could be even larger. It might therefore be in Ken's interest to negotiate a slightly larger financial provision to give himself a little more leeway.

The kind of short-term cash forecast illustrated above, if continuously updated at monthly or even, where appropriate, weekly intervals, can provide a useful early warning of expected deficiencies in finance. Action can then be planned in advance to cover the critical period.

Long-term cash forecasts are normally prepared as part of the long-term corporate planning process. Scheduled investment in growth, whether by expanding production and marketing facilities or by acquiring other businesses, has to be synchronised with the availability of finance.

The forecast will not contain all the fine detail of receipts and payments included in the short-term forecast, and will probably be prepared in yearly periods rather than in months. The sources and application of funds statement produced annually by many companies is perhaps the best format to use; but prepared as a *planning* statement rather than an historic report. It will specify:

- the funds expected to be generated internally from profitable operations;
- funds to be derived from other sources;
- the planned deployment of funds;
- the resultant net increase or decrease in liquidity during the period covered.

The following shows some of the items that will find their way into most forecasts:

Long-term cash forecast years 1–5

Year	*1*	*2*	*3*	*4*	*5*
Planned sources of funds:					
Net profit before tax and dividend					
Add back depreciation					
Funds generated internally					
Sale of assets					
Share issues					
Loan issues					
Government grants					
Total sources					
Planned deployment of funds:					
Repayment of loans					
Purchase of plant and machinery					
Purchase of buildings					
Purchase of other businesses					
Dividends					
Taxation					
Increased working capital					
Total deployment of funds					
Net increase/(decrease) in liquidity					

Note that depreciation is only an accounting adjustment not a cash payment in each year, so it is added back to the planned profit.

If the last line shows a substantial decrease in funds during one or more years, this indicates that extra finance has to be arranged to support the plans reflected in the statement.

The alternative is to revise the plans. They are not sacrosanct. Indeed, as the corporate plan is updated annually, so too will be the long-term cash forecast to take account of changed circumstances.

Self-check

1 George Strumpshaw planned to set up a coal distributing business. He had saved £10,000 and estimated that he would need a further £40,000 for vehicles, premises and initial coal stocks. Would the bank manager agree with George that £40,000 was all the additional finance he needed?

2 Balance sheets for Fido Dogfood Ltd are shown below. Prepare a cash forecast from this information to show the net change in liquidity between next year and this year. Use the format shown in this section for your forecast, but instead of showing working capital changes in one figure, break it down to show the separate effects of changes in debtors, stocks and creditors.

Balance sheets – Fido Dogfood Ltd

	This year		*Forecast for next year*	
	£	£	£	£
Fixed assets	100,000		120,000	
less Depreciation	40,000	60,000	52,000	68,000
Current assets:				
Stocks	10,000		12,000	
Debtors	12,000		13,000	
Cash	3,000		—	
	25,000		25,000	
less Current liabilities:				
Creditors	8,000		9,000	
Bank overdraft	—	17,000	10,000	6,000
		77,000		74,000
Ordinary share capital		60,000		60,000
Retained earnings		17,000		14,000
		77,000		74,000

1 George has probably overlooked the operating expenditure he will incur before he receives any cash from customers. Although his suppliers will probably grant him credit, and this will offset some of his expenditure, there will still be a deficit to be financed caused by the time-lag in receiving payments from customers.

2 *Long-term cash forecast – Fido Dogfood Ltd*

Planned sources of funds:		
Net loss (see reduction in retained earnings)	(3,000)	
Add back depreciation	12,000*	
Funds generated internally		9,000
Planned deployment of funds:		
Purchase of fixed assets	20,000	
Increase in debtors	1,000	
Increase in stocks	2,000	
Increase in creditors	(1,000)	22,000
Net decrease in liquidity (cash plus overdraft)		13,000

*See increase in depreciation.

Review

1 Why does a public limited company have access to a wider financial market than a company without *public* status?

2 What is *bridging* finance? When might it be needed?

3 Current assets will normally be changed into cash within one year. In what sense therefore are current assets permanent?

4 Which of the following influence the amount of capital required by a business?

- **a** The number of directors.
- **b** The amount of tax it pays.
- **c** The lead time between input of resources and payment for goods by customers.
- **d** Production methods and techniques.
- **e** The number of shareholders.
- **f** Planned output and sales.

5 Referring to the Ken Sharp short-term forecast in the last section of this chapter, would it make any difference to the amount of finance required if half the customers who should have paid in month 5, defaulted on their payments?

6 What are the two major differences between the short- and the long-term cash forecasts?

1 Because 'public' implies that a PLC can advertise *publicly* for subscriptions for new share issues it might make.

2 Bridging finance relieves a period of cash shortage. Needed during a time when cash payments *temporarily* exceed cash receipts. For example, when a new product is launched, and up to the time when the first customers pay for their purchases.

3 A business needs stocks of raw materials, work in progress, finished goods and debtors, *permanently*. They change into cash and then back into assets frequently, but a continuing business relies just as much on a permanent stock of current assets as it does on fixed assets.

4 **c**, **d** and **f**.

5 Yes, it would increase the capital required to £56,500.

6 **i** The time periods involved – yearly for the long-term forecast, normally monthly for the short-term.

ii The short-term forecast deals with *detailed* receipts and payments; the long-term with larger changes in funds caused by profit or loss in operating, and planned increases or decreases in assets and liabilities.

8 Types and sources of finance

Introduction

Increasing demand for finance has caused the evolution of an efficient capital market in which different types of finance are available from many sources.

Financing by owners, or borrowed funds

Activity

Harry Bloom is a successful market gardener who a few years ago invested his life savings in his business. It has grown considerably since then, mainly as the result of his 'ploughing back' into the business a large proportion of his profits each year. He now has the opportunity of doubling his operating capacity, but has no cash resources of his own to acquire the necessary fixed and working capital. His present capital invested is £300,000, and his net profit before tax last year was £45,000. He requires £300,000 additional finance for proposed expansion, and estimates that the total profit before tax in the enlarged business will be £105,000.

The improvement in profit will be the result of more efficient operations, and the benefits of bulk buying.

Harry has two main financing options:

a invite a friend, Bill Flowers, who has the amount of capital required, to join him in the formation of a limited company; or

b obtain a loan repayable in ten years' time at an interest rate of 11%. Assuming a tax rate of 40%, calculate the total profit after tax under both options, showing what Harry's share is in each case.

	Limited company £	*Loan* £
Trading profit	105,000	105,000
Interest on loan	—	33,000
	105,000	72,000
Taxation	42,000	28,800
	63,000	43,200
Harry's share	31,500	43,200
Bill's share	31,500	—

Harry is £11,700 better off under the borrowing than under the company option. This is because the cost of obtaining capital from the new shareholder is his half-share of total profit, i.e. £31,500; whereas the loan only costs £19,800 (interest of £33,000 less tax of 40%). It is also worth noting that even under the company option Harry would be entitled to £4,500 (£31,500–£27,000) more than he previously earned.

This example demonstrates that businesses are basically financed from two sources:

- *Use of owners' funds* – such funds are normally permanently invested in the business, only to be repaid if business operations cease.
- *Use of other people's funds* – to be repaid as agreed, unless they are government grants.

Own funds are gleaned from:

a the past and continuing savings of the original proprietor;
b profits earned in the business and retained for reinvestment;
c the savings of people who become part owners of the business, through partnership or shareholdings;
d making more efficient use of the capital already invested in the business.

Once a company has become established and is growing, retained profit provides the bulk of the finance needed but companies will also issue further shares to existing shareholders (i.e. rights issues), or to new shareholders.

We examine the implications of reinvestment and of making further share issues in Part 4.

Other people's funds come from:

a loan providers;
b suppliers' credit;
c instalment credit, hire purchase and leasing arrangements;
d grants and allowances from central and local government.

Self-check

Which of the following relate to funds provided by the owners of businesses, and which to those made available by other people?

a Loans.
b Profit retained for reinvestment.
c Making more efficient use of capital already invested.
d Grants and allowances from central and local government.
e Suppliers' credit.
f Past and continuing savings of the present owners.
g The savings of newly admitted partners and shareholders (new owners).
h Hire purchase and leasing.

Owners' funds: **b**, **c**, **f**, **g**. Other people's funds: **a**, **d**, **e**, **h**.

Loan finance – short-term borrowing (up to three years)

Bank loans are usually for fixed amounts, for specified periods, at fixed rates of interest, although interest governed by changing market rates can be negotiated. Banks normally insist that repayment is secured by the pledging of particular assets – called a fixed charge.

Bank overdrafts are easily arranged and are more flexible than loans because, whilst a top limit of borrowing is specified, the amount of finance required at any particular time may vary, together with interest rates charged, and therefore the average cost of borrowing ought to be lower.

Factoring and invoice discounting usually involve the selling of debtors to a finance house, which advances about 80% of the debts sold. Capital is thus released to be used on other projects. Factoring also includes a sales ledger management service for customers, with or without the advance of finance. The interest rate charged is above the bank's lending rate, and if sales ledger management is included, there is an additional charge for that.

Bills of exchange are equivalent to postdated cheques. A buyer of goods accepts an undertaking to pay the bill in, say, three months' time, by signing (accepting) it. The supplier is then able to obtain immediate payment by discounting (selling) the bill to a bank, and has therefore got early access to much-needed finance. The discount taken by the bank recompenses them for having to wait for payment from the buyer.

Loan finance – medium-term borrowing (from four to ten years)

Term loans are principally made by banks to growing companies. They normally cover projects or assets with lives matching those of the loans. Interest may be at a fixed or a variable rate, and repayment of the capital can be delayed in the earlier years of the loan if desired. The banks normally insist that term loans be secured on tangible assets, but *unsecured* loans may be negotiated at higher interest rates.

Loan finance – long-term borrowing (over ten years)

Mortgage loans are normally made by insurance companies and pension funds for periods of more than twenty years at fixed rates of interest. They are mainly secured by deposit of the title deeds of the property mortgaged. The main recipients are large companies to finance long-term assets, but smaller companies are increasingly being accommodated by mortgage loans from other institutions.

Term loans – similar to medium-term loans, but for longer periods and at higher interest rates. Usually secured on fixed assets.

Debentures and loan stocks are transferrable securities, normally secured on specific assets or by a 'floating charge' on *all* the assets of the business, giving the holder priority in repayment of the debt over the claims of other creditors. The interest rate is fixed, and the securities are repayable on or between certain dates. Unsecured debentures may also be issued, but at higher interest rates.

Convertible loan stock has the added feature of giving the holders the *option* to convert their loan securities into shares on or between specified dates at predetermined prices.

Sale and leaseback is a method of realising 100% of the value of property by selling it mainly to insurance companies and pension funds, but retaining use of it by leasing it back for a long period. The rent is reviewed every five years or so, which can make this a very expensive method of financing.

Trade credit on goods and services

Trade credit is a universal means of financing, especially important to smaller companies which lack access to many sources. Taking *extended* credit without agreement of the supplier is often resorted to these days, but might result in loss of the supplier's goodwill. Where cash discount is offered for prompt payment, delaying payment may secure more finance, but can be very expensive in loss of discounts. Some suppliers will allow arrangements for customers to pay them by instalments.

Hire purchase and leasing

Hire purchase is a method of financing now much used by businesses. The agreement prescribes a deposit payment, the repayment being by instalments over a period of usually less than five years, and a final payment whereupon the goods become the possession of the hirer. Tax advantages include capital cost allowance to be set off against profit and interest charged can be debited against profit of the hirer.

Leasing is similar to hire purchase, save that the lessee never owns the asset. The lease ensures continuous use of the asset, however. Tax capital allowances are passed back to the lessee in lower interest charges, and the lease payments are wholly chargeable as an expense against the profit of the lessee. Leasing is often referred to as 'off-balance-sheet' financing, because neither the asset nor the lease liability appear on the lessee's balance sheet, although this only applies to operating leases. (See Chapter 12.)

Plant hire is similar to leasing, but for shorter daily or weekly periods.

Central and local government grants and incentives

Assistance is available under many schemes in the form of capital for promising new business. Firms moving to government designated 'Assisted areas' are helped considerably with moving costs, grants for plant and machinery and cheap or interest-free loans. (See Chapter 20.)

Tax incentives to invest in plant and machinery, and for non-owners to invest in small and developing companies, are also available.

Self-check

1 What is the difference between a bank loan and an overdraft?
2 Do companies who deal in invoice discounting also offer a sales ledger management service?
3 How does convertible loan stock differ from ordinary loan stock?
4 Hire purchase and leasing are two ways of purchasing assets by instalments. True or false?

1 A bank loan is usually for a fixed amount for a fixed period at a fixed rate of interest; whereas a bank overdraft, although having a top limit, may vary in amount from day to day as required by the borrower, and be subject to a variable rate of interest.
2 No. Factoring includes such a service if required, but invoice discounting relates solely to the provision of finance.
3 Convertible loan stock possesses all the features of loan stock, but has the additional advantage of giving the holder the option of converting the loan stock into other securities – usually ordinary shares – at a prescribed price, on or between specified dates.
4 False. Although it does apply to hire purchase when the last instalment on the hire purchase agreement has been paid. In leasing, the assets do not normally pass into the legal ownership of the lessee.

Who are the main suppliers of finance?

Savings and the institutions

The savings of individuals and businesses supply finance to meet the demands of other individuals, businesses and government who currently have insufficient money for their requirements. These savings are channelled through various institutions.

> *Activity*
>
> Leaf through the pages of the *Financial Times* or a good Sunday newspaper, note and list the different institutions which attract the savings of individuals.

You have probably included the commercial banks in your list; building societies; and the Trustee and national savings bank. But you will also have found that many people's savings find their way into insurance companies as premiums; into pension funds to provide future pensions; and into finance houses, unit trusts and investment trusts as investments.

Because they are under obligation to pay interest, pensions

or insurance claims, these institutions put their savings to work. They do so by reinvesting the funds they receive in shares of, and loans to, businesses; in government securities; in private home loans (building societies and banks); and in hire purchase loans (finance houses).

Financial institutions providing short- and medium-term funds

The commercial banks These are the suppliers of finance known to most people, although they supply little more in total than the insurance companies and pension funds. National Westminster, Barclays, Lloyds and Midland predominate, traditionally taking short-term deposits from their customers, and lending by way of short-term loans and overdrafts. About an eighth of their total funds is kept in cash or relatively liquid form to meet the demands of depositors, leaving a substantial balance to invest in loans, etc. Increasing competition and criticism of the banks in recent years have moved them to expand their traditional role as short-term lenders. Medium-term and even long-term loans may now be negotiated, primarily through their merchant banking subsidiaries, who carry out other functions described below under 'merchant banks'.

Further short-term finance is provide by the banks by discounting and accepting bills of exchange, particularly in connection with overseas trade.

Discount houses There are twelve houses in the London Discount Market Houses Association. Their traditional function is to provide short-term finance by discounting bills of exchange, but they have extended their investing activity to include government Treasury Bills, local authority bonds and certificates of deposit. The latter are negotiable certificates issued by a bank to large depositors of money for fixed periods at fixed rates of interest. The discount houses, together with the commercial banks, the merchant banks which are members of the Accepting Houses Committee and the Bank of England, comprise the short-term *money market*.

Merchant banks These were originally merchants who developed lending businesses.

Hambros, Kleinwort Benson and Rothschild are well known, but there are many more of similar size.

Their funds derive mainly from large company deposits, and they contrive to match the maturity of their lending mainly medium-term, with their borrowing. Long-term investment is considered if complete control over their investment is assured; perhaps by holding a seat on the board of directors of the borrowing company.

Services rendered by merchant banks, but not by all, are extensive, including:

- acceptance of bills of exchange;
- advice on export financing; foreign exchange dealing;
- arranging Stock Exchange quotations and new issues of shares and loan shock;
- advice on financial planning; merger advice; lease financing; hire purchase;
- investment advice and management for clients who have over £50,000 to invest;
- venture and development capital for small businesses.

Foreign banks Branches of overseas banks compete with the UK commercial banks in provision of short- and medium-term finance – particularly for overseas trade and investment.

Finance houses These deal mainly in hire purchase and lease financing. Short-term depositors provide most of their funds, although they will accept longer-term deposits and pay a higher rate of interest on them. Though they take the risk of *borrowing* for the short-term and *lending* over medium-term periods, the lending charges are adjusted upwards to absorb this risk, particularly in connection with hire purchase transactions. Finance houses also arrange short- and medium-term loans, and export finance.

Factoring and invoice discounting companies Although independent companies, many are subsidiaries of the commercial banks. They provide short-term finance by purchasing business debts. Factoring companies also offer debtors' ledger management services for an additional charge.

Leasing companies The majority are subsidiaries of commercial banks, merchant banks and finance houses, though some are independents in the Equipment Leasing Association. They specialise in lease finance.

Financial institutions providing long-term finance

Insurance companies and pension funds Both types of institution invest in long-term assets because their liabilities to policyholders and pensioners respectively are essentially long-term too. As there is a continuous stream of premium and pension contribution cash, immediate liabilities for insurance claims or pensions are met out of current income, the surplus being available for longer-term investment. Both have to plan investments with an eye on *stability* of income and capital, so loans, mortgages, property, sale and lease back, government and local authority stocks are preferred. In recent years, inflation has forced them to invest in the shares of limited companies to maintain the capital value of their funds. However, despite their long-term leanings, insurance companies will now entertain applications for capital from smaller companies.

Unit trusts Money received from investors seeking income or capital growth, or both, is added to a fund invested in securities appropriate to the wishes of investors. The fund is divided into units, each representing a share of the fund. Some funds are specialised in particular industries, e.g. oil-related companies, others have a wide spread of investments to reduce risk further. Many trusts now specialise in overseas investments. The trusts also invest in *new issues* of securities through the Stock Exchange.

A unit trust is called an 'open-ended' fund as new cash is continually being received and paid out. Units can be bought and sold through the unit trust managers at prices quoted daily.

Investment trust companies These are limited companies specialising in the shares and loan stocks of other companies. They obtain capital by issuing their shares, which are traded on the Stock Exchange, and by borrowing. Note that a unit trust is unable to borrow.

If approached by smaller companies they will be willing to invest directly in their shares, subject to a minimum investment of about £25,000.

Building societies These specialise in lending to individuals to enable them to purchase their homes. Funds are borrowed on short-term from savers, and loaned for the long-term to borrowers, the risk in doing this being smoothed out to some extent by the variability of interest rates charged to borrowers.

Other financial institutions

Investors in Industry plc This is the holding company for various UK investment divisions, overseas investment subsidiaries and advisory subsidiaries. It is financed by the commercial banks and the Bank of England, and originated after the Second World War, to provide finance for companies unable to obtain capital anywhere else.

The Industrial and Commercial Finance Corporation (ICFC) and the Ventures Division are the most active of the UK investment divisions, providing a range of financial facilities including term loans, leasing, hire purchase and sale and leaseback finance, as well as offering financial advice to small and medium-sized companies.

Venture and development capital Many agencies, public and private, offer financial assistance to new commercial ventures ripe for exploitation, and to small and medium-sized businesses that require capital for development but are too small to appeal to the public.

Self-check

1 Why do commercial banks mainly supply short-term finance, and insurance companies and pension funds long-term finance?
2 Unit trusts and investment trusts both invest in company shares and loan stocks. How, then, do these two institutions differ?

1 Because they accept short-term funds from their depositors, banks tend to keep their lending short, mainly in overdrafts and loans. About an eighth of their money is kept very liquid, however, to meet the possible needs of their depositors who can withdraw their money at short notice.

Insurance companies and pension funds receive a constant stream of premiums and contributions respectively, but a substantial part of their obligations in respect to these receipts are long-term. Currently maturing insurance policies, insurance claims and pensions can easily be met out of current receipts, the balance being invested in long-term assets such as property.

2 Unit trust funds are invested in a specified range of securities, and the total fund is divided into units allocated to investors. Units can be purchased from, and sold to, the trust managers at any time. The fund is therefore 'open-ended'.

Investment trusts are limited companies which obtain their funds by issuing shares and loan stocks like other companies; and which invest in the stocks and shares of other companies. Trust shares are quoted on the Stock Exchange.

Review

Study the following balance sheet, then answer the questions relating to it that follow.

Leisure Clothing Limited – balance sheet at 31 December 1984

ASSETS EMPLOYED			
Fixed assets:			£
Land and buildings			
(cost less depreciation)			212,000
Plant and machinery			
(cost less depreciation)			362,000
			574,000
Current assets:			
Stocks		35,000	
Debtors		40,000	
Cash		1,000	
		76,000	
less Current liabilities:			
Trade creditors	30,000		
Hire purchase contracts	3,000		
Bank overdraft	5,000	38,000	38,000
			612,000
FINANCED BY			
Ordinary share capital			250,000
Retained earnings			250,000
Shareholders' interest			500,000
Long-term liabilities:			
12% Debentures (1995)		50,000	
14% Mortgage loan (1999)		50,000	
10% Loan (1986)		12,000	112,000
			612,000

Notes:

1 There is a contingent liability for bills of exchange discounted of £2,000.

2 The present value of lease contracts outstanding is £20,000.

1 Briefly indicate which funds are supplied by the owners of the company and which by other people.

2 Which of the sources of funds are short-term, which medium-term and which long-term?

3 Which institutions are likely to have provided the various funds in question **2**?

4 How can **a** land and buildings and **b** debtors be the basis for further financing?

1 The ordinary share capital and retained earnings are owners' funds; the remainder has been supplied by other people.

2 *Short-term*: bank overdraft, trade creditors, bills of exchange.
Medium-term: hire purchase, leasing, 10% loan (repayable 1986).
Long-term: 12% debentures, 14% mortgage loan, share capital and retained earnings.

3 Bank overdraft – a commercial bank.
Trade creditors – suppliers of materials and services.
Bills of exchange – a commercial bank, merchant bank or discount house.
Hire purchase – finance house, merchant bank or a subsidiary of a commercial bank.
Leasing – a specialist independent leasing company, a subsidiary of a commercial bank, merchant bank, ICFC.
10% loan – commercial bank, merchant bank, ICFC.
12% debentures – the public, an insurance company or pension fund, investment trust, ICFC.
14% mortgage loan – insurance company or pension fund, ICFC.
Share capital and retained earnings – private investors, unit trusts, investment trusts, ICFC, insurance company, pension fund.

4 **a** Land and buildings – a second mortgage could raise more funds if and when the property is released from its mortgage; it could also be sold and leased back.
b Debtors – could be sold to a factor or invoice discounting company, which may advance up to 80% of the debts offered.

9 Matching the need to the sources of finance

Introduction

Businesses requiring finance should ensure first that they are making the most efficient use of resources. Capital overinvested in land or machinery, or stocks and debtors, should be released for more profitable investment. The next most readily available source of finance is of course profit, which provides the largest part of business capital.

Continued expansion will inevitably reach a stage when 'ploughed-back' profit and existing shareholders' resources are inadequate. Some control over the business may then have to be relinquished and partners or shareholders invited to join the business. But before then, the advantages of *borrowing* should be explored.

Gearing

The Harry Bloom illustration at the start of Chapter 8 showed how borrowing can be of great value to a business, so long as the return earned on the borrowed money is greater than its cost. Borrowing is referred to as 'gearing' (or 'leverage' in the USA), because changes in trading profit in a geared company have a greater effect on shareholders' return than in an ungeared company.

Gearing is a two-edged sword, however, for whilst it can increase the owner's income, it also adds a further element of *financial* risk to the operating risk of a business.

Activity

The capital structures of Sparks Ltd and Fire Ltd are as follows:

	Sparks Ltd	Fire Ltd
	£	£
Shares of £1 each	50,000	25,000
10% debentures	—	25,000
	50,000	50,000

It is estimated that in the coming year each company has a 50% chance of earning profit of £10,000 and a 50% chance of £2,500.

Ignoring taxation, calculate the earnings per share resulting from each of the possible outcomes, for each company, and the expected value of EPS for each of them in that year. Which company's shareholders fare best? Which company's shareholders' earnings are the more risky? State why in each case.

	Sparks Ltd		*Fire Ltd*	
	50%	50%	50%	50%
Estimated profit	10,000	2,500	10,000	2,500
less Interest	—	—	2,500	2,500
	10,000	2,500	7,500	—
Number of shares	50,000	50,000	25,000	25,000
Earnings per share	.20	.05	.30	0
Expected value of EPS	.125		.15	

Notes:

1 If £10,000 profit is realised EPS is increased by the gearing of Fire Ltd from .20 to .30.

2 There is a higher expected value of EPS in Fire Ltd.

3 On the other hand, if profit is only £2,500, gearing reduces the EPS of Fire from .05 to zero.

4 The *operating* risk represented by the range of estimated profits is the same in both cases, i.e. £2,500 to £10,000. It is only after deduction of interest that the gap between probable EPS of Fire appears wider than Sparks's: a range of zero to .30 compared with .05 to .20 respectively.

5 The *wider dispersion*, which you remember could be compared by calculating standard deviations, illustrates that the possibility of additional income through gearing has its price in additional risk in the case of Fire Ltd.

Lenders take little risk. They get a fixed return on their capital, leaving it to the business owners to accept possible volatility in *their* earnings. In compensation for taking this higher risk, owners expect a higher return, although they do receive the benefit of tax relief on the interest paid on loans, and this takes the edge off the financial risk to some extent.

Apart from fluctuating profit, the main risks attending borrowing are:

- the obligation to repay or renew the loan – the long-term risk;
- the commitment to pay interest on the loan – the short-term risk.

Firms will consequently take on an amount of borrowing that will not evidence too high a reliance on repayable funds, and whose interest charges can be adequately covered by expected future cash flows.

You will recall the borrowing capacity ratios in Chapter 2. The long-term debt to net assets ratio measures a firm's dependence upon capital that has to be repaid; and the interest cover ratio, the number of times that earnings before interest covers interest payable. In calculating both these ratios we must take account of other forms of *continuing* debt such as renewable overdrafts and lease contracts, which increase the capital to be repaid, and the fixed charges to be met out of profit.

Activity

Advice: before working the following, refer to Chapter 2 and the ratios in the section 'Has the business over-borrowed?'

Yachting Supplies Ltd expect turnover, and therefore net assets, to treble in the next two years. Net assets are currently valued at £50,000, financed by 25,000 £1 (nominal) shares. Given the expansion in assets, what *value* of capital could be borrowed at 10% interest if the owners require a long-term debt to net assets ratio at 1 : 3?

What minimum annual profit before interest and tax will have to be realised to meet an interest cover ratio of 6?

Capital to be borrowed: $(£50{,}000 \times 3) \div 3 = £50{,}000$.
Profit before interest and tax: $(10\% \times £50{,}000) \times 6 = £30{,}000$.

The weakness of using ratios to decide borrowing capacity is that they have to be subjectively assessed, or gleaned from somebody else's experience, and this is not very satisfactory.

Unfortunately, there is no exact way of deciding what amount of money a company can borrow. Patently, the essence of the decision is the same as that applying to private borrowing – an assessment of the risks of having to repay the loan, and to pay interest in the meantime.

One way for a company is to analyse the effect on earnings per share of obtaining additional capital by borrowing or issuing further shares. If interest has to be paid, then profit has to be at least sufficient to cover that interest before shareholders start to gain. Once interest is covered by profit, any additional profit generated by the loan capital belongs to shareholders, and this will increase the EPS on the shares they already hold.

Activity

Using the data in the last activity, assume that the company has the financing alternatives of:

a issuing 50,000 shares at £2 each; or
b issuing 25,000 shares at £2 each, and £50,000 10% loan stock.

Calculate the EPS under both alternatives if earnings before interest and tax (EBIT) is £50,000. Assume corporation tax at 50%.

	All shares £	*Shares and loan stock* £
EBIT	50,000	50,000
less Interest	—	5,000
	50,000	45,000
Corporation tax	25,000	22,500
	25,000	22,500
Number of shares	75,000	50,000
EPS	33p	45p

Note the much higher EPS under the loan stock issue.

From the above information we can now construct a chart to show EPS at different levels of EBIT, and this is shown in figure 17.

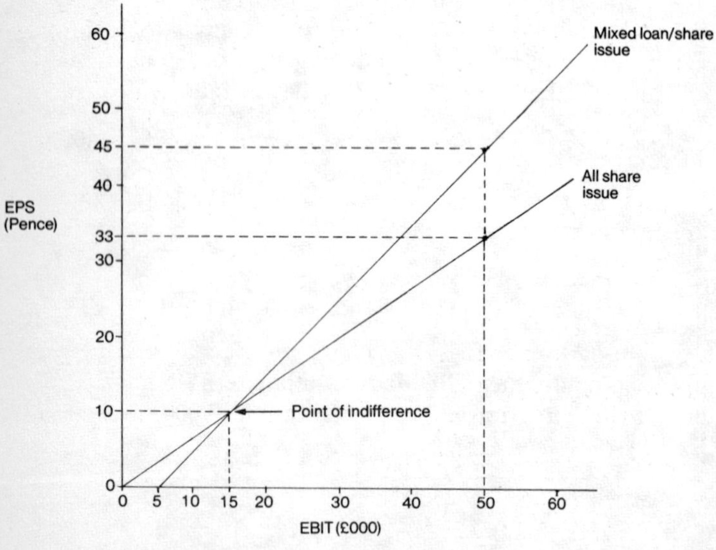

Figure 17. EBIT/EPS analysis chart

Activity

Obtain a sheet of graph paper, continue reading and draw the chart yourself.

The vertical axis shows EPS and the horizontal, EBIT. First plot the coordinate for EPS 33p at £50,000 EBIT for the share option; then draw a line from the origin through this point. The line represents EPS at all levels of EBIT if an all-share issue is made.

Now plot the EPS for the mixed capital option at £50,000 EBIT, i.e. 45p. Draw a further line through this coordinate, but this time commencing at a point of £5,000 along the EBIT axis. Recall that interest of £5,000 has to be paid first before EPS commences.

Observe the crossover point at £15,000 EBIT, where EPS of 10p is the same under both options. Below that level of EBIT the share option shows the higher EPS; above it, the mixed capital option is superior.

This point of indifference between either financing option can also be calculated algebraically by using the following simple equation:

$$\frac{X\,(1-T)}{\text{total number of shares if only shares issued}} = \frac{(X-I)\,(1-T)}{\text{total number of shares if mixed capital issue}}$$

where X=EBIT at the indifference point
T=corporation tax rate
I=interest payable on loan

The left-hand function represents the EPS for an all-share issue, the right-hand one for a loan and share issue. At the indifference point they should be equal – hence the equation.

Applied to the above example we have:

$$\frac{X(1-T)}{75{,}000} = \frac{(X-5{,}000)\,(1-T)}{50{,}000}$$

or $$\frac{X}{75{,}000} = \frac{X-5{,}000}{50{,}000}$$

and $50{,}000X = 75{,}000X-375{,}000{,}000$

and $25{,}000X = 375{,}000{,}000$

to give $X = 15{,}000.$

This can also be checked by calculating EPS at £15,000 EBIT:

	All shares	*Shares and loan stock*
	£	£
EBIT	15,000	15,000
less interest	—	5,000
	15,000	10,000
Corporation tax	7,500	5,000
	7,500	5,000
Number of shares	75,000	50,000
EPS	10p	10p

The next step is to estimate the probability that future EBIT will be in excess of £15,000 in most future years. If it is estimated to be so, then the mixed issue is preferable; if it is not, the all share issue should be made.

Self-check

The following data relates to two companies of equal size in the same line of business, Aqua Ltd and Foam Ltd.

Capital structure	*Aqua Ltd*	*Foam Ltd*
	£	£
Ordinary shares of 25p each	50,000	25,000
Retained earnings	150,000	115,000
10% debentures	20,000	80,000
	220,000	220,000
EBIT	40,000	40,000

Required

1 Calculate the long-term debt to net assets and interest cover ratios of both companies.

2 Which company is more highly geared?

3 Assuming a corporation tax rate of 50% calculate the present shareholders' EPS.

4 What would shareholders' EPS be if earnings (**a**) trebled and (**b**) fell to £10,000?

5 If Aqua Ltd needed £50,000 additional capital, at what level of EBIT would be shareholders be indifferent between issuing shares at £2 each, and further 10% debentures?

6 How would you use your answer in **5** to make your financing decision?

1 Long-term debt/net assets: Aqua 20,000÷220,000=1 : 11 or 9%; Foam 80,000÷220,000=1 : 2.75 or 36%.
Interest cover: Aqua 40,000÷2,000=20 times; Foam 40,000÷8,000=5 times.

2 Foam is the more highly geared because it has more debt to equity capital than Aqua.

3 and **4**

	A	*F*	*A*	*F*	*A*	*F*
EBIT	40,000	40,000	120,000	120,000	10,000	10,000
Interest	2,000	8,000	2,000	8,000	2,000	8,000
	38,000	32,000	118,000	112,000	8,000	2,000
less Tax 50%	19,000	16,000	59,000	56,000	4,000	1,000
Shareholders' earnings	19,000	16,000	59,000	56,000	4,000	1,000
Number of shares	200,000	100,000	200,000	100,000	200,000	100,000
EPS (pence)	9.5	16	29.5	56	2	1

Note that the highly geared Foam produces a better EPS in good profit conditions, but does badly when profits slump.

5

$$\frac{(X-I)(1-T)}{225{,}000} = \frac{(X-I)(1-T)}{200{,}000}$$

$$\frac{(X-2{,}000)}{225{,}000} = \frac{(X-7{,}000)}{200{,}000}$$

$$200{,}000X-400{,}000{,}000=225{,}000X-1575{,}000{,}000$$

$$25{,}000X = 1{,}175{,}000{,}000$$

$$X = 47{,}000.$$

6 Estimate the prospects for future levels of EBIT being substantially above the indifference point.

Further factors influencing the choice of finance

If you were to visit your banker and ask him for a personal loan, he would ask you what you wanted the money for, how much you wanted and for how long. There would be other questions, of course, including your present borrowing commitments. Your banker deals with businessmen in much the same way, and the work you have completed in Chapter 7 on how business finance requirements might be determined, and the first section of this chapter on gearing, would help you to present your case. There are, however, at least four other factors that greatly influence the financing decision. These are:

- *cost*;
- *flexibility*;
- *accessibility*;
- *control*.

We will examine each of these in turn.

Cost

The expected profitability of an investment project can be ascertained by comparing its yield with the company's cost of capital, as shown in Chapter 3. It follows that the cost of capital is the minimum rate of return a businessman must earn on his investments to satisfy the requirements of the capital providers, whether lenders or shareholders. In Chapter 15 we will examine how a company's overall cost of capital might be determined; but it will help at this stage to consider the economic and other influences bearing on the costs of individual types of finance. These include:

- The term-structure of interest rates, which relates interest to the length of the borrowing period; traditionally short-term loans carry a lower rate of interest than long-term because of the promise of earlier liquidity, and lower risk of non-repayment.
- Forecast rates of inflation; the rates at which money is loaned must include some compensation for the expected fall in its purchasing power when it is eventually repaid. If inflation is expected to fall, then long-term rates of interest may be temporarily below short-term rates.
- Government policy; e.g. a higher borrowing requirement by the government will add to the demand for money and tend to raise interest rates.

- If overseas rates of interest are high, then UK rates may have to follow suit, otherwise the value of sterling may be affected by the flight of money abroad.
- The cost of money to the lender; e.g. a finance house must charge its borrowers rates of interest on their hire purchase contracts that more than cover the deposit account interest paid by them.
- Risk – the higher the risk to which the finance is exposed, the higher the rate of return expected.
- Taxation – if there is an interest element in the cost, this is chargeable against profit for tax purposes, effectively reducing the cost of such finance.
- The costs of arranging the finance – can be as high as 8% of the value of a share issue.

Financing policy must be directed at reducing capital costs.

Flexibility

Flexibility in financing means 'keeping one's options open' in relation to borrowing and lending.

> *Activity*
>
> How do building societies build flexibility into their various savings schemes?

By offering progressively higher rates of interest to depositors who are willing to lock their funds away for lengthening periods of time. Depositors can thus keep as much 'instant' cash as they need in the easily accessible ordinary savings account, and as long as they match their requirements for cash at longer intervals with giving the required notice of withdrawal, can earn higher interest in longer-term deposit accounts. Withdrawals can even be made from the latter but with some interest penalty imposed. Further, building society interest rates are not fixed; they vary with market rates, adding more flexibility to their schemes.

If a business becomes shut in by *long-term* borrowing at a fixed rate of high interest, it suffers two disadvantages:

- it will have to pay interest on all the finance, even if there are surplus funds from time to time;
- it will be obliged to continue to pay the same high rate of interest, even though interest rates generally may be falling.

So long-term borrowing has become rarer, aided by lenders' reticence to commit themselves to long-term lending contracts during periods of high uncertainty and inflation. In addition, the introduction into borrowing arrangements of interest rates that *vary* in sympathy with the general level of rates has made short- and medium-term more attractive than long-term.

Building more flexibility into financing should make it cheaper in the long run, since:

- borrowing only as much capital as required in the short-term is cheaper than paying for surplus funds;
- borrowing short-term is generally cheaper than long-term;
- borrowing short-term at high rates of interest, when interest rates are expected to continue to fall, may be worthwhile to take advantage of lower long-term rates in the future;
- borrowing over short or medium periods perhaps at variable interest rates, or leasing, or hire purchasing, to match fast obsolescing plant or machinery, could be more sensible than borrowing expensive fixed-interest long-term funds.

As you would expect, however, there are risks associated with flexibility of short-term borrowing, since:

- loans can be called in by the lender at fairly short notice;
- loans may not be renewable at a time when finance is tight;
- loans are subject to more volatile interest rate changes than long-term borrowing, making cash planning difficult;
- if interest rates fall considerably, long-term borrowing becomes more attractive; more especially if inflation is forecast to rise in the medium to long-term.

Accessibility

Accessibility of finance does not worry the large, well-established companies, which can probably rely on internally generated funds for most needs.

It is the small- to medium-sized growing companies which find their way blocked to the full range of financing available to larger companies. Paradoxically, sole trader and partnership businesses may find it easier than limited companies to obtain finance, as the *personal* assets of the owners underpin any borrowing. Shareholders' liability by comparison is limited.

Generally, smaller firms find finance for expansion not only harder to access but also comparatively dearer than larger companies, since the latter are reckoned lower risks.

Reasons for their difficulties came out in the report of the Bolton Committe on Small Firms in 1971:

- they may have little past business record on which to base an application for finance;
- management may be inexperienced or incompetent, and have little knowledge of sources of finance;
- interest rates asked are higher than for established firms, and security for loans may be inadequate;
- sources of capital are fewer, because some institutions will only accommodate larger firms;
- financial management is often given scant attention inside small firms, production and sales being deemed all-important;
- large customers tend to treat small suppliers badly by delaying payment of their debts, thus aggravating the small firm's financial problem;
- lenders are reluctant to lend to firms with no obvious management succession plans, and where risk of insolvency is greater because of their size.

The Wilson Committee which reported on the workings of the financial institutions in 1979 stated that small firms were at a disadvantage not only regarding accessibility to finance but also in relation to cost and security impositions placed on them. Consequently, many schemes are now available to aid the financing of small companies, which will be discussed in Chapter 20. The most significant of these measures have been (a) the introduction of lower corporation tax rates for small companies and (b) tax relief offered to investors in small companies, subject, however, to such investors being prevented from taking part in the management of the enterprises.

Control

Imagine you started a business five years ago, which you have nursed through good years and bad, to a healthy and still growing state. Considerable further growth may now be possible, quite beyond the financial capability of the firm, through either reinvesting profit or further borrowing. You are presented therefore with the alternatives of stagnating, but keeping complete control over your company, or 'going public', that is becoming a plc, and advertising publicly for more finance through an ordinary share issue.

You will inevitably lose some control, depending upon the amount of capital required, but to retain a majority interest (at least 50%), and continue to see your dreams of growth being realised, may meet your objectives for the business more than retaining complete control.

Obviously, if there is borrowing capacity left, this will be used to maintain control. Preference shares are another financing alternative. They are normally non-voting shares, which help to retain control, but the dividend cost will be relatively high to compensate for this. More to the point, preference dividend is not chargeable as an expense against profit, as is interest, which makes it comparatively more expensive still.

Self-check

1 What are the *benefits* and *risks* attending flexible financing arrangements?

2 'All business firms have equal accessibility to the capital market.' True or false?

3 'The need for more finance may lead to some loss of control by the present owners.' Explain this statement. How might this be avoided?

1 *Benefits* of flexibility:

- cheaper borrowing costs because short-term interest rates are generally lower than long-term, and only the amount of capital required from time to time will be borrowed; even though finance is required for permanent assets, borrowing short-term is more sensible whilst interest rates are falling rapidly.

Risks of flexibility:

- short-term loans may be called in and perhaps not renewed;
- short-term rates are more volatile than long-term, making cash planning more difficult.

2 False. Small firms have more difficulty in obtaining finance than large firms, mainly because of their lack of proven business record, the inexperience of their managers and the risks connected with small businesses.

3 If the only place to obtain more capital is the *share* issue market, then some control will have to be sacrificed. This can be obviated by borrowing, as long as this does not increase financial risk inordinately.

The Financing Decision

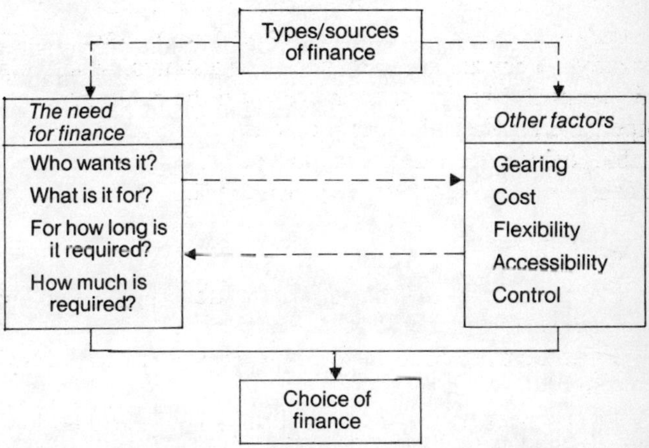

Figure 18. The financing decision

No universal model may be applied to all financing problems. Businesses differ in size and activity, and a particular choice of finance at one time may not be appropriate at another.

Consider Simon Poacher, who channelled his genius for producing succulent pies and pâtés into a thriving business.

Early days

With his degree in catering management Simon was determined to 'go it alone' from the start but he had only £3,000 in personal savings.

Unfortunately his cash forecast covering the first six months of planned business operations revealed a start-up requirement of £6,000, including fixed assets costing £4,000 and working capital of £2,000.

Never at a loss for ideas, Simon gradually softened up his family by introducing game pie and delicious duck and orange pâté into their diet. Father soon gave in and contributed £2,000 towards the share capital of the embryo business.

However, this still left Simon £1,000 short of total requirement, and, with no past business record, he found sources of finance very inaccessible. Even suppliers insisted on cash on delivery in early months.

Fortunately, his bank manager not only lent a sympathetic ear, but was sufficiently impressed by Simon's presentation of cash forecast, and production, sales and profit plans, to grant him an overdraft facility of up to £2,000, secured by his father's personal guarantee.

Activity

Explain why the overdraft would be more flexible than the fixed loan.

The overdraft would probably be cheaper than a loan, because the amount owing would be *variable*, that is, *up to* £2,000, rather than a *fixed* amount of £2,000. However, if interest rates increased, a variable interest rate would be more expensive than a fixed rate. In addition, flexibility could work against him should the bank manager decide to call in the overdraft at any time.

Thus Simon started business, his balance sheet showing that his commencing debt capital to equity capital ratio (gearing) of 1 : 5 was not excessive.

Simon Poacher Pie and Pâté Co. Ltd.

	£		£
Share capital	5,000	Fixed assets	4,000
Overdraft	1,000	Working capital	2,000
	6,000		6,000

Early success and growth

Simon Poacher worked hard during the next three years at every task in production, selling, delivery and administration. His pies and pâtés became gastronomic legends and, soon, he was hard-pressed to meet demand.

Consequently, the business moved to an industrial trading estate after two years, where Simon was fortunate to acquire rented premises, eliminating the need to invest in land and buildings. Indeed, the local authority granted him rent-free use for the first year of his tenancy.

However, an extensive range of ovens, implements and other equipment, together with three more delivery vans and two motorcars, additional stocks and debtors, considerably enlarged his requirement for permanent finance. This was largely satisfied by reinvesting profit but, because the business now had a successful track record, other types of finance became available.

> *Activity*
>
> Given the types of finance discussed in Chapter 8, what types of finance do you think became available to Simon?

Additional types and sources would probably include:

- *Trade credit from suppliers* – a facility that can be expected to extend proportionately to operating activity.
- *Bank overdraft* – an increased limit, possibly unsecured if the bank considered Simon to be sufficiently creditworthy; although essentially short-term, because it is renewable, it might be effectively considered to be long-term finance.
- *Term loan* – for, say, three to five years, from a commercial bank, merchant bank or the ICFC.

- *Hire purchase* – of equipment or vehicles through a finance house.
- *Leasing* – ovens from a leasing company.
- *Selling debts* – through a factoring or invoice discounting arrangement.

Simon had made full use of trade credit and tax payable, and his investment in stocks and debtors was efficient and optimal. He had negotiated a five-year term loan of £30,000 with ICFC secured by a floating charge on all his assets. Equipment, delivery vans and cars had been bought on hire purchase, and were now paid for. The bank overdraft was a modest £15,000, leaving some scope for this to be extended should the need arise.

By now the financial position looked like this:

	£		£
Share capital	5,000	Plant and machinery (net)	90,000
Retained earnings	105,000	Motor vans and cars (net)	19,000
	110,000	Motor vehicles (net)	6,000
Term loan	30,000	Stock	30,000
Bank overdraft	15,000	Debtors	50,000
Tax payable	10,000		
Trade creditors	30,000		
	195,000		195,000

Given the rapid and continuing growth of the company, the balance sheet shows a reasonably sound position. A total borrowing ratio of .75 : 1 is rather high, but to be expected at this stage. Liquidity, currently at .91 (50,000/55,000), could be a problem if assets require early replacement.

Further growth

Four years later, with an order book bursting at the seams and enquiries flooding in Simon felt he had outgrown his trading estate premises. Enquiries were made of a property agent, and suitable freehold land and buildings purchased for £150,000, financed partly by a mortgage loan of £110,000 arranged with a pension fund, and partly out of retained earnings. Some additional and replacement equipment and vehicles were leased, the remainder being financed by renegotiating the term loan with ICFC, and retained earnings. Factoring debts was considered too expensive, especially as the company had a very efficient debtors control system.

Simon knew that a wider range of sources of finance had become accessible as his business grew, enabling his family to retain 100% control of the company.

Activity

A food distributor on holiday from France calls on Simon out of curiosity. He is so impressed by the company's products that he signs a contract immediately for a weekly shipment of pâté to his warehouse in France. However, he asks for three months' credit.

How can Simon secure early payment in this country for the shipments?

Simon could draw bills of exchange at three months on the French importer, have them accepted by an agent of that firm in this country, and then discount them with his bank. Export finance will be discussed more fully in a later chapter.

Expansion

One of the major problems connected with the continuing growth in orders was product distribution. It was therefore decided to open a production and distributing centre in the south of England. This would require additional finance of £150,000.

The balance sheet at this time was as follows:

	£		£
Share capital	5,000	Land and buildings (net)	150,000
Retained earnings	265,000	Plant and machinery (net)	120,000
Equity interest	270,000	Motor vans and cars (net)	60,000
Mortgage loan	110,000		330,000
Term loan	25,000	Stock	50,000
Trade creditors	40,000	Debtors	80,000
Tax payable	25,000	Cash	10,000
	470,000		470,000

Activity

1 Calculate:
  a the current and acid test ratios in the above balance sheet;
  b the long-term debt to equity ratio;
  c the total liabilities to equity ratio.

2 Do the above ratios show a satisfactory financial position?

1 a Current ratio: 140/65=2.15 : 1; acid test ratio: 90/65=1.4 : 1.
  b Gearing ratio: 135/270=.50 : 1.
  c Total liabilities: 200/270=.74 : 1.

2 Liquidity as shown by current and acid test ratios is adequate, but the gearing ratio leaves little room for further borrowing, without broadening the equity share capital base of the company.

Simon pondered whether to 'go public' and make a share issue. He decided against, for he considered the company too small to be attractive to general investors and also because he did not welcome the idea of giving up much control of his business.

Further discussions were held, therefore, with the Industrial and Commercial Finance Corporation. The ICFC had already helped the company with term loans, was most impressed by its performance and management and was prepared to assist with further *development* capital.

After the negotiators had considered the long-term cash and profit forecasts, Simon agreed he would subscribe a further £50,000 from his private resources as additional share capital, which the ICFC agreed to match and to supplement with a ten-year loan of £50,000, secured on the premises of the new branch.

The capital structure was now:

	£
Equity capital	370,000
Mortgage loan	110,000
Loan (10 years)	50,000
Term loan	25,000

This retained the same relatively high gearing ratio as before, .50 : 1. It was rather high for a little-known company, but the kind of development capital situation that ICFC was created to support – a fast growing, successful company, unable to appeal elsewhere for funds.

Going public

Simon Poacher's company would inevitably reach a point at which retained earnings and further borrowing were insufficient to support expansion, and the only solution would be to appeal to the public by an issue of shares. Simon and his family would lose part control, but could still retain a substantial majority interest. From a broader equity base, more loan capital could be obtained to replace the more expensive leasing arrangement. But medium- rather than long-term loans might be more attractive to borrower and lender given the uncertainty of long-term interest rates.

Review

The Rainyday Garment Co. Ltd was expanding rapidly after four years' existence, and required further finance. One new machine costing £60,000 was needed immediately. The balance sheet and profit and loss account for the company for the year just ended arc shown below:

Balance sheet

	£		£
Share capital	60,000	Land and buildings (net)	156,000
Retained earnings	136,000	Plant and machinery (net)	58,000
	196,000	Vehicles (net)	12,000
Term loan	70,000		226,000
Trade creditors	26,000	Stock	58,000
Bank overdraft	2,000	Debtors	40,000
Dividend payable	10,000		
Tax payable	20,000		
	324,000		324,000

Profit and loss account

	£
Sales	240,000
Cost of sales (including depreciation £12,000)	150,000
	90,000
Taxation	20,000
	70,000
Dividend payable	10,000
Retained profit for the year	60,000

Additional information:

1 As a result of the additional investment, turnover is expected to increase by one-third next year, with further growth in future years.

2 Average stock turnover in the industry based on sales is six times, and average debtors outstanding 45 days.

3 The 8-year term loan which is secured on the property was arranged with the company's bank one year ago. The balance is repayable by equal instalments over the next seven years with interest at 12% per annum on the outstanding balance at the beginning of each year. Last year's interest of £9,600 is included in cost of sales.

4 It can be assumed that cost of sales (excluding depreciation and interest), as a percentage of sales, will be the same next year as this.

5 It is planned to maintain dividends at the same amount next year.

Required

a Calculate and comment on the current, acid test, stock, debtors and gearing ratios of the company.

b Suggest how Rainyday might finance their expansion, assuming more efficient management of working capital.

Hint: a funds flow forecast for next year will help you in making your decision.

a Ratios

Current	98/58=1.69 : 1
Acid Test	40/58= .69 : 1
Stock T/O	240/58=4.14 times
Debtors	40/240×365=61 days
Gearing	70/196= .36 : 1.

The bank would be happier if the current ratio were nearer to 2:1, and the acid test at less than 1 : 1 could be potentially dangerous for a young, fast-growing business. However, taxation is probably not payable until October next, by which time cash flows resulting from growth should alleviate the liquidity problem (see cash forecast below).

Stock turnover at 4.14 times and debtors outstanding of 61 days' sales compare unfavourably with the industry norms of six times and 45 days respectively. However, most of the over-investment will be absorbed by next year's business expansion.

Debtors ought to be 45/365×£240,000=£29,589; and stock £240,000÷6=£40,000. The difference of £28,411 between these figures and those in the balance sheet can be released for investment.

Given the fast growth of Rainyday, the gearing ratio of .36 : 1 is to be expected, and the existing term loan is adequately secured on property.

b A cash flow forecast for the coming year is shown below:

		£
Sales (£240,000×1⅓)		320,000
Cost of sales (54%×£320,000) (see Note 1 below)		172,800
Funds generated by operations		147,200
Working Capital:		
	£	
Debtors 45/365×£320,000	39,452	
Stock £320,000÷6	53,333	
	92,785	
less: credit from suppliers .26*×92,785	24,124	
	68,661	
less current investment in stock, debtors, less creditors	72,000	
Working capital released		3,339
		150,539
less Taxation	20,000	
Dividend	10,000	
Loan repayment – bank	10,000	
Interest 12%×£70,000	8,400	48,400
Estimated increased in liquidity		102,139

*Percentage of debtors and stock as last year

Whilst the estimated increase in liquidity appears adequate to cover the new £60,000 machine, cash would not be available immediately, and resources would be needed for future replacement of fixed assets and for further expansion.

The bank would probably extend their overdraft to accommodate any temporary loss of liquidity caused by increases in stocks and debtors, but might be unwilling to increase longer-term lending to Rainyday. In any case, it would be advisable to leave the bank facility in reserve in case of need. This would provide more *flexibility* in future financing.

Even if existing shareholders are willing to provide the additional finance (say 20,000 shares at £3 each), it would still appear to be to their advantage to negotiate a further loan on terms similar to the current one, as the EBIT analysis in Note 2 below shows. Assuming a tax rate of 50%, EBIT above £117,200 increases their earnings per share with the loan option, and this level of earnings is shown to be attainable in the cash forecast.

A £60,000 term loan repayable over eight years, together with interest at 12% per annum, has therefore been arranged with the ICFC, secured by a floating charge on all the company's assets. This *development* loan immediately worsens the gearing ratio, but the cash flow statement indicates that retained earnings will build-up fairly swiftly to correct that situation, and to provide a broader equity base for future borrowing. The modest dividend policy is evidence of the owners' intention to 'plough-back' the bulk of the earnings available to them.

Alternative arrangements, to lease the machinery or to factor debts could be acceptable, but their *costs* would have to compare favourably with the term loan.

Note that Rainyday has reached the stage in its development when types and sources of finance become more *accessible*, although the owners will have to consider going public and giving up some control if growth continues at its present rate.

Note 1 Calculation of cost of sales percentage

£	£	
Cost of sales last year		150,000
less: Depreciation	12,000	
Interest	9,600	21,600
		128,400
128,400/240,000)	= 54% (approx.)	

Note 2 EBIT Analysis

Let X=indifference EBIT between loan and equity capital

Loan option — Share option

$$\text{Then: } \frac{(X-\text{Interest})(1-\text{tax rate}) - \text{loan repayment}}{\text{No of shares}} = \frac{(X-\text{Interest})(1-\text{tax rate}) - \text{loan repayment}}{\text{No of shares}}$$

$$\frac{(X-15{,}600)(1-.5)-17{,}500}{60{,}000} = \frac{(X-8{,}400)(1-.5)-10{,}000}{80{,}000}$$

$$\frac{.5X-7{,}800-17{,}500}{60{,}000} = \frac{.5X-4{,}200-10{,}000}{80{,}000}$$

$$8(.5X-25{,}300) = 6(.5X-14{,}200)$$

$$4X-202{,}400 = 3X-85{,}200$$

$$X = 117{,}200$$

Part 4
Long- and medium-term finance

10 'Going public' and the securities market

Introduction

The financial markets bring together those who require short-, medium- and long-term funds, and the suppliers of those funds.

'Going public'

Colin Pike, chairman and managing director of Pike Electronics Ltd, was discussing with his bank manager, James Thorburn, his company's need for a large injection of additional capital. Latest accounts of the company showed it had a net asset value of £3 million, and that pre-tax profit last year was about £1 million.

'Most private companies that experience the rapid growth that your company has achieved over the last five years have reached the stage when existing shareholders' private resources are exhausted, and retained profit is insufficient to cope with the rate of expansion,' the bank manager began. 'Further borrowing on top of your current £1 million of loans will probably be resisted by lenders until you have a more substantial layer of equity capital.

'One solution to your financial problem,' continued the bank manager, 'is to retain the services of a financial intermediary –

usually a merchant bank, to find a financial institution such as an insurance company or an investment trust that is willing to subscribe more capital. This is known as a *private placing*.'

'Isn't such a method expensive?' queried Colin.

'Well, the administrative costs would not be too onerous,' replied Mr Thorburn, 'but the *private* nature of the arrangement, which renders the investment less liquid, and the inherent uncertainty associated with a relatively unknown business will cause the investor to look for a higher than normal rate of return. In addition, the subscribing institution might insist upon representation on your board of directors, and would probably expect the company to convert to *public* status and apply for a Stock Exchange listing within two or three years, in order to provide a wider market for the sale of their investment.'

'How would going public affect our company?' questioned Colin.

'You would first have to register Pike Electronics as a *public limited company* (plc) with the Registrar of Companies. You simply add that you are a public limited company to your memorandum of association which sets out your constitution. That you already have the required minimum issued capital of £50,000, leaves the way open to you to publicly advertise your shares for sale.'

The bank manager handed Colin a note he had drawn up in anticipation of their discussion, listing the advantages and disadvantages of going public.

Advantages

- access to the capital market and to larger amounts of finance becomes possible by having shares quoted on the Stock Exchange;
- institutions are more likely to invest in a public listed company, and additional borrowing becomes possible;
- a market price for the company's shares is established, providing a recognised value for sale purposes, and for capital transfer tax valuation;
- shareholders will find it easier to sell their shares in a wider market;

- the purchase of other companies is made easier by being able to offer the vendors shares instead of cash;
- the company attains a higher financial standing.

Disadvantages

- costs of a public flotation of shares are high – as much as 4% to 10% of the value of the issue;
- because outside shareholders are admitted, some control may be lost over the business;
- publicly quoted companies are subject to more scrutiny than private;
- the risk of being taken over is introduced by making it easier for the company's shares to be purchased on the Stock Exchange.

'What chance do we have of obtaining a quotation for our shares?' asked Colin.

'In my opinion, an excellent chance,' replied James, 'You will be required to reveal your last five years' trading record; have a minimum market capitalisation of £500,000; make at least 25% of your equity shares available to the public; and sign a Stock Exchange *listing* agreement which binds you to disclose specified information about your company in future.'

Self-check

1 Give two advantages each accruing to **a** an individual shareholder **b** the company, when a company goes public and obtains a Stock Exchange quotation.
2 Why does a public quotation increase the risk of a company being taken over?
3 What additional pressures are created against a company when it goes public?

1 a A market price for the shares is established; shareholders find it easier to sell shares in a wider market.
b Access to wider sources of finance; purchase of other companies is made easier by being able to offer shares instead of cash.

2 Because it is relatively easy to purchase the company's shares on the Stock Exchange.
3 Some control may be lost to new shareholders; the company's affairs are more closely scrutinised because more information about it is made public.

Types of shares

Presuming that a public quotation could allow more flexibility into his company's capital structure, Colin wanted to know a little more about the different types of shares that can be issued by a company.

'The two main classes of shares are *ordinary* and *preference*,' said Thorburn. '*Ordinary shares* (sometimes referred to as the "equity" shares) are those held by the highest risk-takers in the company. This implies that the holder's claims upon profit – for dividend, and assets – if the company is liquidated, are deferred to the prior rights of creditors and other security holders. However, the capital liability of ordinary shareholders is limited to the amount they have agreed to subscribe on their shares; therefore they cannot be called upon to meet any further deficiency that the company may incur.

'In your company the ordinary shares are the voting, controlling shares, but in some companies, when a significant proportion of the shares is held by the directors, and the remainder are widely held by a large number of small shareholders, the directors may effectively control the company.

Preference shares are attractive to risk-averse investors because of their fixed rate of dividend, which normally must be at higher level than the rate of interest paid to lenders, because of the relatively greater risk of non-payment of dividend. Whilst they are part of the share capital, the holders are not normally entitled to a vote, unless the terms of issue specify otherwise, and even then votes are usually only exercisable when dividends are in arrears.

'Preference shareholders have a prior right to dividend before ordinary shareholders, but it may be withheld if the directors consider there are insufficient resources to meet it.

There is an implied right to accumulation of dividends if they are unpaid, unless the shares are stated to be non-cumulative. Payment of such arrears has priority over future equity dividends.

'If the company goes into liquidation, preference shareholders are not entitled to payment of dividend arrears or of capital before ordinary shareholders, unless their terms of issue provide otherwise. They would thus rank equally with ordinary shareholders to share any surplus remaining after creditors have all been paid.

'Three varieties of preference shares have been issued by companies from time to time, to confer special rights, these are redeemable preference shares, participating preference shares and convertible preference shares.'

'*Redeemable preference shares* are similar to loan capital in that they are repayable, but they lack the advantage enjoyed by *loan* interest of being able to charge dividend against profit for taxation purposes. *Participating preference shares* enjoy the right to a further share in the profits beyond their fixed dividend, normally after the ordinary shareholders have received up to a stated percentage on their capital. *Convertible preference shares* give the option to holders to convert their shares into ordinary shares at a specified price at a specified time.'

Colin interrupted: 'Why is it that preference shares seem to be so unpopular nowadays?'

'There are four main reasons,' replied Thorburn. 'First, their dividends are not chargeable against profits for taxation purposes; second, the dividends can be passed over in years of poor profitability; third, their permanence and fixed return are subject to the ravages of inflation from the investors' point of view; and fourth, holders take greater risks than debenture holders but do not enjoy the higher returns and voting control of ordinary shareholders.

'However, preference shares may still be attractive as company investments because dividends from them are not subject to corporation tax, and because advance corporation tax on their own dividends may be reduced by the ACT already paid on dividends received by them. A further reason for issuing preference shares may be because debt capital is too risky if the company has already got a high gearing ratio; and the alternative of an issue of ordinary shares would pass control of the company to outsiders.'

Self-check

1 'The difference between loans and shares is that the return to investors on the former is fixed, but on shares it is not.' True or false? Explain.
2 'Only ordinary shareholders are entitled to vote at meetings.' True or false? Explain.
3 Why have there been few preference share issues in recent years?

1 False. *Ordinary* share dividend is not fixed; it is dependent upon there being profit available after all prior rights are satisfied. However, *preference* share dividend is normally fixed.
2 False. Although this may be normally true, it is sometimes the right of preference shareholders to vote if their dividend is in arrears.
3 Preference share issues are now few because:
a unlike interest, dividends cannot be deducted from profit for corporation tax purposes;
b dividends can be passed over in years of poor profit;
c inflation reduces the real value of dividends, and the preference capital value.

The Stock Exchange

'You stated earlier, James, that a Stock Exchange listing provides access to a wider capital market. Can you please tell me something about the functions of the Stock Exchange?' queried Colin.

'Quite simply the major role of the Exchange is to provide a well-regulated second-hand market in ordinary and preference shares, British government and local authority stocks, loan stocks and some foreign stocks, that are all included in its listings,' began Thorburn.

'Without this market facility, buyers for new issues of securities would be difficult to find as it would be harder for them to sell their holdings. The Stock Exchange is self-regulated by a council elected by its members (over 4,500), who are themselves either *stockbrokers* or *stock jobbers*, belonging to about 350 firms.

'The council acts through committees who:

- consider applications for listing of securities;
- decide on the admission of new members, or the expulsion of existing members;
- supervise the solvency requirements of members;
- enforce the general rules and discipline of membership.

'*Stockbrokers* act as agents on commission for clients who wish to buy or sell securities, and they deal with *jobbers* who are principals and own and specialise in certain classes of stocks and shares, e.g. property. The jobber is remunerated by selling a share at a price slightly higher than that paid for it, this being known as the "jobber's turn".

'When approached by the broker, the jobber, who does not know whether the broker is a buyer or a seller at that stage, quotes two prices, say 75–77; the lower is the price at which he will buy, and the higher his selling price; *but he is obliged to buy or sell* if the broker wishes to deal with him. This gives the investor an assured market for buying or selling shares.

'Not all securities are dealt with through brokers and jobbers. In 1974, a computerised system was set up by large institutions to match buyers and sellers, and thus reduce the expense connected with frequent high-volume transactions in securities. It is known as ARIEL (Automated Real-time Investments Exchange Ltd).

'Three developments strengthened the role of the Stock Exchange, and widened its services:

- The setting up of the computerised Talisman system which has speeded up transactions between buyers and sellers of securities.

- The setting up of the *Unlisted Securities Market* (USM) by the Stock Exchange in 1980.
- The introduction of the traded options market in 1978 by the Stock Exchange.'

Colin interrupted his bank manager: 'The USM sounds intriguing. Would it be a suitable vehicle through which to launch our company on to the market?'

'It is certainly a *cheaper* way than a *full* listing to establish a market for your shares, but your requirements for a *large* amount of finance, and the fact that your reputation is already established in the industry, points the way to full listing.

'The USM is essentially for small to medium-sized companies desiring to retain substantial control over their own destiny, but wishing to secure a market value for their shares, and access to the capital market, without the expense of a full listing. Its main features are:

- no lower limit on the company size as there is with a full listing;
- companies should normally have a three-year trading record;
- 10% of the equity capital (instead of 25% for a full listing) must be in public hands;
- *placing* is the normal method of marketing shares, with a £3 million limit;
- the prospectus and advertisements giving details of the share issue need only be in abridged form;
- companies must sign the general undertaking of the Stock Exchange covering the arrangements for keeping the shareholders and the market regularly informed.'

'If we obtain a full listing and the capital we require, how will the *traded options market* that you mentioned earlier affect us?' queried Colin.

'It would not directly affect your company, but it is a facility that you as an investor could use.

'An option is the right to buy or sell something at an agreed price within a stated period of time. With reference to shares, a premium is paid to a broker for a *put* option (giving the right to *sell* shares at some future date), or a *call* option (giving the right to *buy* shares at a future date).

'Because traded options cost much less than the underlying securities, an investor is able to back an investment opinion without risking too much money. For example, an investor might buy a call contract for 1,000 shares traded in the options market, at 20 pence per share, the option being exercisable in July. At the time the contract is taken out the market price is £2.80, but the agreed exercise price is £2.95.

'Should the share price move up to £3.30, the investor does not necessarily have to buy the share to take a profit. Instead, he can sell the option for the difference between the market price and the exercise price, i.e. £3.30 less £2.95=35 pence. Having paid 20 pence for the option in the first place, he has realised a profit of 35 less 20 pence on 1,000 shares=£150, which is a 75% return on his original outlay of £200. Thus the risk of loss by the investor is limited to the amount paid for the option contract, whilst the profit on traded options can be quite substantially more than trading in shares.'

New issues of securities

Turning to the question of going public, the bank manager handed Colin another note on various ways in which a company can make new issues of shares:

Stock Exchange introduction

1 This method is used when all that is needed is a stock market quotation by a public company whose shares are already widely held, to create a market and thus a value for the company's shares. Valuation might be required for capital transfer tax purposes, or to facilitate a sale.
2 The company has to be of substantial size, and will supply jobbers with sufficient shares to create a free market in them.
3 No new capital is required but a prospectus is prepared and advertised for information purposes only. A *prospectus* is the document issued by a company to persuade investors to buy the company's shares. It contains details of the securities to be issued, past trading record, and future prospects, and has to comply with the Companies Acts and Stock Exchange regulations.

Stock Exchange placing

1 A small, not very well known company with a capital of about £1 million, which wishes to obtain a market quotation *and* capital of up to £500,000, would use this method. It is a combination of an introduction and a private placing. The placing letter will contain the same information as a prospectus, and the issue will be advertised.

2 25% of the shares are made available to the market through jobbers and brokers, the remainder probably going to institutional investors. Any issue larger than £500,000 would have to be dealt with as a direct public issue (see below), as the Stock Exchange discourages the restrictions on marketability associated with placings.

Public issue by prospectus

1 A relatively low percentage of funds are raised in this way by public companies, only the largest issues, by well-known companies, being able to support the high issue costs.

2 Companies advertise in the press, inviting offers at a price intended to attract sufficient purchasers to absorb the whole issue in one day. Timing of the issue is therefore of obvious importance, and the price fixed so as to secure the whole of the finance required with the issue of the least number of shares.

3 The prospectus and procedure of issue must comply with the stringent requirements of the Companies Acts and the Stock Exchange.

4 Issues are sometimes grossly oversubscribed, in which case the company has to scale down applications. This is usually effected by allotment to the widest spread of subscribers possible. When an issue is undersubscribed, shares not taken up by the public are allotted to the underwriters.

5 Oversubscribed issues are caused by 'stags', i.e. applicants whose intention is to sell their shares at a profit immediately after allotment. The share price of an oversubscribed issue will usually go to a considerable premium, and this helps 'stags' in their operations.

Offers for sale

1 This method enables the shareholders or the company to obtain immediate cash for their existing or new shares respectively.
2 An issuing house will act as the principal rather than as agent, by purchasing all the shares from the company at an agreed price, and then offering them to the public by advertisement at the same price or at a slightly higher price. The remuneration of the issuing house is either by way of a fee or the difference (or 'turn') between the buying and selling prices of the shares.
3 Smaller issues, by lesser-known companies, tend to be dealt with in this way. Otherwise, the procedure is the same as for an issue by prospectus.

Offers for sale by tender

1 Shares are offered to the public by a company or issuing house at a minimum price, applicants stating how many shares they are willing to take up and at what price. Allotments may then be made at a price which will just clear all the shares. This method is used when the issuing house finds it difficult to predetermine an issue price, because the company has no equivalent on the stock market, because its operations are unique, or because the market does not appear sympathetic towards the proposed issue.
2 As the Stock Exchange requires there to be an adequate market in the shares, and the company normally desires a good spread of shareholdings, the 'striking price' at which the shares are eventually allotted may be less than the price at which all shares offered can be cleared.
3 If there is heavy demand for the shares, the company takes advantage of the premium resulting from this, and 'stags' are discouraged by the unknown striking price.
4 Whilst this method has been used by public companies since 1961, especially by companies in whose shares public demand is uncertain, it has not been widely popular.

'In your circumstances, an offer for sale will probably be the most effective way of marketing your new issue of shares, but one of our subsidiary companies, which is an issuing house, will confirm this,' said Mr Thorburn. 'In the meantime, here is another paper to take away and read. It outlines the procedure for an issue of securities.'

Colin glanced through the document:

Outline procedure for an issue of securities

Issuing houses

Although companies may be able to assess their own financial requirements and carry staff able to advise on the raising of capital, it is probable they will call on the services of an outside specialist in this field; that is, either an issuing house or a stockbroker. Issuing houses belong to the Issuing Houses Association (about fifty members), and many of them are well-known merchant banks. The main functions of issuing houses are to advise upon the amount, type, timing, marketing, underwriting and issue prices of new or existing securities.

Acceptability of clients

The reputation of issuing houses depends on the success or otherwise of the securities they market, and the subsequent market performance of those securities. It is essential, therefore, that they satisfy themselves as to the suitability of clients, to ensure that issues have a good chance of success.

In this respect issuing houses will:

a examine the memorandum and articles of association of the company, and the terms of issue of any existing securities, for possible restrictions upon the raising of further capital;

b assess the efficacy of management, and the organisational structure of the company;

c ensure the adequacy of working capital for present and future operations;

d evaluate the future profitability of the company, particularly in respect of the project for which new capital is required;

e assess the proposal to issue securities and to seek a stock market quotation.

Timing of the issue

Where the amount of money to be raised is to exceed £3 million, the sponsoring broker will apply to the government broker at the Bank of England for an 'impact' date; that is, the first day on which the size and terms of the issue may be known. This is to ensure an orderly new issues market.

It is essential that the issue is made when the market is receptive to the particular type of share and its offer price. The more favourable the market conditions, the less likely that equity dilution will be caused by a resultant low issue price, and the more likely that the issue will succeed.

If, for example, interest rates are falling, perhaps because of a fall in inflation, equity share prices tend to increase. Should this trend be forecast to continue, investors will probably be receptive to an early issue of shares in the belief that share prices will continue to rise.

General procedure

The preliminary enquiries specified in paragraph 2 above will have satisfied the issuing house as to the viability of the proposal.

With the assistance of a sponsoring broker, who must be a member of the Stock Exchange, the type of issue to be made (i.e. prospectus, offer for sale, placing, tender or introduction) will be agreed and, with the guidance of the quotations department of the Stock Exchange, application will be made to the department at least fourteen days before the publication of the prospectus.

An underwriting agreement will be completed in the case of a prospectus issue, between the issuing house (probably involving sub-underwriters) and the company. Underwriting is an assurance that, if the public does not take up all the shares, the underwriter will take up the balance. The issue price will not be determined at this stage.

Copies of the prospectus, definitive certificates, memorandum and articles of association, and trust deed (in the case of an issue of debentures), will accompany the application to the Stock Exchange for *initial approval.*

The prospectus or offer for sale must be published in two leading London newspapers, and circulated by Exchange Telegraph Ltd and Moodies Service Ltd, investment service agents.

Having gained initial approval of the Stock Exchange, the company will either receive the agreed amount per share from the issuing house in the case of an offer for sale, or offer the securities to the public themselves on a planned date, at a price determined as close as possible to the issue date. Allotment will then follow.

At least two days prior to the hearing of the application by the committee of the Stock Exchange quotations department, the final formal application must be made, together with signed and certified copies of the prospectus, advertisements and other documents specifying information required by the Stock Exchange and complying with the Companies Acts.

The company is also required to sign and submit a Stock Exchange listing agreement which binds the company to maintain a regular supply of information to the Stock Exchange, shareholders and the investing public.

Provided the Stock Exchange finally approves the issue, a quotation will be granted.

Pricing the issue
Must be fixed at a level that will ensure the success of the issue. A low price would do this but would not satisfy the company as more shares would have to be issued to obtain the same amount of finance.

When shares of the same type are already on issue, the current market price will be a guide but there will normally have to be some underpricing as the natural reaction of the market is to mark down the shares in anticipation of some earnings dilution.

New securities, especially those issued by private companies going public, will be priced by reference to the P/E ratios of similar companies. Where comparison is difficult to make, estimated profit plus growth, capitalised at an appropriate rate of return, will provide a guide to value. (See Chapter 13 on share valuation.)

Self-check

1 What is the main function of the Stock Exchange?
2 Briefly differentiate between the functions of stockbrokers and stockjobbers.
3 What are the implications of jobbers' prices reading 89p–94p?
4 A Stock Exchange introduction is a method used by small companies to obtain further capital.' True or false? Explain.
5 When investors state the price that they are willing to pay for a share this relates to:
a a placing;
b an offer for sale;
c an offer for sale by tender;
d a public issue by prospectus.
Which is the appropriate method?

1 The Stock Exchange is the official second-hand market for all industrial, commercial, government and corporation securities quoted in its daily official listings.

2 A *stockbroker* acts for investment clients, whereas *stockjobbers* are wholesale dealers in certain types of securities, dealing only with other jobbers or brokers. When brokers wish to buy or sell shares for a client, they approach the appropriate jobbers who trade in that type of share.

3 The *lower* price is that at which the jobber will *buy*, and the *higher*, that at which he will *sell*. The broker does not inform the jobber whether he is a buyer or a seller until after he is aware of the price 'spread'.

4 False. An introduction is a means whereby a large, public company, whose shares are already fairly widely held, obtain a Stock Exchange listing, to improve the marketability of its shares.

5 **c** an offer for sale by tender.

Who are the investors in shares?

Colin asked his bank manager who the major investors were. The manager replied:

'The Wilson Committee Report on the Functioning of the Financial Institutions showed that, in 1975, 62.5% of shares were held by the institutions, which include insurance companies, pension funds, investment and unit trusts. This percentage has probably risen since then.'

'Does that mean that the institutions will be the dominant applicants for our shares?' queried Colin.

'Not necessarily. Although individuals have found it more tax-efficient and secure to invest their savings *indirectly* through pension fund contributions and unit trusts, more encouragement has been given to them to invest directly in companies. The investment income surcharge has been abolished, there is now no government restriction on dividends, and the limit beyond which capital gains tax becomes payable has been raised, and will be inflation-indexed in future.

'In any case, when shares are allotted, the issuing house will probably advise a policy of allotting *in full* to individuals, and scaling down those to institutions. This would strengthen your controlling interest, as shares would be more widely held and constitute less of a threat than if dominated by the institutions.'

Review

1 Explain **a** Stock Exchange listing agreement; **b** share issue prospectus.

2 'Preference shares, along with ordinary shares, are part of the permanent capital of a company.' Is this statement true?

3 Which of the following is retained by a company to guide it through the process of going public?

a Stock Exchange.
b Merchant bank.
c Issuing house.
d Stockbroker.
e Registrar of Companies.
f Finance house.

4 The USM is the official name given to the US Wall Street securities market.' True or false? Explain.

1 a The Stock Exchange listing agreement must be signed by all companies wishing to obtain a quotation for their shares. It prescribes the information that listed companies are obliged to disclose to the Stock Exchange and to the public.

b A prospectus is issued by a company to inform and persuade the public to invest in its shares. It specifies the purposes for which the capital to be raised is required, reports on the company's past profit record, discloses the current financial position of the company and its future prospects. Its contents have to comply with the requirements of the Companies Acts and Stock Exchange regulations.

2 Not true. Some preference shares are redeemable, on specified terms; otherwise they do have the characteristics of straight preference shares.

3 c Issuing house.

4 False. The USM is the unlisted securities market operated by the Stock Exchange for relatively small companies who do not yet satisfy the conditions for a full quotation.

11 Long-term finance for expansion

Introduction

To rapidly expanding companies such as Pike Electronics, going public opens up many new sources of finance. This is largely because a public company is subject to more public scrutiny than a private company, through the rigorous statutory and Stock Exchange disclosure requirements. As a result, suppliers of finance are able to apply more informed judgement to their investment decisions.

From the company's viewpoint, although the improved availability of finance will be welcome, financial planning has still to take account of the following four factors:

- Availability of internally generated profit for reinvestment within the company; about two-thirds of new sources of finance in industrial and commercial companies comes from retained earnings, which of course increases the proportion of equity capital.
- Injection of additional debt capital when required and when borrowing capacity permits.
- The need to keep an acceptable balance between borrowed and equity capital.
- Whether existing shareholders will be willing to dip into their pockets for further finance when retained earnings and borrowed capital are insufficient to finance expansion. This is done by way of a 'rights' issue.

Rights issues of shares

A 'rights' issue is an offer to existing shareholders enabling them to subscribe for additional shares in the company in proportion to their current holdings. For example, a 1 for 4 offer made to a shareholder of 1,000 shares would entitle him to subscribe for a further 250 shares. Both the Companies Act 1980 and Stock Exchange listing regulations require companies to offer new issues of shares to *existing* shareholders before offering them to the public. It is the main method of making new share issues.

The attractions of making a 'rights' over a public issue are:

- the proportionate ownership rights of existing shareholders are preserved, and therefore their control over the company;
- the issue is more likely to be successful because it is being offered to committed shareholders;
- costs of issue are much less than for a public issue; underwriting is not normally required, but if it is, it will cost less because there is more certainty of the issue succeeding, no prospectus is required, and administration costs are less;
- a broader equity capital base provides further scope for borrowing.

A rights issue is made in the following circumstances:

- to finance further investment;
- to replace short-term debt capital that has caused the company to become overgeared;
- to take advantage of favourable market conditions to obtain equity finance; fewer shares will have to be issued when share prices are buoyant and there is a greater chance the issue will be taken up fully.

When the issue is agreed, each shareholder is sent a 'rights' letter outlining his entitlement to new shares. He may then accept the offer, or renounce his privilege and sell his 'rights' through a broker or to the company. A renounceable allotment letter is enclosed with the offer to the shareholder, and a time limit is placed upon the receipt of acceptances.

Subscription price

One of the main features of a 'rights' issue is its price. This is usually substantially below the current market price of the share and is kept as low as possible to ensure the success of the issue.

Obviously, if the market price of the share, subsequent to the issue, were to fall below the rights subscription price, the issue would fail. A discount of between 15% and 30% on the current market price has been made on past issues.

Activity

Alpha Printing plc has 400,000 £1 ordinary shares in issue. The current market price of the share is £3. The company is to raise further capital of £250,000 by a rights issue. If the issue price is fixed at £2.50:

a How many shares would have to be issued?
b How many shares does a shareholder have to hold currently to have the right to subscribe for a further share?

a £250,000÷£2.50=100,000 shares.
b A shareholder has to hold 400,000÷100,000=4 shares to subscribe for one new share.

Note that the rights share is priced at a discount of 16.6% of the current market price, which will result in there being more shares relative to capital than there are at present, and consequently a reduction in earnings per share. In theory, a lower EPS should not really matter as long as the new capital earns the same return as existing capital.

Activity

Alpha Printing currently earns 20% on the market value of its shares, and this rate is expected on the new capital. Calculate:

a earnings per share on the existing capital;
b earnings per share after the rights issue.

a EPS=equity earnings÷number of equity shares=(.20×£1.2 million)÷400,000=60 pence.
b EPS=equity earnings÷number of equity shares=(.20×£1.45 million)÷500,000=58 pence.

The EPS of Alpha is reduced even though the return on capital is still 20%. This may have a depressing effect on market price, which however could be countered by maintaining the original dividend per share.

Valuing rights

There is a *natural* fall in market price of a share after a rights issue because of the relatively low subscription price; the fall occurs at a time shortly before the final closing of the rights offer. Up to that time a buyer of the shares is entitled to the rights and the share price (*cum rights*) paid by him, reflects this; subsequently, a seller of the shares keeps the rights to sell or to exercise, and the share price falls to its *ex rights* value.

Activity

Given that a holder of four shares in Alpha exercises his right to apply for a further share at a price of £2.50, what should the *ex rights* price of the share be?

		£
Value of shares held previously	4@£3=	12
Add rights share	1@£2.50=	2.50
		14.50
Theoretical ex rights price £14.50÷5=		2.90

The shareholder now holds five shares at £2.90, instead of four shares @ £3 and cash of £2.50. His *total* wealth has therefore not changed as a result of exercising his right.

What if a shareholder does not want to subscribe for further shares? Does this mean that his shareholding after the rights issue is worth only 4×£2.90=£11.60 – a loss of 40 pence? As indicated earlier, this apparent loss can be offset by the shareholder renouncing and selling his rights to further shares. An Alpha shareholder ought to be able to sell his right for 40 pence, because when the buyer exercises it he will have paid a total of £0.40+£2.50=£2.90, which, as you have already seen, is the ex rights value of the share. Thus the seller is compensated for the 40 pence fall in the value of his share. However, if the holder of a right does not exercise it, he will not lose value, as the Stock Exchange require companies to sell rights not taken up by the acceptance date, and compensate the shareholders concerned.

The *theoretical value of a right in each share* is the difference between the cum rights share value and the theoretical ex rights value, i.e. £3 less £2.90=10 pence in Alpha's case. This is sometimes expressed as the *nil paid value of a right to take up another share*, and is the difference between the theoretical *ex rights price* and the *subscription price*. For Alpha, this is £2.90 less £2.50=40 pence, and is simply the 10 pence right in each of four shares.

Of course, should the market not be very enthusiastic about the purpose of the issue, the share price could fall and affect the value of a right.

A shareholder with sufficient cash should subscribe for rights shares if he believes that the expected return on the additional investment makes it worthwhile. In making his decision, he will compare alternative investment opportunities, and the composition of his present portfolio. Investors do not always act rationally, however, and misconceived loyalty may persuade him to take up his rights instead of diversifying.

Self-check

Trident Hire Cars plc are expanding their operations and require additional capital of £200,000. A 1-for-3 rights issue is offered to shareholders at £2.00 per share. The current market price of the share is £2.80. Calculate:

a the theoretical ex rights price of each Trident share;
b the value of a right in *each* existing share;
c the nil paid value of a right to take up a further share.

a Theoretical ex rights price=((3×£2.80)+£2.00)÷4 =10.40÷4=£2.60.
b Value of the right in each share=£2.80−2.60=20 pence.

c Nil paid value of a right to take up a further share =£2.60−2.00=60 pence.

The characteristics of long-term debt capital

'Long-term' in this context is over 10 years but rarely longer than 30 years. Companies try to match financing terms with the lives of their assets, those having long lives tending to be financed with long-term capital, to ensure that vital operating capacity is undisturbed, with property attracting *mortgage loans* of 20 to 25 years' duration, and plant and machinery and permanent working capital, loans of between 10 and 20 years.

The general features of long-term debt capital are as follows:

- Lenders are *creditors* whose debts are subject to specific repayment dates.
- Lenders have no control over borrowers other than is provided for in the loan agreement covenants.
- Loan agreements can include fairly onerous conditions to protect the lender, including restrictions on further borrowing and pledging of assets; restrictions on dividends; the right of a lender to appoint a director to the company's board; disclosure of financial information by the borrower to the lender; and an obligation to consult the lender regarding exceptional transactions such as acquiring, or merging with, other companies.
- A fixed rate of interest is normally payable, although variable rates can be negotiated.
- Interest is a prior charge against profits before any dividends are payable and is treated as an expense for corporation tax purposes; loans are usually *secured* either by a *fixed charge* on a specified asset, are a *floating charge* on all the company's assets, or both, giving the lender priority in repayment of his debt in a liquidation of the company, over other creditors.
- Loan stocks may include a *call* feature which enables the company to repay the debt before its maturity date at a specified price. The call would be exercised if interest rates fell and the company wished to renegotiate the loan to take advantage of the lower rates.

- Capital is committed to a project for a long period during which circumstances could change (e.g. interest rates) to the advantage or detriment of the borrower.

Since the mid 1960s conditions have militated against long-term borrowing and it is now a negligible proportion of total financing. The greatest influences in this respect have been:

- a deteriorating economic position both at home and abroad, resulting in lower profits, unable to support a high level of interest payment;
- a consequent reduction in industrial capital investment, particularly in property, which has traditionally been financed long-term;
- the traumatic reduction in property values in 1974, with its consequent reduction in security for loans;
- high inflation, causing interest rates to reach their highest levels for years; rates that borrowers are not prepared to commit themselves to pay when economic conditions and financial markets are so uncertain, given that insolvency is the penalty for overborrowing;
- lenders are loathe to lend long-term knowing that the *real* values of their loans diminish with inflation;
- the willingness of banks to continue lending for short and medium terms.

The main factor governing borrowing is the rate of interest. There is little doubt that, if interest rates in general are low, there is more long-term borrowing and consequently a higher level of economic activity.

However, inflation is not the only factor causing high interest rates. Government borrowing, caused by high government spending in both the UK and the USA, has pushed interest rates higher, and because investment in gilt-edged securities (government, local authority and Commonwealth bonds) is risk-free, investors prefer them as safer homes for their savings.

Interest rates on industrial long-term securities take their cue from similarly dated gilt-edged securities but with the addition of risk premiums to compensate for the higher operational risks and restrictive covenants.

Self-check

Cover up the answers given below. Read through the previous section again. Now summarise the conditions conducive to borrowing long-term.

a General economic stability and growth.
b Growth in the particular industry.
c Stable and growing, company turnover and profit.
d Current *low* interest rates.
e Forecasts of future high inflation rates, and thus higher interest rates.
f Share prices currently depressed – making debt capital cheaper.
g If the current gearing ratio of a company is low.
h Substantial mortageable assets available – not already charged.
i The need to convert a present high volume of short-term borrowing into more permanent capital, to avoid the risk to liquidity of having to repay loans at short notice.
j A high corporation tax liability against which to charge debt interest.
k Recognition that borrowing within limits can reduce the cost of capital.
l The desire of existing shareholders to retain control of their company will encourage them to borrow rather than make a public issue of shares.
m Costs of obtaining debt capital are less than for shares.

In Chapter 8 a brief description was given of the various types of loan capital. They fall broadly into three categories:

- loans arranged with one or a small consortia of lenders, including mortgage and term loans;
- loan stocks issued as *securities* that are readily saleable on the market, including debentures, unsecured loan stock and convertible loan stock;
- sale and leaseback.

Mortgage loans

This is finance obtained on the security of specific property, and is usually negotiated through a merchant bank with an insurance company or a pension fund. These institutions follow a policy of matching their long-term insurance and pension commitments with stable, long-term income, and will lend mainly to large established companies on the security of specific property. As much as two-thirds of the lender's valuation of the property will be advanced, for up to 35 years on *commercial* property (because of their rentable value), with a review of interest rates after 20 years; and up to 20 years for industrial assets.

The agreement is normally to repay the loan by instalments at a fixed rate of interest, although variable rates are increasingly used because of the uncertainty of inflation. The borrower also normally pays the lender an arrangement fee of about 2% of the loan.

Finally, a trustee is usually appointed to watch over the rights of each lender, to foreclose upon and sell the property should anything go wrong and repay lenders out of the proceeds. Trustees are often banks or insurance companies.

Term loans

For periods of over 10 years, loans can be negotiated with commercial banks, the ICFC and investment trusts, insurance companies and pension funds, on the security of fixed assets. The rate of interest is normally fixed, and is determined by reference to an appropriate gilt-edged security of equal life.

Information on the past financial and operating performance of the prospective borrower has to be supplied to the lender, who charges to the borrower the costs of the investigation and arrangement of the loan.

Debentures

A debenture is a bond under seal issued to a lender acknowledging a debt. It states the interest payable, the nature of the security (if any), the restrictive covenants and the timing and circumstances leading to repayment of the loan. Only large, established companies can issue debentures; the institutions being the chief investors. They may be listed on the Stock Exchange but there have been few issues in recent years.

Secured debentures are charged either on specific assets (a fixed charge), or upon all the assets, where these are predominantly current assets (a floating charge).

Trustees are appointed to represent the interests of the debenture-holders. Should the terms of the trust deed not be met, or the company go into liquidation, the debenture-holders would be entitled to repayment of their debt out of the sale proceeds of the security before any other class of creditor is paid.

Unsecured debentures are mere promises to repay a loan, and therefore have no prior right to repayment over other classes of creditors. Only extremely creditworthy companies are in a position to issue unsecured debentures, which will probably carry a higher rate of interest to compensate for the lack of security.

Debentures may be *repayable* at the end of their stated life; by instalments over the period of their issue or after a specified period; by conversion into some other form of security – usually equity shares (see convertible securities, below); or purchase by the issuing company on the open market where this right has been reserved, usually to take advantage of falling interest rates.

Subordinated debentures are issues whose rights as to interest and capital repayment are deferred to those of other debenture-holders and, very often, to unsecured creditors as well.

As with all loans, inflation erodes the real value of the amount repayable at maturity, and although the rate of interest includes a provision for expected inflation over the life of the debenture, this obviously will not cover unanticipated inflation.

Debentures commonly have nominal values of £100, although they may be issued at a lower price to make them attractive to investors. The rate of interest charged (known as the *coupon* rate), will be the yield currently being earned on securities of similar risk.

Valuation of debentures If a £100 debenture is redeemable in 20 years at £100 (par) value, then providing general interest rates and the level of risk associated with the debenture, do not change, its market value at any time should remain at £100. If for example a £100 10% debenture matures in three years' time, its present value can be shown to be:

$$D_O = \frac{I}{1+r} + \frac{I}{(1+r)^2} + \frac{I}{(1+r)^3} + \frac{100}{(1+r)^3}$$

Where D_O=present market value of the debenture
I=interest payable per annum
r=current expected yield on this class of debenture (assumed to be 10%)

$$\text{Then } D_O = \frac{10}{1.10} + \frac{10}{(1.10)^2} + \frac{10}{(1.10)^3} + \frac{100}{(1.10)^3}$$

$$= (10 \times 2.4868) + (100 \times .7513)$$

$$D_O = £100.$$

If interest rates or risk change, however, the *expected yield* on this debenture will also change, and the market value of the security will increase or decrease accordingly.

Activity

If the expected yield on the above debenture increased to 12%, what would its current market value be with only three years to run to maturity?

$$D_O = \frac{10}{1.12} + \frac{10}{(1.12)^2} + \frac{10}{(1.12)^3} + \frac{100}{(1.12)^3}$$

$$= (10 \times 2.4018) + (100 \times .7118)$$

$$D_O = £95.19.$$

The lower market value indicates that investors are only willing to pay £95 for a 10% debenture, for which they now require a 12% yield.

The market values of *all* fixed interest securities move up or down with changes in expected yields. Given that the market value and the coupon rate of a debenture are known, its expected market yield can be ascertained by calculating the rate of return (using the 'trial and error' method illustrated in Chapter 3), that discounts future interest payments plus capital repayment to the current market value of the debenture. In the last activity, £95.19 is the current market value, and 12% would be the yield rate derived by trial and error.

The rate derived in this way is known as the *yield to redemption*.

Convertible securities

Norfolk Agrimek plc, agricultural engineers, have 400,000 ordinary shares in issue, market price currently £3.50, and their present gearing ratio is in line with the company's target.

The company is expanding and requires £500,000 additional long-term capital. The directors are considering the alternatives of a 'rights' issue of ordinary shares, or a secured loan.

The company's finance director has given the following information regarding the current state of the financial markets:

- *The company's share price is depressed* – partly the result of the economic recession and in line with other shares, but also, in his opinion, because the market is undervaluing the company's earnings growth potential.
- *The company's profit forecast promises substantial growth* – especially taking expansion into account, but this growth will not materialise for three to four years because of delays in building construction.
- *Interest rates are currently very high* – which is another reason for low share prices.

He explained to the board that if a rights issue were made more shares would have to be issued at present low prices, than later, when profits and share prices would be higher. As a consequence, earnings per share would be considerably diluted during the next two or three years, and this could depress share prices even further.

On the other hand, high interest rates do not encourage more long-term loan capital.

The finance director suggested the current situation was conducive to the issue of *convertible securities*, and went on to explain that these were fixed-interest loan stock or preference shares giving an option to the holders to convert them into ordinary shares on or between predetermined dates, at predetermined prices. Convertibles are therefore loans with delayed equity options and, because of this option, can be issued at lower interest rates than ordinary debentures. Should the option to change the loan stock for ordinary shares not be exercised within the prescribed time, the stock reverts to being a pure loan, redeemable on a specified date.

The present yield on a straight 15 year debenture is 14½%, but Norfolk Agrimek could issue 5,000 13% convertible debentures of £100 each, giving the holders the option to convert each debenture into 25 ordinary shares in four years' time. The option could be held open for, say, four years, after which the debentures would be ordinary debt repayable 15 years from the date of issue.

The *conversion ratio* of 25 shares for each £100 debenture implies a *conversion price* of £4 per share. To be of advantage to the company this price has to be higher than the current market price of £3.50, but has also to be realistically attainable before the date of conversion, to encourage investors to convert.

The *conversion value* of the convertible debenture on its date of issue is 25×£3.50=£87.50, indicating that each £100 convertible is issued at a *conversion premium* of £12.50 (12½/87½×100=14%).

By issuing convertibles the company obtains the advantage of low-cost debt capital (remember the corporation tax advantage of interest) and is able to issue ordinary shares, via conversion, at a price higher than the present one. Investors have the surety of a *fixed* income initially, with the prospect of higher equity earnings later. They also have some protection against capital loss because the convertible will never fall below the market value of straight debentures of the same risk. As a consequence of this, and the possibility of high equity gain, a convertible may have a market value higher than its conversion value.

Activity

Assume that there are three more years to run before expiry of Norfolk's conversion option. The market price of the ordinary share is now £3.70, and the present yield on a non-convertible debenture is 15%. Calculate:

a the market value of the convertible debenture as equity, i.e. calculate its conversion value;
b the value of a £100 convertible as a non-convertible debenture (ignore taxation).

Hint: there are 10 years remaining before redemption, and therefore 10 years' interest of £13 plus £100 at the end of ten years.

a Conversion value: £3.70×25=£92.50.
b Value as a simple debenture, discounted at 15%:

$$D_O = \frac{13}{1.15} + \frac{13}{(1.15)^2} + \frac{13}{(1.15)^3} \ldots \frac{13}{(1.15)^{10}} + \frac{100}{(1.15)^{10}}$$

$$= (13 \times 5.0188) + (100 \times .2472)$$

$$= £65.2444 + 24.72$$

$$= £89.96.$$

Although the conversion value of £92.50 is higher than the straight debt value of £89.96, a holder of the convertible might be wiser to hold than to convert, especially if interest rates are expected to remain high. The share value has grown from £3.50 to £3.70 (1½% per annum) in five years, and even if the growth only continued at 1% p.a. during the next three years, conversion value would remain higher than debenture value.

Warrants

A warrant is an option to purchase a stated number of shares at a specified price (the exercise price), usually within a specified time. They are attached to debt or equity issues to make the latter more attractive to investors, or to lower the interest rate payable on debt capital. If the company succeeds in its operations and its share price goes ahead of the warrant exercise price, holders will either apply for shares at the exercise price or sell their options. In these circumstances, the value of an option will be the difference between the share market price and the exercise price. Warrants may be sold separately from their parent securities but only provide additional capital for a company if they are exercised.

For example, in January 1981, the New Darien Oil Trust Ltd issued 10,000,000 25 pence ordinary shares at £1 each with warrants attached. Each warrant entitled the registered shareholder to subscribe for one share in respect of every ten ordinary shares held, at £1 each, between 1982 and 1988.

Sale and leaseback

A company owning property may sell it to an insurance company, pension fund or other leasing finance company, and simultaneously arrange to lease it back for a substantially long period, subject to periodic rent reviews – usually every five years. The company thus continues in occupation and releases capital for investment.

The obvious alternative finance, utilising the same property, is a mortgage loan, which is cheaper, ensures that the company retains property which may increase in value, and will continue to provide security for further loans. The drawback to a mortgage loan is that only between 50% and 60% of the value of the property may be borrowed.

Properties suitable for sale and leaseback are shops and offices in prime areas which will generate a steady and inflation-proofed rental income to institutions which require stable, certain revenue.

When a company requires a large amount of capital and is unable to obtain it any other way, sale and leaseback offers a convenient way of obtaining it.

Review

1 Phoenix Holidays plc has 500,000 ordinary shares in issue, the current market price of each share being £2.60. The company requires £400,000 of new capital and it proposes to make a rights issue of one new share for every five shares currently held, at a price of £2 per share. Calculate or explain:

a how many shares would be issued;
b the theoretical ex rights value of the share;
c the value of the right in each share;
d if the actual ex rights value of the share before expiry of the rights offer was £2.30, the nil paid value of a right to take up another share;
e why the ex rights price of the share has fallen below its theoretical level calculated in **b**.

2 a Instead of the rights issue, the Phoenix Company issued 13% convertible debentures of £100 each, with the option to convert each debenture into 30 ordinary shares commencing in two years' time. At the date of issue what would be: **i** the conversion ratio, **ii** the conversion price, **iii** the conversion value and **iv** the conversion premium?
b What advantages do convertible securities confer to a holder over ordinary loan stock?

3 'The options conferred by both warrants and convertibles are the same in that cash is subscribed for further shares in both cases.' True or false?

4 Both mortgage loans and sale and leaseback arrangements result in annual payments being made by the company arranging the finance. What is the nature of the payment in each case, and why might the amounts differ?

1 a £400,000÷£2 . . . =200,000 rights shares.
b ((5×£2.60)+£2.00)÷6 . . . =£2.50.
c £2.60−£2.50 . . . =10 pence.
d £2.30−£2.00 . . . =30 pence.
e The rights value is less than its theoretical level mainly because investors consider that the new capital will not yield as high a return as the existing capital. Consequently EPS would be diluted, and dividends may fall. The fall in value could also be attributable to a general fall in share prices or an increase in the risk of the Phoenix operations.

2 a i Conversion ratio – as stated – 30 shares for each £100 convertible.

ii Conversion price: £100÷30=£3.33 (approx).

iii Conversion value: 30×£2.60=£78.

iv Conversion premium: £100−78=£22 (or 22÷78×100=28%).

b
- As a loan stock, a specific rate of interest is receivable.
- The risk of capital loss is lessened because of its 'floor' value as loan stock.
- It is marketable, and because of its equity connection, may sell at a premium over loan stock value.
- It enables investors to share in the growth of a company.
- The conversion right is optional, should the equity prove to be a disappointment.

3 False. Convertibles are simply *exchanged* for shares; only warrants require the payment of additional cash.

4 Interest is payable on loans, whereas rent is payable on leases. The rent is normally subject to periodic (about five-yearly) review, and will also vary with the site location and type of property. The interest on mortgage loans will vary according to the quality of the risk associated with the loan.

12 Medium-term finance

Introduction

The different types of finance under the heading 'medium-term' cover periods of between three to ten years.

Medium-term financing has grown considerably in the last twenty years to fill the gap which has widened between short- and long-term facilities. Among the reasons for this gap are:

- reluctance of *borrowers* to commit themselves to long-term loans at high interest rates during a period of economic uncertainty, and with the possibility that interest rates might fall during the term of the loan;
- conversely, *lenders* have been reluctant to lend at other than high interest rates, given the level of inflation and general uncertainty;
- borrowing medium-term offers more stability as regards term, interest and amount than short-term borrowing;
- in the face of political and competitive pressure, clearing banks have been more willing to lend medium-term;
- competition from overseas banks, particularly branches of US banks, who are able to lend at keener interest rates because of their lower overhead costs in this country;
- growth of *leasing* to help overcome the liquidity problems of companies;
- growth of the Euroloan market, making it possible to borrow European and other international currencies for medium terms, at competitive interest rates.

Term loans

Whilst the clearing banks are the largest providers of term loans, they operate in a highly competitive market. Branches and subsidiaries of foreign banks, insurance companies, merchant banks, the Industrial and Commercial Finance Corporation and finance houses are all willing to consider applications for term loans. Even the government, under its selective assistance scheme, offers medium-term loans at concessionary rates (see Chapter 20).

Negotiations for a medium-term loan will cover the following:

- The lender will have to be satisfied about the *commercial standing* of the applicant, the efficacy of its management, and the forecast adequacy of future cash flows to service the loan repayments.
- *Security* for a loan is infrequently required, but this will be entirely dependent upon the credit status of the applicant.
- *Terms* of between five and seven years are predominant.
- The *interest rate* on term loans is usually 1% to 4% over the interbank rate depending upon the customer's standing, security and loan agreement covenants. Rates are normally variable, being adjusted every six months on average. If a fixed interest rate is agreed, there may be provision for the borrower to renegotiate the rate, although a penalty clause may deter him from doing so.
- *Repayment terms* can be extremely flexible. Loans can be paid back in a lump sum at the end of the loan period, but more frequently repayment by instalments is the arrangement. An agreed delay before repayment commences will give a business time to generate cash flows.
- The lender charges an *arrangement fee* to cover the costs of credit status investigation and administrative and legal costs.

Negotiations for medium-term loans are smoother than for long-term. The period of negotiation is shorter; it is easier to deal with one lender than hundreds of security holders; terms can be renegotiated informally.

Term loans are particularly useful for:

- assets whose lives can be matched with the term of the loan, such as plant and machinery; swiftly changing technology may now render long-term finance unsuitable for such purposes;

- financing additional working capital for a self-liquidating project;
- funding short-term overdrafts that have virtually become hardcore borrowing;
- periods when conditions do not favour the issue of long-term debt;
- providing flexibility in financing when future needs are uncertain;
- small to medium-sized companies, for whom long-term funds are not available.

Activity

If a term loan of £50,000 has to be repaid by equal annual instalments over four years we are in effect paying the lender an annuity. You will recall that Appendix B gives the present value of an annuity of £1 for different periods, at different rates of interest. Using the table, and assuming an interest rate of 10%, calculate the annual repayment instalment on the £50,000 loan.

Loan÷PV annuity factor=50,000÷3.1699=£15,773.

Self-check

'The trouble with medium-term loans is that they can be called in at any time at the whim of the lender.' True or false? Explain.

False. A medium-term loan is one made for a fixed period of between three and ten years, although its terms can usually be renegotiated during that time.

Eurocurrency loans

These originated in the mid-1960s, when there were large deposits of US dollars (known as Eurodollars) in European banks. It was more profitable to hold deposits in Europe when US interest rates were low, and also because US Federal authorities had placed restrictions on borrowing in the US for overseas investment, by either overseas or US companies.

Eurocurrency deposits and loans are not only denominated in dollars. These may include any currency deposited with a bank outside the country of the currency's origin; but it is still generally referred to as Eurocurrency. The market is mainly European, centred on London, but is also an important international market for finance in any currency.

Eurocurrency is available to large international companies of good credit standing for short periods ranging from overnight to three months, and for medium-term borrowing. Medium-term Eurocurrency loans of between five and ten years are issued in the form of '*notes*', whilst ten- to fifteen-year *Eurobonds* are issued.

Borrowers include the UK government, public corporations, nationalised industries and very large international companies. The amounts borrowed are large and rarely less than £500,000.

Interest rates vary according to the term of the loan and the credit standing of the borrower. Medium-term loan rates are based upon the London interbank borrowing rate (LIBOR). They are usually fixed but can be variable, and security for the loan is not normally required.

Eurobond issues are sold simultaneously in more than one country, with one bank, perhaps acting for a consortium of banks, taking a lead in the arrangements. Issue costs are high, but because loans tend to be for over £10 million, the size of the loan can easily absorb them.

The *major problem* with borrowing or lending international currencies is the risk of exchange rate losses.

Loans must normally be repaid in the currency originally borrowed; so if sterling deteriorates against the borrowed currency, the cost of interest and repayment of the loan could be exorbitant. Companies operating in the country whose currency has been borrowed can overcome this difficulty by using cash flows and assets in that country to meet their liabilities for interest and repayment.

Self-check

1 'A Eurocurrency loan is one arranged in a European country.' True or false?
2 What is the difference between Euronotes and Eurobonds?

1 False. The term 'Eurocurrency' embraces *any currency* deposited with a bank outside the country of the currency's origin. Loans are therefore available in any currency on an international scale, though London dominates the market.
2 A Euronote evidences a medium-term loan of between five and ten years; whereas Eurobonds are issued for longer terms of between ten and fifteen years.

Hire purchase

For the small to medium-sized business unable to negotiate further bank credit, this is a second line of finance offering use of productive assets upon payment of a relatively small initial downpayment, followed by an agreed number of instalments which include both interest and capital repayment.

The assets do not become the possessions of the hirer until the final instalment is paid.

Finance houses are the usual suppliers of credit, either acting through the supplier or, more likely, dealing direct with the hirer following investigation of his credit status.

Agreements are commonly between one and five years but may be longer. They will always be shorter than the life of the asset, with asset disposal value greater than outstanding instalments at any time.

The required deposit is dependent upon current government credit regulations, but instalment repayments can be arranged to match the hirer's cash flows.

The rates of interest charged, commonly between 20% and 40%, are relatively high, to compensate finance houses for the risks of borrowing short-term from the banks and the money market, whilst being committed to longer-term lending. Variable rates of interest may be adopted for long-term agreements.

Advantages of hire purchase are:

- capital is released for alternative investment;
- it is readily available, easily negotiated finance, when other credit is restricted;
- the most up-to-date equipment can be utilised to increase profit out of which instalments can be paid;
- VAT is recoverable in full against outputs at the time of payment of the initial deposit;
- *real* cost of instalments will be reduced in times of high inflation;
- after sales service is often more forthcoming when instalments are still outstanding than if an asset is owned and fully paid for.

The major drawback of hire purchase finance is that it commits the hirer to a contractual payment that he may find difficult to meet.

Hire purchase is now referred to as 'lease purchase', presenting a more respectable image in the financial markets.

> *Self-check*
>
> If you buy an asset on hire purchase, can you offer it as security for another loan?

The property in the asset does not pass to the hire purchaser until the final instalment is paid, therefore it cannot be pledged as security for another loan until after that time.

Leasing

Nature of leasing

Term loans and hire purchase give businesses the chance to use equipment and other assets, even though they may not have the necessary finance to pay for them immediately. *Leasing* is yet another way of financing the *use* of an asset without having to pay its full cost immediately. Unlike borrowing and hire purchase, however, the leased asset does not normally become the property of the lessee; this should not be seen as a disadvantage for it is the *use* not the *ownership* of the asset that is important.

Leasing is generally less expensive than hire purchase but is highly competitive with term loan borrowing and buying.

Most people think of leasing in connection with property, and up to about 1960 this was so. Since then there has been a significant growth in the provision of lease financing for plant and machinery, computers, business cars, agricultural machinery, ships, aircraft, telecommunication and hospital equipment.

Statistics produced by the Equipment Leasing Association reveal £20 million of leasing contracts in 1967, rising to well over £2½ billion in 1983. This growth is attributed to three influences:

- It affords a means of financing when further borrowing is impossible; though this should be considered in the context of gearing, which is subject to further discussion below.
- capital allowances granted to the lessor in respect of the equipment are substantially passed on to the lessee in the form of lower rentals.
- From the capital provider's viewpoint, there is less risk in leasing than lending as it is much easier to repossess a leased asset than one used as security for a loan; operationally risky firms will be more attractive therefore to a lessor than a lender.

A lease is a contract between the owner of an asset, the *lessor*, and the user, the *lessee*, for the hire by the latter of a specific asset selected by the lessee from a manufacturer or vendor of such assets. The lessee has possession and use of the asset on payment of specified rentals over an agreed period but ownership remains with the lessor.

It is similar to borrowing in that it imposes a continuing financial obligation on the lessee.

Types of lease

Lease financing is mainly offered by subsidiary companies of clearing banks, finance houses, merchant banks, independent specialist leasing firms and the ICFC. It is a competitive business so terms of leasing are comparatively very similar.

Activity

What main points would you expect a lease agreement to cover?

The essential aspects will be the period of hire, the periodic amount payable, the frequency of the payment, insurance and maintenance. But they will vary depending upon whether the lease is a *financial* or an *operating* one.

A financial lease is a non-cancellable contract providing for payment of specified rentals over an obligatory *primary* period, aimed at repaying the capital outlay of the lessor and to give him a margin of profit. The lessee is responsible for maintenance and insurance of the equipment.

This arrangement is, therefore, a way of financing use of an asset over its useful life. Five-year contracts are typical of this type of lease but 10 to 15 year leases for assets such as aircraft are not unknown.

Rentals are commonly payable quarterly in advance during the primary period but can be timed to match the lessee's cash flows arising from using the asset. At the end of the primary period, the lessee has the option to renew the lease for a *secondary* period at a reduced rental, and if the asset is sold, the lessee and lessor generally share the proceeds with the major part going to the lessee. Some leases do provide for cancellation before expiry of the obligatory period upon payment of an onerous penalty by the lessee.

An operating lease refers to contracts for assets, whereby the total rentals payable during the period of the lease do not fully repay the capital outlay of the lessor. The latter relies upon higher rentals, further lease contracts in respect of the same asset or a high residual value after the initial contract to enable him to recover his costs and realise a profit.

Operating leases are cancellable upon the lessee giving a short period of notice, which makes the arrangement attractive to users who anticipate rapid technological change, or who may cease to require the asset. The lessor is responsible for maintenance and insurance.

Taxation and leasing

One reason for growth in lease financing has been the facility it affords to companies and public bodies which are in a temporary or permanent non-taxpaying position to take advantage of the capital allowances claimable by the lessor. Trading losses may reduce taxable profit. Insurance companies, building societies and some public bodies whose liability to corporation tax is relatively low or non-existent are in a similar position of being unable to take full advantage of the capital allowances available on the purchase of industrial plant and equipment. Leasing makes these allowances available through reduced rentals.

Even if taxable profit does exist and thus weakens the advantage of leasing over purchasing, the fact that rentals are chargeable against profits for tax purposes gives a further advantage to leasing.

A choice between leasing and borrowing and buying

Lease rentals are known with *certainty* when the lease contract is written, so the risk that rental payments will vary is almost nil. The natural alternative to leasing is borrowing and buying; therefore the net of tax *borrowing* rate of interest is both the opportunity and the risk discounting rate to apply to the appraisal of the leasing cash flows, when comparing leasing with borrowing and buying.

Activity

Simon Poacher's Pie and Pâté Company need to replace a machine which is part of the pâté production line. Without it the line would grind to a halt. A suitable replacement has a cash cost of £80,000, with no residual value at the end of its useful life of five years.

It could be leased for £19,000 per annum over five years, each rental being payable in advance. Show whether the company should (**a**) borrow £80,000 from its bank on a five-year term loan at 12% interest or (**b**) opt for the alternative of leasing.

The machine attracts a 100% capital allowance in the year of purchase. Assume corporation tax at 50%, with a tax payment/receipt time-lag of one year. The company is currently earning sufficient taxable profits to absorb capital allowances or lease payments.

Hints:

1 Because the company is currently paying tax, the net of tax discounting rate to apply to the cash flows is 12%−(.50×12%)=6%.

2 The loan interest on the instalments to repay a bank loan is allowed as an expense for tax purposes. If the resulting *net* repayments, after the interest tax relief, are discounted at 6%, this will give a present value approximately equal to the amount borrowed of £80,000. In your appraisal of the term loan therefore, you need only show £80,000 as the purchase price of the machine at the commencement of year 1, rather than a schedule of instalment repayments.

a

Five-year term loan	*Purchase price* £	*Tax saving 50%* £	*PV factor @ 6%*	*Present value* £
Year 0	−80,000		1.000	−80,000
2		+40,000	.890	+35,600
Net present value				−44,400

b *Leasing*

Year	*Lease rental* £	*Tax saved* £	*Net cash flow* £	*PV factor @ 6%*	*Present value* £
0	−19,000		−19,000	1.000	−19,000
1	−19,000		−19,000	.943	−17,917
2	−19,000	+9,500	− 9,500	.890	− 8,455
3	−19,000	+9,500	− 9,500	.840	− 7,980
4	−19,000	+9,500	− 9,500	.792	− 7,524
5		+9,500	+ 9,500	.747	+ 7,097
6		+9,500	+ 9,500	.705	+ 6,698
			NPV		−47,081

Notes:

1 Borrowing and buying has the lower NPV cost, and is therefore preferred.

2 If the lease agreement had been extended beyond the primary period to include secondary period rentals, leasing would have been comparatively even more expensive.

3 A residual value for the machine would probably have had the same effect on both alternatives.

If we assume that the company will be in a non-taxpaying position over the life of the asset, we must discount the pre-tax cash flows at the pre-tax rate of 12%.

Activity

Now compare the alternative methods of financing, ignoring taxation, and discounting the cash flows at 12%

a *Five year term loan*
Purchase price – present value . . . £80,000.

b

Leasing

Year	*Lease rentals*	*PV factor @ 12%*	*Present value*
	£		£
0	– 19,000	1.0000	– 19,000
1–4	– 19,000	3.0373	– 57,709
			– 76,709

The decision is now reversed, and leasing is preferred to borrowing and purchasing. Further, even if the delayed tax allowances applicable to the alternatives of £40,000 and £38,000 respectively, are brought into account in the fifth year, the decision is not affected.

This activity illustrates that the combined effect of rentals reduced by passed-on capital allowances, and delay in taxation allowances, favours leasing. When a company has ample taxable profit, however, the borrow and buy alternative is a serious competitor to leasing.

The above illustrations relate purely to the *financing*

decision. The investment decision is presumed to have been pre-empted by the *necessity* to replace the machine as being an essential part of a whole production line. In other cases the investment decision may be forced for health or safety reasons.

When the investment decision is not pre-empted by circumstances, however, *it must take account of how the investment is to be financed.*

The investment decision and leasing

Investment and financing decisions are always inextricably linked, for the decision to proceed with a project will depend, not only on the benefits arising, but also on the discounting rate applied to the cash flows. As stated in the last section, the cash ouflows connected with leasing are known with certainty and the same applies to borrow and buy, and hire purchase financing. But the *project* net revenues or cost savings will be riskier cash flows, and should therefore be discounted at an appropriately higher rate.

Activity

Pike Electronics were considering the purchase of a machine that would yield cost savings of £12,000 per annum for the next five years. The machine could be leased at a primary rental of £15,000 for each of the first three years, and a secondary period rental of £500, all rentals payable in advance.

Assuming a corporation tax rate of 50%, an overall cost of capital for Pike of 12% and a five-year life for the machine, show whether the project should proceed.

Operational cash flows

Year	*Cost savings* £	*less Tax* £	*Net cash flow* £	*PV factor @ 12%*	*Present value* £
1	+ 12,000		+ 12,000	.893	+ 10,716
2	+ 12,000	− 6,000	+ 6,000	.797	+ 4,782
3	+ 12,000	− 6,000	+ 6,000	.712	+ 4,272
4	+ 12,000	− 6,000	+ 6,000	.636	+ 3,816
5	+ 12,000	− 6,000	+ 6,000	.567	+ 3,402
6		− 6,000	− 6,000	.507	− 3,042
			NPV		+ 23,946

Lease rentals

Year	*Rentals* £	*Tax saving* £	*Net cash flows* £	*PV factor @ 12%*	*Present value* £
0	– 15,000		– 15,000	1.000	– 15,000
1	– 15,000		– 15,000	.893	– 13,395
2	– 15,000	+ 7,500	– 7,500	.797	– 5,978
3	– 500	+ 7,500	+ 7,000	.712	+ 4,984
4	– 500	+ 7,500	+ 7,000	.636	+ 4,452
5		+ 250	+ 250	.567	+ 142
6		+ 250	+ 250	.507	+ 127
NPV					– 24,668

Note that, *discounted at 12%*, the present value cost of the lease exceeds the present value of the cost savings. Based upon this data, the project would not proceed.

Activity

Now discount the lease cash flows at a net of tax borrowing rate of 5%, which is appropriate to its more certain cash flows.

Year	*0*	*1*	*2*	*3*	*4*	*5*	*6*
Net cash flows	– 15,000	– 15,000	– 7,500	+ 7,000	+ 7,000	+ 250	+ 250
PV factor @ 5%	1.000	.952	.907	.864	.823	.784	.746
	– 15,000	– 14,280	– 6,803	+ 6,048	+ 5,761	+ 196	+ 187

NPV = – £23,891

The present value cost of leasing, discounted at 5%, is now revealed to be less than the present value of the cost savings. The project should therefore go ahead, subject to analysing the *sensitivity* to change of the operational cash flows.

This activity shows how important it is:

- to link the financing and investment decisions, because the way a project is financed will directly affect its viability;
- to apply appropriate risk rates to *operational* as distinct from *financing* cash flows;
- to appraise financing alternatives separately, with the objec-

tive of choosing the lowest cost alternative to compare with the present value of the operational cash flow benefits.

Summary of advantages of leasing to the lessee

- *Additional credit* is obtained above normal debt capacity.
- *No capital outlay is required*, which enables a company to obtain the use of up-to-date equipment in times of tight credit restrictions.
- *Grants* payable to firms in special development areas are claimable by the lessor and are invariably passed on to the lessee, in the form of either a lump sum or reduced rentals. These do not affect the taxation capital allowances.
- *Availability* of certain assets may only be possible through leasing, which may be easier to arrange than a loan, because the property in the leased asset remains with the lessor, giving him great security.
- *Tax allowances*. Capital allowances are included in the rentals, which themselves can be written off against profits for tax purposes.
- *Inflation*. Rentals are normally fixed, which provides a hedge against rising prices.
- *Fixed contract*. Unlike an overdraft, the financial lease contract cannot be withdrawn.

Review

Norfolk Mushrooms plc decided to replace one of their spawning machines, the current new cash price of which is £100,000. The new machine should have at least a five-year life, but because of its specialised construction, will have a negligible residual value at the end of that time.

The company is considering three alternative ways of financing the replacement:

a A £100,000 *term loan* arranged with their bank, to be paid off by equal annual instalments over five years. The bank lending rate is 12% gross.

b A *hire purchase contract*, requiring an initial deposit of £30,000, followed by five equal annual instalments of

£22,000, paid at the end of the each of the years 1 to 5. The interest included in the five annual instalments is respectively £12,000, £11,000, £9,000, £6,000 and £2,800.

c *Leasing* the machine by paying five annual rentals of £23,000 at the commencement of each year.

If purchased, the machine will attract a first year capital allowance of 100%. Corporation tax is to be taken as 50%, and it can be assumed that there is a one year time-lag in paying corporation tax. Which financial alternative will be preferred? Show workings.

a *Borrow and pay*

Year	*Loan*	*Tax saving*	*PV factor @ 6%*	*Present value*
	£	£		£
0	– 100,000		1.000	– 100,000
2		+ 50,000	.890	+ 44,500
NPV cost of borrowing				– 55,500

b *Hire purchase*

Year	*Instalments*	*Tax saving*	*PV factor @ 6%*	*Present value*
	£	£		£
0	– 30,000		1.0000	– 30,000
1–5	– 22,000		4.2123	– 92,671
2		+ 50,000 + 6,000	} .890	+ 49,840
3		+ 5,500	.840	+ 4,620
4		+ 4,500	.792	+ 3,564
5		+ 3,000	.747	+ 2,241
6		+ 1,400	.705	+ 987
NPV cost of hire purchase				– 61,419

c *Leasing*

Year	*Rental*	*Tax saving*	*PV factor @ 6%*	*Present value*
	£	£		£
0	– 23,000		1.000	– 23,000
1–4	– 23,000		3.465	– 79,695
2–6		+ 11,500	3.974	+ 45,701
NPV cost of leasing				– 56,994

The five-year term loan has the lowest present value cost, and is therefore preferred on this basis. However, because the decision is marginal between borrowing and leasing, it would pay Norfolk Mushrooms to 'shop around' in the highly competitive leasing market in case a better offer is available.

Part 5
Share valuation, dividends and cost of capital

13 The investor and share valuation

Introduction

An investor with a building society savings account knows precisely the rate of interest receivable on his savings and can make direct comparisons with *current* returns on alternative 'safe' investments. He is not concerned about the underlying or future earnings of the building society.

By comparison, an investor in ordinary shares has to forecast the *future* returns from his investment. He normally expects to receive a continuing, fairly stable but growing annual dividend and a progressive increase in the value of his shares. He should therefore subject proposed investments to the same principles of appraisal as those applied to businesses and dealt with in Chapter 3.

Theoretically, the *current* market value of his shares should represent the present value of future dividends, plus the expected proceeds of their sale some time in the future. But, as these cash flows are the product of company investment projects, it follows that share values represent the present value of future cash flows from these projects. We discuss share valuation in more detail later in this chapter.

An investor's judgement about the future prospects of a company will inevitably take account of its past and present earnings record evidenced partly by the profitability ratios discussed in Chapter 2. But he will particularly want to know how much of the company's profits relate to shareholders, and how much has been distributed as dividends.

Dividends are the *annual* reward to shareholders, whilst the profit retained and reinvested provides the prospect of future growth in earnings. The ratios used by investors to assess the performance of their investments are the subject of the first section of this chapter.

How investors evaluate the performance of their shares

Shown below is the profit and loss account of Norfolk Agrimek plc, manufacturers of agricultural machinery and implements, which has 10,000,000 £1 ordinary shares in issue, at a current market price per share of £4.

Norfolk Agrimek plc
Profit and loss account for the year to 19X3

		£000s
Net trading profit		3,100
less Corporation tax		1,000
		2,100
add Extraordinary profit on the sale of property		100
Earnings applicable to shareholders		2,200
less Dividends:		
Preference	100	
Ordinary	1,000	1,100
Earnings for the year carried forward		1,100

How can a shareholder use this information to appraise his investment? One way would be to compare this year's figures with those for last year, to determine whether there is any deterioration or improvement. Another approach would be to calculate the return on total capital employed illustrated in Chapter 2. However, neither of these measurements is close enough to the requirements of the individual shareholder. Only *earnings* and *dividends per share*, related to share market price, can do this.

Earnings per share

This is calculated by dividing total earnings after tax, before adding extraordinary items but deducting preference share dividends, by the total number of ordinary shares in issue.

> *Activity*
>
> From the above information calculate Norfolk's earnings per share (EPS).

(Shareholders' earnings − extraordinary profit − preference dividend) ÷ number of shares in issue = (2,200,000 − 100,000 − 100,000) ÷ 10,000,000 = 20 pence.

Given the number of shares does not change, this is an *absolute* measure of profit earned for ordinary shareholders, out of which their dividend is paid. A growing EPS will be expected if profits are withheld and reinvested in the company.

The number of shares in issue can change from year to year, however, and it is important to recognise this when comparing EPS this year with other years. Shares can increase in number when a 'rights' issue is made, which can dilute EPS. Another way in which earnings per share can be diluted is to make a 'bonus' issue of shares. Such an issue does not increase a company's total capital value; it merely increases the *number* of shares issued. For example, if Norfolk Agrimek had reserves of £20 million, it could *capitalise*, say, £10 million of this by issuing one new share for each share already held. The result would be that issued ordinary share capital increases to £20 million, and there are now twenty million shares in issue. Each shareholder has twice as many shares as he held before, but the value of each is half of what it was. Because shares have a lower market price they are more marketable.

If a bonus issue is made during a year, therefore, due recognition should be given to this when comparing with the previous year's EPS.

Price/earnings ratio

The opinions of investors as to whether past growth in EPS,

together with other factors, will lead to more growth in the future, are reflected in the market price of the share. Investors will pay a higher price both for growth and for a share whose earnings are thought to be subject to a relatively low level of risk.

The price/earnings ratio (PE) is a widely accepted measure of the relative growth and risk rating of a share. It is calculated by dividing the share market price by the last reported EPS.

> *Activity*
>
> Calculate Norfolk Agrimek's PE ratio.

Market price÷EPS=400÷20=20.

Note that the *last reported EPS* is used in the calculation, in harness with a market price which reflects expected *future growth.*

Generally, a high PE rating indicates a high growth expectancy; and a low one, a company that is dragging its feet. This does not imply that low PE companies should be ignored. For example, a company with a current low PE may be in the process of being reorganised under new management, and may be attractive as a speculative investment. Remember that the market price of a share is only as good as the information made available to the market and that, possibly, internal management has more faith in the future of the company than the stock market.

Earnings yield

This is the reciprocal of the PE ratio, i.e. current EPS as a % of market price.

> *Activity*
>
> Calculate Norfolk's earnings yield.

EPS÷market price×100=20÷400×100=5%.

A high market price will result in a low earnings yield, and be a signal of high growth potential; conversely, a high earnings yield indicates that investors are more uncertain about *future* growth and require a higher *current* yield to compensate for this.

This ratio has largely been superseded by the PE ratio in recent years, and is not published in the list of daily share prices.

Dividend yield

Dividends mean much more to small investors than earnings, because they can be compared with yields on alternative investments. Consequently, they will be more interested in *gross* dividends (i.e. dividends before tax), as a percentage of share price. Most investment yields are quoted gross, that is, before deduction of standard tax rate (currently 30%); therefore, dividend yield is calculated on the same basis. But because dividends are paid net of an imputed tax rate of 30%, their gross value is found by applying × (100÷70).

> *Activity*
>
> Calculate: **a** Norfolk Agrimek's gross dividend per ordinary share; **b** the company's gross dividend yield.

a Net dividend per ordinary share=1,000,000÷10,000,000=10 pence.
Gross dividend per share=(10÷70)×100=14.28 pence.
b Gross dividend yield=(14.28÷400)×100=3.6%.

Why is it that investors will accept such a low return compared with the higher yields on other shares, and fixed interest securities? It can only be that investors expect a compensating high growth rate in future dividends, and this is reflected in a high share price. When future growth is not expected to be so high, investors look for the safety of the higher dividend yield.

Dividend cover

This measures the number of times that dividend paid is

covered by earnings. It is an indicator of growth through retained earnings, and also of the company's ability to maintain the current dividend.

> *Activity*
>
> Calculate Norfolk Agrimek's dividend cover. Hint: use the earnings figure from the EPS calculation.

Earnings per share (EPS)÷dividend per share (DPS)=20÷10=2.

Each £1 of dividend paid by Norfolk is being matched by an equivalent reinvestment of £1.

Asset backing

> *Activity*
>
> **a** Obtain a recent copy of the published annual accounts of a limited company, and from the balance sheet calculate the value of each ordinary share. This is done by dividing the share capital and reserves appropriate to ordinary shareholders by the number of ordinary shares in issue.
>
> **b** Now compare this value with the quoted market price.

Theoretically the values should be the same, but in most cases will not be. This is because shares tend to be valued on an expected dividend basis whereas balance sheet values depend on the accounting conventions applied in the valuation of assets and liabilities.

Although a share can be sold at its stock market value at any time, the balance sheet may indicate a considerably higher value (i.e. asset backing). In these circumstances, an investor might be advised to hold on to his shares as they could be undervalued. If this is so, and a potential purchaser appears on the horizon, the market price is likely to increase.

Whilst asset value is not so important as earnings and dividends when investment in shares is being considered, it is a factor that cannot be ignored, as assets may have an intrinsic value quite apart from their earning capacity.

Self-check

1 The number of shares issued by Consolidated Plastics plc is 5,000,000. Its earnings per share are 30 pence. What is the profit applicable to ordinary shareholders?
2 If the PE ratio of Consolidated Plastics is 25; what is the market price of its shares?
3 What is the earnings yield of Consolidated Plastics?
4 The net dividend yield of Consolidated Plastics is 2%. Calculate **a** dividend in pence per share, **b** dividend cover.
5 Do you consider Consolidated to be a high growth share? Explain.

1 £1,500,000.
2 PE×EPS=25×30 pence=£7.50.
3 (30÷750)×100=4%.
4 **a** 2%×£7.50=15 pence
b EPS/DPS=30/15=2.
5 Yes. It has a relatively high PE ratio, although this would have to be confirmed by comparison with other companies in the same industry. The low dividend and dividend cover also indicate growth.

The efficient market theory of share valuation

Constant dividends and share valuation

In the introduction to this chapter it was implied that the current market price of a share represents the present value of expected future dividends on that share. In other words, it is the amount that an investor is prepared to pay now for the flow of future dividends. The *process* of transferring shares does not affect their market price. The company's share register merely records that a share now belongs to someone else, and the transfer simply diverts the dividend on that share to the new holder. The total dividend paid by the company remains unchanged.

You will recall from Chapter 3 that the amount someone will be prepared to pay now (i.e. the present value), for an amount receivable in one year's time is $A_1 \div (1+r)$, where A_1 is the amount receivable, and r is the investor's required rate of return, incorporating both the costs of waiting and risk. Thus the present value of £100 receivable in one year's time at 10% is $100 \div 1.10 = £90.91$.

It can also be shown that the present value of a *perpetual* annual amount receivable (a perpetuity) is $A \div r$, where A is the perpetuity, and r the investor's required rate of return.

Activity

Assuming that a company pays a constant dividend (a perpetuity) of 30 pence per share, and the shareholder's required rate of return is 20%, what is the present value of the share?

$V_0 = D \div r = £0.30 \div .20 = £1.50$.

where V_0=value now
D=perpetual dividend
r=shareholder's rate of return

Investment of retained earnings and share valuation

Where a company uses retained profit for reinvestment, this should increase future dividends, and the total value of the company's shares should increase by the net present value of the investment project, *as soon as shareholders are aware that the project is to go ahead.*

For example, where a company pays a constant dividend of £10,000, the total value of its shares before acceptance of a project is:

$D \div r = 10{,}000 \div .10 = £100{,}000$

where r is 10% – the investor's required rate of return.

Should £5,000 of the next dividend payable be invested in a project at the end of year 1 to yield £4,000 in each of years 2 and 3, and the dividend be increased accordingly in those two years, then the market value of the company after acceptance of the project will be:

$$V_O = \frac{5{,}000}{(1.10)} + \frac{14{,}000}{(1.10)^2} + \frac{14{,}000}{(1.10)^3} + \frac{10{,}000}{(1.10)^4} \ldots \frac{10{,}000}{(1.10)^\infty}$$

$$= 4{,}545 + 11{,}570 + 10{,}518 + \frac{100{,}000}{(1.10)^3}$$

$$= £101{,}763. \ (\infty = \text{infinity.})$$

Which shows an increase in total value of £101,763−100,000=£1,763.

Note that dividend is reduced in year 1, increased in years 2 and 3, but resumes its normal pattern again from the end of year 4. Note also that the £100,000 discounted at the end of year 3 represents the present value at that time of the constant dividend of £10,000 from year 4 onwards.

Activity

Now check that the investment project NPV agrees with the £1,763 increase in market value.

	Cash flow	*PV factor @10%*	*Present value*
Year 1	−5,000	.909	− 4,545
2	+4,000	.826	+ 3,304
3	+4,000	.751	+ 3,004
NPV			+£1,763

Dividend growth and share valuation

Assuming that shareholders expect that a company's dividend grows at a constant rate, then the present value of the future dividend stream can be found as follows:

$$V_O = \frac{D_O(1+g)}{1+r} + \frac{D_O(1+g)^2}{(1+r)^2} + \frac{D_O(1+g)^3}{(1+r)^3} + \ldots \frac{D_O(1+g)^\infty}{(1+r)^\infty}$$

where D_0=the current dividend
g=the constant growth rate expected
r=the shareholders' expected rate of return.

It can be shown that this simplifies to:

$$V_O = \frac{D_O(1+g)}{r-g} \text{ or } \frac{D_1}{r-g}$$

where D_1 is the dividend payable in a year's time.

Activity

A company has just paid a dividend of 25 pence per share, which is expected to grow in future at a constant rate of 8%. Assuming a shareholders' discount rate of 13%, calculate the present value of the company's share.

$$V_O = \frac{D_O(1+g)}{r-g} = \frac{.25(1.08)}{.13-.08} = £5.40.$$

Efficient stock markets

The concept that price is the present value of a future stream of dividends inherently assumes that investors have *full knowledge* of:

- all investment opportunities available to companies;
- general economic trends;
- the overall state of the financial markets;

and that they react immediately to this information by buying or selling shares because they believe them to be worth more or less than their current prices. If this is the case, the stock market can be said to be 'efficient' in that it reflects the intrinsic value of this information in the market prices of shares.

New information made public regarding prospective investments by a company *ought* to change the intrinsic value of its shares but because investors interpret the information differently the price will fluctuate randomly around the intrinsic value. Thus the price of a share is said to 'take a random walk' around its intrinsic value.

If we accept that the 'efficient market' and 'random walk' theories are broadly true, as research seems to bear out, then stock market analysts are in no better position than anyone else to predict share price movements. Despite this, analysts do exist in very large numbers, adopting either *technical* or *fundamental* analysis in assessing investments.

Technical analysis or *charting* examines long-, medium- and short-term trends of past share movements, assumes that the same patterns will repeat themselves and attempts to *predict* future share prices. However, the 'random walk' theory would appear to dismiss the validity of technical analysis.

Fundamental analysis is roughly in tune with the efficient market theory, for its adherents analyse all available information past and present, to calculate the 'intrinsic' value of a share, and advise investors accordingly.

Self-check

1 Given a required rate of return of 10%, what is the maximum price you would pay for a share that is currently paying 30 pence dividend if: **a** dividend is expected to remain constant; **b** dividend is expected grow at 5% per annum for ever.

2 What are the conditions associated with an efficient capital market?

1 a

$$V_O = \frac{D}{r} = \frac{£.30}{.10} = £3.00.$$

b

$$V_O = \frac{D_O(1+g)}{r-g} = \frac{.30(1.05)}{.10-.05} = £6.30.$$

2 An efficient capital market is one in which stock prices reflect all publicly available information regarding individual companies and the economy at large, and which *immediately* adjusts to this information.

Why value shares?

This may seem a strange question to ask following a statement that the Stock Exchange is an efficient market for shares. However, because there is usually a wide spread between share buying and selling prices, and because trading in certain shares may be limited, it cannot be guaranteed that the listed prices will always represent their true value.

You will recall that the efficient market theory is founded on *publicly known information*. However, this information may not be complete in that:

- company investment plans will not all be public information;
- the value placed upon a company's assets by a potential buyer may be different from the value based upon share price;
- the majority of companies, mainly private, are not listed on the Stock Exchange;
- holders of a large number of shares in a company may be in a strong bargaining position to insist on a higher than listed price;
- a company seeking fresh capital may have to price a new issue of shares below market price to make them attractive.

Circumstances requiring the valuation of shares include:

- proposed amalgamation of two or more businesses;
- purchase of shares in a company by another company;
- sale of shares in unquoted, mainly private companies;
- valuation for tax purposes;
- nationalisation of a company;
- flotation of a fresh issue of shares.

Methods of share valuation

If a share is listed, its quoted price always provides a value reference point. In other cases, a company's articles of association may specify the basis to be used to value its shares.

Valuation bases used include:

- Net asset values – **i** as a 'going concern', **ii** at break-up values.
- Capitalised earnings – **i** using an implied rate of return, **ii** using an appropriate PE ratio.

- Imputed dividend yield.

Each of these methods is discussed below, drawing on the following information relating to Compact Containers Ltd, a private limited company.

Compact Containers Limited
Balance sheet at 31 December 19X4

Fixed assets:	£000s	£000s
Land and buildings (net)	600	
Plant and Machinery (net)	500	1,100
Current assets:		
Cash	90	
Debtors	220	
Stocks	330	
	640	
less *Current liabilities:*		
Trade creditors	120	
Taxation	40	
	160	480
		£1,580
200,000 ordinary shares of £1 each		200
Retained earnings		980
		1,180
100,000 12% preference shares of £1 each		100
10% loan (repayable in 8 years)		300
		£1,580

Year	*Profit applicable to ordinary shareholders* £000s	*Dividends paid* £000s
19X4	248	80
19X3	200	60
19X2	180	60
19X1	160	50

Net assets basis

Bearing in mind that asset values in a balance sheet are usually stated at *historic cost*, and that even those values depend upon the accounting policies of the company, it will be necessary to adjust them to current values.

With increasing property values *land and buildings* could be under-valued; excepting perhaps for *leasehold* properties that may be subject to contingent liabilities for renewing dilapidations at the end of the terms of the leases.

Plant and machinery should be revalued at replacement cost less appropriate depreciation, and *investments* valued at current market prices.

Stock is valued at cost or realisable value, whichever is the lower, and a provision for bad debts made against debtors where this is thought necessary.

Assuming the net assets of Compact Containers Ltd are under-valued by £100,000, the value of its ordinary shares would be:

		£000s
Net assets value per balance sheet		1,580
add Revaluation of assets		100
		1680
	£000s	
less Preference shareholders	100	
10% loan	300	400
Net asset value attributable to ordinary shareholders		£1,280
Number of shares		200
Value per share: £1,280/200		£6.40

Break-up or liquidation value would be considerably below the going-concern value, and would be the minimum price payable. In most cases it would only be used if the business is not worth continuing. Businesses are sometimes purchased with the sole objective of selling off all or part of its assets. This is referred to as *asset-stripping*, and the asset-stripper would fix his maximum price at a level that takes into account the potential sales and operating values of each of the separate assets.

Capitalised earnings – using an implied rate of return or PE ratio

This approach is the most logical to use if one agrees that an investment in the shares of a company is made in the expectation that the resources purchased will generate sufficient earnings to repay the price paid within a reasonable time and yield a satisfactory rate of return on capital invested.

It is the basis most appropriate to a prospective purchaser of a *controlling* interest in the company, as he will be able to influence trading policy and thus total profit.

The two basic factors in capitalising earnings are:

- expected level of earnings;
- required rate of return or PE ratio to apply to those earnings.

The appropriate level of earnings will be the ordinary shareholders' *future maintainable profit*; and if the profits of the most recent years are used as a guide for this purpose, adjustments will have to be made for non-continuing and extraordinary income and expenditure, and changes in accounting principles.

The *rate of return* to apply to future maintainable earnings will be that appropriate to the risks inherent in those earnings. The average *earnings yields* or PE ratios (discussed earlier in this chapter) of *quoted* companies with similar risks will be a guide here, subject to the chosen earnings yield being adjusted upwards, or the PE downwards, by up to as much as 25% if it is a private company whose shares are being valued. This is because a private company may be little known to the investing public and therefore riskier as an investment.

If we assume that the most recent Compact Containers profit of £248,000 represents a reasonable figure of future maintainable annual earnings, and that an earnings yield of 20% is appropriate, the capitalised earnings value of its shares is: £248,000÷.20=£1,240,000.

If the PE ratio of the company whose earnings yield has been applied above, is used instead, it will be the reciprocal of the earnings yield, i.e. 1÷.20=5, and the value of the Compact shares is the same: £248,000×5=£1,240,000. In each case the value per share is £1,240,000÷200,000=£6.20.

Dividend yield valuation

Although a *small investor* in an unquoted company would look for good dividend cover to provide growth, he has little management influence over total earnings which may, in any case, fluctuate considerably. He will therefore tend to value his shares on the basis of dividends rather than earnings, and for this purpose will seek out the dividend yield on the shares of a *quoted* company of comparable size, risk and growth potential. It will be impossible to discover an exactly similar company so an average of the yields of two or three companies of similar size will be a reasonable proxy.

A low dividend yield normally implies high growth prospects and would be accompanied also by a relatively high dividend cover. A potential investor may, therefore, take a sceptical view of an unquoted company which is currently distributing high dividends (i.e. low dividend cover), even though it may have growth potential, and adjust his expected dividend yield upwards accordingly. He would make a further adjustment if the company was little known and therefore risky.

As dividend yields are quoted gross, the dividend paid by Compact Containers must be grossed up by a factor of 100/70, assuming a standard rate of tax of 30%. If an expected dividend yield of 8% is used, the value of Compact's shares using the latest dividend of £80,000, is:

$$(80{,}000\times100)\div(70\times.08\times200{,}000)=£7.14.$$

General considerations affecting share valuation

- Before attempting to value shares, a close scrutiny of the company's memorandum and articles of association will reveal how such valuation may be influenced by special capital, dividend and repayment priorities, as well as any special rights reserved for the benefit of directors.
- It should be confirmed that there is adequate liquid capital either existing or readily available to continue and develop the business effectively, and that there will be no early liability to repay capital.
- Adequate asset and earnings cover for capital and dividends is of prime importance.
- Valuation is what a willing buyer and seller agree it is, and whichever methods are used initially, the valuations emerg-

ing will merely serve as starting points and as a basis for negotiations. The value eventually agreed will, at best, be a compromise of subjective judgement and strategic adjustments on both sides.

- Because valuation is made for different purposes, different methods or a combination of them will probably be used. For example, the assets method may be adopted when the main interest is in securing and eventually disposing of certain assets. Where assets have high intrinsic value, for example property, this method will tend to dominate. The assets basis will also be appropriate when the bulk of the assets is of the liquid type, and therefore probably realistically valued already; for example those of investment trusts, banks and insurance companies.
- On the other hand, the capitalised earnings basis is the logical approach to valuing 'going concern' assets, for without a continuing stream of future earnings, assets are only worth their break-up values.

Review

One of the directors of Alton Engineers Ltd, a private company engaged in the manufacture of small machine tools, wishes to sell some of his shares and has requested you to advise him regarding the price that he might ask for them. He provides you with a copy of the last balance sheet and other financial information given below:

Alton Engineers Ltd
Balance sheet at 31 December 19X5

	Cost £	Aggregate depreciation	Net £
Fixed assets:			
Land and buildings	750	90	660
Plant and machinery	1,000	470	530
Furniture and fixtures	50	30	20
	1,800	590	1,210
Current assets			
Stock	350		
Debtors	280		
Short-term investments	50		
Cash	20		
	700		
less *Current liabilities*			
Trade creditors	200		
Net working capital			500
			£1,710
Shareholders' capital and reserves:			
Called-up share capital – ordinary shares 50p			400
Profit and loss account			1,010
			1,410
Creditors falling due after more than one year:			
13% term loan (repayable in 5 yrs)			300
			£1,710

Note:
Because of increased property values, land is thought to be worth £100,000 more than its balance sheet value. All the above figures are £000s.

Operating results for the last three years (£000s)

	19X5	*9X4*	*19X3*
Turnover	4,000	3,500	2,800
Net profit after tax	256	210	154
Ordinary dividend paid	101	90	80

Information gleaned from the financial press regarding the recent performances of two companies in the same industry, and of approximately equal size, is as follows:

	P/E ratio	*Gross Dividend yield*	*Dividend cover*
Zena Corporation	12	5%	3.0
Yani Engineers	10	6%	2.8

Assume that the current standard rate of income tax is 30%.

Required: advise the director regarding the valuation of his shares.

Report on the valuation of Alton's ordinary shares

To: Director

From: Financial adviser

Overall considerations

1 Small machine tool shares are currently favoured by the market, therefore you should have no difficulty in disposing of your shares.

2 Some companies' articles of association set down a basis for the valuation of shares, but there is no such provision in your articles.

3 Potential investors will be looking for a good profit to capital employed record; will expect the company to have adequate liquidity; and to have an acceptable level of gearing. In all these areas, your company appears to be quite sound.

Bases for valuation

1 Three methods of valuing your shares are illustrated below; implying that valuation is partly subjective and subject to negotiation and compromise between buyer and seller.

2 The bases used are:

a *Net assets value* – not the most satisfactory method, as balance sheet values are usually stated at historic cost; and net value, particularly in regard to plant, machinery and stocks, is so much dependent upon the accounting valuation bases used by the business.

b *Price/earnings ratio* – applied to future expected maintainable earnings. This is the basis upon which a person interested in securing a substantial holding of shares would depend, as he would be in a strong position to influence policy and therefore earnings.

c *Dividend yield* – the basis more applicable to purchasers of small numbers of shares, because they are not in a strong enough position to influence earnings. What decision a small investor makes, hangs upon whether he wants income or capital growth from his investment. If the former, a high yield would be expected; if the latter – a low yield.

In each case, *asset backing* is important, but the investor looking for capital growth would also expect to see a relatively high *dividend cover.*

Assets valuation

The only information regarding *revaluation* is that concerned with land but further enquiries might reveal the existence of obsolescent machinery or stock, or debtors that may be of doubtful value. Subject to any such further adjustment, asset valuation is:

		£000s
Total net assets		1,710
less Term loan		300
		1,410
add Revaluation of land		100
		1,510
Value per share: £1,510,000÷800,000	=	£1.89 (approx.)

Price/earnings valuation

Similar risk quoted companies have an average PE ratio of 11 but because Alton is a little-known private company, investors will probably give it a lower rating – perhaps by up to 25%.

Alton's *earnings per share* for the most recent year are £256,000÷800,000=32 pence. Assuming that this level of earnings will continue, and an appropriate PE ratio is 8, Alton's share value is 8×32 pence=£2.56.

Dividend yield valuation

Using the latest dividend paid, Alton's gross dividend per share is: (101,000×100)÷(70×800,000)= . . . 18 pence.

Dividend cover is 256÷101=2.57.

Because Alton is not known to the financial market, and also because its dividend cover does not match up to its competitors', investors will look for a higher than average yield – say, 7% – and its dividend yield valuation would then be: .18÷.07= . . . £2.57.

Conclusion

The earnings and dividend valuations are approximately the same; therefore given that £2.57 reflects the future prospects of Alton this should be the initial asking price for the share, with a 'floor' value of £1.89, the net asset valuation.

14 Dividend policy and share valuation

Introduction

Retained profit provides a significant proportion of new finance. This is not surprising for, apart from borrowing, the alternatives are:

- that existing shareholders dig more deeply into their own pockets by way of a rights issue; or
- the company makes a public issue of shares.

Only when all other sources are exhausted will the latter course be followed for this would dilute existing shareholders' control over the company.

Regarding a rights issue, it would be illogical for a company requiring finance, and having profit readily available, to distribute it all as dividends and then ask for some of it back. However, companies *do* continue to pay dividends whilst making issues of shares, so how are their dividend, financing and investment policies reconciled? This question has exercised the minds of academics and financial managers in recent years but without any completely satisfactory answer being produced.

Dividends as a residual profit decision

It would seem sensible for a company to continue to reinvest profit as long as projects can be found that yield returns higher than its cost of capital. In this way, the company can earn a higher return for shareholders than they can earn for themselves by reinvesting dividends. Such a policy can only be optimal, however, if the company maintains its target gearing ratio by adding an appropriate proportion of borrowed funds to the retained earnings. If not, the company's cost of capital would increase because of its disproportionate volume of higher cost equity capital; this would be reflected in a reduced share price.

Activity

Laser Engineering Ltd has the chance to invest in the five projects listed below:

Project	*Capital outlay*	*DCF yield rate*
A	70,000	18
B	100,000	17
C	130,000	16
D	50,000	15
E	100,000	14

The company's cost of capital is 16%, its optimal debt to equity ratio is 30%. and the current year's profit available to equity shareholders is £350,000.

Required

a State which projects would be accepted, and what is the total finance required for those projects?

b Assuming that the company wishes to maintain its gearing ratio, how much of the required finance will be borrowed?

c How much of this year's profit can be distributed?

a *A*, *B* and *C*, with yields greater than or equal to the company's cost of capital; total finance required £300,000.

b Amount to be borrowed: 30% of £300,000=£90,000.

c This year's profit:

This year's profit:	£350,000
less amount to be reinvested – £300,000 – 90,000:	210,000
Profit for distribution:	140,000

Laser shareholders obtain the best of both worlds. They can invest the £140,000 received as dividends to earn a higher rate of return than the company could earn for them; and the £210,000 retained by the company is reinvested to shareholders' advantage. Shareholders' wealth is optimised, and the dividend paid is simply the *residual profit after investment policy has been approved.*

If companies look upon dividends as what remains after investments are decided then the search for an optimum dividend policy is pointless. Shareholders wanting dividends can always make them for themselves by selling some of their shares.

Further support for the 'residual' theory of dividends, and the argument that a change in dividend policy does not affect share values, was advanced by Modigliani and Miller in 1961. They contended that the increase in total value of a company after it has accepted an investment project is the same, whether internal or external finance is used.

We can look again at the dividend valuation model discussed in Chapter 12, which showed that $V_0=D \div r$, where V_0 is the present value of a share; D is an assumed constant dividend; and r the shareholder's required rate of return.

Thus if D is £2,000 then $V_0=£2{,}000 \div .10=£20{,}000$, where $r=10\%$.

Activity

Given the above data, if a dividend is *currently* due, but not yet paid, what would the present value of the company be?

$V_0=£2{,}000+(2{,}000 \div .10)=£22{,}000$ – which simply shows the value to include the current, unpaid dividend.

Activity

If the dividend currently due was invested in a project yielding £300 per annum in perpetuity, what would be the net present value of the project if the shareholders' required rate of return is 10%?

	£
Value of £300 in perpetuity at 10%=£300÷.10=	3,000
less Capital invested	2,000
Net present value	£1,000

The value of the company should therefore increase by £1,000.

Activity

Assuming that the £300 additional earnings from the internally financed project is used to increase the annual dividend, show the revised present value of the company.

V_0=£2,300÷.10=£23,000 – i.e. an increase of £1,000 over the previous value, this being the net present value of the new project. The dividend foregone is, of course, still included in the total value.

Activity

Now assume that the current dividend is paid to shareholders, and the new project is financed by an issue of shares, on which 10% is still the required rate of return. What is the present value of the company, and how much of that value relates to the shares held before the new issue?

V_0=£2,300÷.10=£23,000 – of which a capitalised expected annual dividend of £200÷.10=£2,000 relates to the new shares; leaving £21,000 appropriate to the original shares – the same as before.

One deficiency in the Modigliani and Miller hypothesis is that they ignore costs associated with an issue of shares which can be quite considerable.

Self-check

1 'The residual theory of dividends assumes that a stable dividend policy is followed, with the residue of profit being reinvested within the company.' True or false? Explain.

2 'Retained earnings and external finance are interchangeable for investment purposes' (M. and M.). Did they mean by this:
a that they are both sources of cash;
b that existing shareholders' wealth is unchanged whatever the choice of finance; or
c that the cash required would come from the same source – shareholders?

1 False. The residual theory of dividends implies that companies should continue to use profit for reinvestment purposes, as long as the return earned on company projects exceeds its cost of capital. When investment needs are satisfied, the residue of profit can then be distributed as dividends.
2 b M. and M. contend that dividend policy does not affect the wealth of shareholders.

Costs associated with dividend policy

Capital flotation costs are a deterrent to substituting external finance for retained earnings but there are other costs affected by the dividend decision.

If shareholders are left to make their own dividends by selling some shares, this involves brokerage and other selling costs which, on a small number of shares, can be extremely uneconomic. In addition, if they have to be sold during a period of low share prices, capital losses may be suffered.

Another important factor is *taxation*. Firstly, when a company distributes dividend it has to pay an advance instalment of corporation tax (ACT), currently 3/7ths of the amount paid. But the offset against the mainstream liability to pay corporation tax will be delayed by at least one year. Indeed, if the company does not currently pay corporation tax, the delay in setting off ACT will be even longer, and this will tend to restrain extravagant dividend distributions.

Secondly, from the investors' viewpoint, profitably invested retained earnings should increase share values, enabling shareholders to create their own dividends. Selling shares creates a liability to capital gains tax, currently 30%, but subject to a fairly generous exemption limit. By comparison, dividends in the hands of shareholders attract higher rates of income tax (up to 60% at 1984 rates). Thus, higher rate taxpayers may prefer comparatively low dividend payouts to minimise their tax burden.

Thirdly, *financial institutions* confuse the taxation picture even more, through their major holdings in the shares of quoted companies. They are able to set off dividends received against dividends paid for tax purposes but some may be liable to capital gains tax if they sell shares to make dividends. Pension funds welcome dividends for they can reclaim the advance corporation tax paid at source on the dividends they receive. They are not liable to capital gains tax on shares they sell.

The effect of taxation on dividend decisions is difficult to analyse. It may be argued that companies attract investors who can match their personal taxation regimes to company dividend policy, and that those who do not want to join a particular 'taxation club' will invest elsewhere. If this is true, however, a change in a company's dividend policy would probably not find favour with its shareholder clientele, and would consequently affect share values, which seems to support the argument that dividend policy matters.

Self-check

List, in two columns, the costs and taxes incurred by shareholders in financing investment by **a** retained earnings and **b** external finance.

Retained earnings	*External finance*
Cost of selling shares to make dividends.	High tax rates on dividends.
	Share issue costs.
Capital gains tax on shares sold to make dividends.	Delayed recovery of ACT.

Other arguments supporting the relevance of dividend policy

> *Activity*
>
> As a potential investor, how would you react to the following questions?
>
> **1** Would you prefer cash dividends now, against the promise of future, perhaps uncertain dividends?
> **2** Would you prefer a stable, growing dividend, to one that fluctuates in sympathy with company investment needs?
> **3** If a company, in whose shares you invest, increases or decreases its dividend, would this change your personal investment policy?

In answer to question **1** you probably opted for cash now rather than cash you may never see. The future is uncertain and most people take much convincing that it is in their interests to postpone income. Although the equity shareholder by definition is the risk-bearer, he is also entitled to a reasonable resolution of dividend prospects to compensate for the additional risk he carries. An investor will almost certainly pay a higher price for earlier rather than later dividends.

By definition, a fluctuating dividend is more risky than a stable dividend. Investors will pay more for stability, especially if it is linked with steady growth. Research has shown that, in general, dividends follow a pattern of stability with growth. Maintenance of the previous year's dividend is the first consideration, with growth added when directors feel that a higher plateau of profitability has been consolidated.

As regards question **3**, you would no doubt be very happy about an increase, and might even be prompted to buy more shares – thus helping to push the market price up. Conversely, a decreased dividend would cause you to review your investment, perhaps even to sell your shares to take advantage of better investment opportunities elsewhere. Investors tend to believe that dividend changes provide information regarding a company's future prospects, and they react accordingly. For example, in 1980 ICI cut its dividend for the first time in years, and this harmed the market price of its shares considerably. The directors were reacting to the continuing recession, expecting that future earnings would not be sufficient to support a continuation of the previous dividend payout.

Dividend policy does therefore appear to be relevant to share valuation, but as stated in the introductory section of this chapter, it is left to the individual company to reconcile this policy with uncertainty, costs, taxation and other factors to be discussed in the next section.

Practical factors affecting dividend policy

Whatever dividend policy is thought to be best for a company in theory, certain practical factors influence the decision.

Availability of profit The Companies Act 1980 provides that dividends can only be paid out of accumulated *realised* profit less *realised* losses, whether these are capital or revenue. Previous or current years' losses must be made good before a distribution can be made. If an asset is sold, any *realised* profit or loss arising can be distributed; but any profit or loss arising from a revaluation of an asset cannot be distributed – unless and until the asset is sold.

The additional cost of replacing productive assets at inflated prices should be provided for in determining profit available for distribution.

Availability of cash Profit may be earned during a year and yet it may not be possible to pay a dividend because of lack of cash. This can arise for various reasons. It may already have been expended or be needed to replace fixed and working assets, perhaps at inflated prices. Large customers may not yet have paid their accounts or cash may be needed to repay a loan.

Government restrictions Dividends may be restricted by government prices and incomes policies.

Other restrictions The company's articles of association may limit the payment of dividends or a lender may insert a condition into a loan agreement to restrict the level of dividends.

Similar firms' policies A company's dividend policy cannot be so outrageously different from policies followed by similar companies in the same industry, otherwise the market price of its shares could fall.

Review

1 A company has just made a profit after tax of £350,000. Its investment schedule shows that £300,000 could be invested in projects yielding more than the company's cost of capital. Assuming that the company has a target gearing ratio of 33⅓%, how much dividend could be paid this year?

2 Which of the following support the argument that dividend policy is relevant to the optimisation of shareholder wealth?

a the certainty of dividends now is preferred to dividends later.

b directors have the power to change dividends.

c dividends provide information regarding the expected future fortunes of the company.

d shareholders prefer stable, growing dividends.

e dividends are only payable to registered shareholders.

f dividends should be reconciled with the taxation position of shareholders.

g shareholders would prefer that all profit be distributed as dividends.

3 Given the following information, what dividend can be paid by each company?

	Alpha £	*Beta* £	*Gamma* £
Profit/(loss) brought forward from the previous year	(1,000)	2,000	(3,000)
Trading profit/(loss) for the current year	5,000	4,000	2,000
Loss suffered on sale of property	—	(1,000)	—
Revaluation of property	—	—	10,000

1 Investments financed with *borrowed* capital=⅓×£300,000 =£100,000. Remaining £200,000 being financed out of retained earnings. Dividend that could be paid=£350,000−200,000=£150,000.

2 **a**, **c**, **d**, **f**.

3 Alpha – £4,000 . . . realised profit less accumulated realised losses.

Beta – £5,000 . . . realised profit less accumulated realised losses – including those of a capital nature.

Gamma – nil . . . realised accumulated losses exceed realised gains. The revaluation of property is not a realisation (sale) of the property.

15 Cost of capital

Minimum acceptable rate of return

When appraising investments we need to know the investor's *required rate of return* (see Chapter 3). This is the discounting rate applied to cash flows to ascertain their *net present value.* If NPV is positive a project is deemed to be acceptable; if negative, it would normally be rejected. Alternatively, a project should not proceed unless its DCF yield rate is higher than the required rate of return.

This 'cut-off' point, below which proposed investments should be rejected, is the minimum acceptable to investors. It is their *cost of capital.*

> *Activity*
>
> Jim Crow has surplus cash which he wishes to invest in an easily accessible savings account. He is a non-taxpayer. He ascertains that the rates of interest by three savings institutions are 7½% net of tax, 8½% net of tax, and 12% gross of tax respectively. In his continuing search for a better return, which of the above rates would he consider as his 'cost of capital'?

Jim does not pay tax, therefore the gross yield of 12% would be the yardstick guiding his search. It is the best opportunity discovered to date, the one that he would call his *opportunity cost.*

The concept of opportunity cost applies to all investors. The *owner of a small business* would not continue trading indefinitely if his profit did not measure up to that obtainable on an investment of similar risk. A *lender* expects a rate of interest equivalent to that obtainable on an alternative investment of similar risk. Likewise a *shareholder* would sell his shares if the combined dividend and capital growth on them was less than he could obtain on another share of equivalent risk.

The affect of gearing on cost of capital

Traditional view – weighted average cost

In Chapters 8 and 9 we discussed the benefits to a business of borrowing. Most firms adopt a 'geared' capital structure, using borrowed as well as own funds but rarely take borrowing to an extreme point. This is because they fear that a high burden of interest, and capital that has to be repaid, puts at risk not only the interest and capital of lenders but also the income and capital of its owners. Further, the more variable its operating income, the higher this risk will be.

If a company employs various types of finance, the required rate of return on investments will be a mix of their various costs, weighted in proportion to the amount of each in the total pool of funds.

For example, if a company is financed with £1,500 ordinary shares, and £500 loan stock, the after-tax costs of each being 16% and 8% respectively, its weighted average cost of capital is:

	Capital proportion		*Cost*		*Weighted cost*
			%		%
£1,500 ordinary shares	.75	×	16	=	12
£500 loan stock	.25	×	8	=	2
					14

Assuming that capital is obtained in these proportions, and that their costs remain the same in future, providing investment projects yield a return at least equal to the weighted average cost of capital of 14%, shareholders' and lenders' costs of capital will be satisfied.

On the supply side, shareholders who sense that the risks inherent in high gearing are greater than the extra income derived from using loan capital will sell their holdings and cause share prices to fall. This automatically forces up the rate of return required by investors in those shares. Likewise, lenders will charge more for excessive borrowing and will eventually refuse to supply more finance because of the risk of loss through bankruptcy of the borrower.

Activity

1 Complete the weighted average cost column in the following schedule by adding together the proportionate costs of share and loan capital for each of the five capital mixes.
2 What is the optimum level of gearing?

Share capital		*Loan capital*		*Weighted average*
Cost	*Proportion*	*Cost*	*Proportion*	*cost*
£	%	£	%	£
9	90	5	10	
9	80	5	20	
9	70	5½	30	
10	60	6	40	
12	50	8	50	

1 8.6; 8.2; 7.95; 8.4; 10.0.
2 At the lowest cost point, i.e. 70 : 30 share to loan capital.

The above schedule illustrates the traditional and most widely held view that the weighted average cost of capital of a company will fall with increased borrowing until a point is reached when the higher costs of share and loan capital force the average up. The optimum gearing ratio is achieved when the weighted average cost of capital is at its lowest point.

The Modigliani and Miller view

In a research paper published in 1958, Modigliani and Miller (M.M.) argued that the cost of capital of a company is not affected by the way it is financed. They agreed that capital gearing adds financial risk to a company's normal operating risk and thereby forces up the return required by investors in shares, but they claimed that this increased rate is *exactly* compensated by the additional income accruing to shareholders as a result of the gearing. They concluded, therefore, that there is no difference in the costs of capital, nor the values, of a geared and an ungeared company of equal operating risks.

To illustrate the M.M. theory let us examine two companies, *A* and *B*. *A* is all-share-financed, and *B* has a mixed share/loan capital structure. Both companies' shares are valued at £2 each, and both make a trading profit of £20,000. The capital structures and profit and loss accounts of both companies are shown below. Taxation has been ignored at this stage.

	A		*B*
Share capital 100,000 shares		50,000 shares	
@£2 each	200,000	@£2 each	100,000
Loan capital 5%	—		100,000
	£200,000		£200,000
Net operating profit	20,000		20,000
less Interest	—		5,000
Shareholders' profit	£20,000		£15,000

Note that the return required on the shares of *A* is 20,000÷200,000=10%; and in *B* it is 15,000÷100,000=15%; although the share prices are both the same at £2 each.

B's share holds its value despite the risk of gearing, because of the additional £5,000 income accruing to *B*'s shareholders from the use of the loan capital (i.e. ½×£20,000 less interest of £5,000=£5,000).

The *weighted average* costs of capital are the same as shown below:

		A			*B*
20,000÷200,000	=	10%	Shares .5×15%	=	7½
			Loan .5× 5%	=	2½
					10%

M. M. supported their arguments by showing that if the share prices of two similar risk companies drift apart, investors will see the chance of making money by switching investment from the high-priced share in one company to the low-priced share in the other. This process of switching is called *arbitrage*.

For example, if *B*'s share price increased to £2.40 because of market imperfections, a holder of say 2% of the shares in *B* would realise that company *A* is making the same profit as *B*, but on a smaller capital value. He would therefore:

- sell his 1,000 shares for £2,400;
- create his own gearing by borrowing an amount equal to his previous proportionate shareholding×*B*'s loan capital, i.e. 2% of £100,000=£2,000;
- buy 2% of the shares of *A* for £4,000

A comparison of this investor's income *after* these transactions, with what he previously received shows:

		£
Share of profit from *A* on 2,000 shares (2% of £20,000)	=	400
less Interest on loan 5%×£2,000	=	100
Net income (the same as his previous income from *B*, i.e. 2% of £15,000)		£300

Therefore his income remains unchanged, but he realises a *capital gain* of £400 comprising:

	£
Sale of shares in *B*	2,400
Amount borrowed	2,000
	4,400
less Invested in *A*	4,000
	£ 400

Investors will continue the arbitrage process until both shares have the same value.

However, the M. M. hypothesis was based on the assumption that capital markets are perfect.

- They ignored the impact of taxes on interest paid.
- They assumed that individuals and companies can borrow at the same rates of interest, regardless of differing credit ratings.
- They assumed that investors are perfectly informed and that they always act rationally.

- They ignored companies' fears of bankruptcy costs at high levels of gearing.
- They ignored the costs connected with share transactions.

M. M. later relented on the effects of taxation and agreed that the effective Inland Revenue subsidy on interest payments does reduce a firm's cost of capital. They stand firm on their basic theory, however.

Controversy continues over the effect of gearing on cost of capital and valuation but the traditional view of an optimum capital structure for each company prevails, fear and costs of bankruptcy being the limiting factors on the extent of borrowing.

Self-check

1 The investment 'cut-off' rate of a company is **a** the highest rate of return on investment projects, **b** the planned level of capital expenditure, **c** the investor's cost of capital, **d** the dividend yield. Which of these statements is correct?

2 What is the opportunity cost of funds supplied by ordinary shareholders?

1 **c** the investor's cost of capital.

2 The rate of return obtainable on a comparable share of equal risk.

Self-check

1 'The weighted average cost of capital is less than the cost of a company's equity capital.' True or false?

2 The yield rate of a project is 9%. The company's weighted average cost of capital is 12%. If the project goes ahead, **a** will the suppliers of the company's loan capital be satisfied and **b** will the ordinary shareholders be satified?

3 Jerome Ltd is currently financed wholly by share capital, and its shareholders' required rate of return is 14%. If it obtained a 9% loan, its cost of share capital would increase to 15%, and the loan to equity ratio would be 1:2 What would be the company's cost of capital after obtaining the loan, **a** taking the traditional view of the effects of gearing and **b** assuming the M. M. theory of cost of capital. Ignore taxation.

1 True. The addition of loan capital reduces the weighted average cost below the cost of equity capital.

2 a Loan providers will probably be paid interest out of the 9% yield because they have a prior right to be paid their interest. They will be highly sceptical of present company investment policy, however, of accepting projects below its weighted average cost of capital.

b Ordinary shareholders will only receive satisfactory dividends if investment returns are at least equal to the weighted average cost of capital; they will therefore not be satisfied if present company investment policy continues.

3 a

	Proportion	*Cost*	*Weighted average*
		%	%
Shares	⅔	15	10
Loan	⅓	9	3
			13

b The M. M. view is that the cost of capital is not affected by the way a business is financed, therefore Jerome's cost of capital will remain at 14%.

Ascertaining the cost of each type of finance

Determining the cost of each type of finance employed by a company is not easy for two reasons:

- As we are concerned with the appraisal of *future* investment cash flows, we have to estimate *future* costs of capital covering the investment period.
- Although *explicit* rates of interest are associated with new issues of loan capital, other costs of capital will have to be *imputed* from stock market information; this is particularly so in the case of equity capital.

Cost of borrowed funds

New loans The cost of loan capital is basically the rate charged by the lender. On *new loans* this will be the explicitly agreed rate of interest (known as the 'coupon rate'). If a variable interest rate is charged, the expected average rate over the loan period will be more appropriate.

However, because loan interest can be deducted from profit for tax purposes its effective cost is I (1 − t), where I is the gross interest rate, and t the company's tax rate. For example, interest of 10% with a 50% tax rate, will reduce to 10(1−.50)=5%.

In addition, there are usually administrative costs associated with an issue of loan stock or debentures and possibly also a discount allowed on issue. A £100 unit of loan stock might be issued at £99 to make it attractive, and issue costs of 1% incurred. The net proceeds of each £100 stock are therefore £98, and the cost of this capital changes to (10÷98)(1−.50)=5.1%.

Imputed cost of loan capital

> *Activity*
>
> If you can buy a £100 nominal value 5% debenture on the stock market for £50, what is the effective gross rate of interest receivable by you? What does this tell you about the effect on market prices of loan stocks of a general change in interest rates?

The effective rate of interest is (5÷50)×100=10%. When the general level of interest rates increases, market prices of existing fixed interest stocks fall; when rates decrease, fixed interest stock prices rise.

It follows that, if a company has 8% debentures in its present capital structure, and the current market price of each £100 debenture is £80, the market rate of interest is (8÷80)×100=10%. A new issue of similar debentures would have to be offered at this rate; therefore this is the cost to include in the weighted average cost of capital.

Another way to illustrate that 10% is the imputed cost of debenture capital is to point to the company's right to purchase its own debentures on the market. At £80, they present an investment opportunity to the company of 10%, by reason of interest saved; therefore this opportunity cost is the effective cost of debenture capital.

A final point regarding cost of existing loan capital is that the market price of such capital is increased by accumulating interest. For example, a £100 10% debenture, interest payable half-yearly, might be quoted at £105 just before a half-yearly interest payment is due. In calculating the cost of loan capital, the accumulated interest should be deducted from the market price to leave only the capital value of the stock. Thus the cost of our 10% debenture would be $(10(1-t))\div(105-5)$.

Imputed cost of redeemable loans When a loan is scheduled to be repaid at a relatively early date, and interest rates have changed since the loan was first contracted, the current interest rate on the loan is ascertained by calculating the DCF yield rate that equates the present value of all future payments on the loan to its current market value. The resultant rate is known as the 'yield to redemption'.

A short-cut arithmetic calculation of the yield to redemption is given by:

$$r=\frac{I(1-t)+\frac{1}{n}(V_n-V_0)}{\frac{1}{2}(V_n+V_0)}$$

where r=yield to redemption
t=the company's tax rate
n=years to final redemption date
V_n=loan value payable in n years
V_0=market value of loan stock now

This might look fearsome at first glance, but it simply expresses the *annual* interest and capital cost as a percentage of the *average* value of the loan up to the repayment date.

For example, a £100 10% debenture, with a current market value of £80, repayable in five years' time, assuming a tax rate of 50%, has a yield rate of:

$$\frac{10(1-.50)+\frac{1}{5}(100-80)}{\frac{1}{2}(100+80)}=\frac{5+4}{90}=10\%.$$

Activity

Check the last calculation by applying 10% DCF factors to the five-year interest and capital cash flows. Their present value should approximately equal £80 – the current market price.

Year	*Interest less tax*	*Loan repaid*	*10% DCF factors*	*Present value*
	£	£		£
1	5		.909	4.545
2	5		.826	4.130
3	5		.751	3.755
4	5		.683	3.415
5	5	100	.621	65.205
				£81.050

The small difference is due to the use of *simple* interest in the short-cut method, as against *compound* interest in the DCF calculations.

Cost of preference capital

Few preference share issues have been made since 1965, because in that year loan interest became deductible as an expense for business tax purposes. Preference dividend is not chargeable as an expense.

However, where they do feature as part of the planned capital structure of a firm, their cost is the explicit rate payable expressed as a percentage of the *current market price* of the share. For example, the cost of an 8% £1 preference share, with a market price of 60 pence, is (8÷60)×100=13% (approx).

Cost of equity capital

The holders of the equity shares, normally the ordinary shares, in a company are those entitled to the profits after the fixed obligations to lenders and preference shareholders have been met. No fixed amount is payable but shareholders do expect to receive dividends. In addition, as most companies retain and reinvest a part of their profits, shareholders also expect the market value of their shares to grow. If their expectations are not satisfied – that is, if the return from their investment is not equal to that obtainable on a share of similar risk – they will probably sell their shares causing the market price to fall.

The return expected by ordinary shareholders will be higher than that on borrowed capital because of the higher equity risk but, because the *express* wishes of its many shareholders are impossible to discover, a company may simply adopt an equity rate of return that reflects this higher risk.

From a company's viewpoint *dividends* are all that shareholders are paid and a change in ownership of a share does not alter this. At any time, therefore, the price an investor is prepared to pay for a share must represent the present value of all future dividends. It follows that the rate of return expected by shareholders can be imputed from the relationship between dividends and share market price.

Cost of equity capital assuming no growth in earnings

If all shareholders' earnings are distributed, there will be no growth and the cost of equity capital is the rate of return that discounts all dividends paid to infinity to the present market value of the share. This can be represented by the following equation:

$$V_o = \frac{D}{(1+r)} + \frac{D}{(1+r)^2} \cdots \frac{D_\infty}{(1+r)^\infty}$$

where D = dividend paid each year

V_0 = present market value of the share

r = shareholders' expected rate of return

∞ = infinity

which simplifies to $V_0 = \frac{D}{r}$

therefore $r = \frac{D}{V_o}$.

Activity

If the current market price of an ordinary share is £2.36, and the company expects to pay a constant dividend of 26 pence per share, what is the company's cost of equity capital?

$$r = \frac{D}{V_0} = \frac{26 \times 100}{236} = 11\%.$$

Cost of equity capital with growth

The assumption of a constant dividend is rather unrealistic because most companies retain profit for investment. Growth in dividends must therefore be provided for in the share valuation model as shown below:

$$V_0 = \frac{D_0(1+g)}{(1+r)} + \frac{D_0(1+g)^2}{(1+r)^2} \cdots \frac{D_0(1+g)^\infty}{(1+r)^\infty}$$

where V_0=the present market share value
D_0=current dividend
g=expected growth rate
D_1=next dividend payable

which simplifies to $V_0 = \frac{D_0(1+g)}{(r-g)}$

therefore $r = \frac{D_0(1+g)}{V_0} + g$

and $r = \frac{D_1}{V_0} + g$

which recognisably satisfies the equity shareholder's requirement for dividend yield plus growth.

Activity

The current market price of the Fortune plc ordinary share is £1.87. The company has just paid a dividend of 9 pence per share, and expects future dividends to grow at a constant rate of 10% per annum. Calculate the company's cost of equity capital using the dividend growth valuation model.

$$r = \frac{D_0(1+g)}{V_0} + g = \frac{9(1+.10)}{187} + .10$$
$$= \frac{9.9}{187} + .10$$
$$= .053 + .10$$
$$= 15\% \text{ (approx.)}$$

The most difficult factor to forecast is the growth rate. Recent experience may be a guide to future growth if it is thought that it will continue into the future and, of course, the company's corporate plan should incorporate the company's growth forecast.

Another factor is the cost of issuing shares which includes not only the administrative costs but also any reduction in the current market price that is normally made to make the issue attractive. These costs will reduce the amount received per share and thus add to the required rate of return.

Cost of equity capital and the capital asset pricing model (CAPM)

When changes in the national or international economic or political outlook occur, share market indices, such as the Financial Times Index, also change according to whether the forecasts are optimistic or gloomy. Such indices reflect the general movement in share prices.

Activity

Obtain a recent copy of a financial newspaper which lists share prices daily (e.g. the *Financial Times*), if possible for a day following one on which some bright or pessimistic news was announced. Which way did prices move in general?

Calculate the percentage increase or decrease in the FTI 30 share index. Now calculate the percentage increases or decreases in the prices of several shares chosen at random from different sectors of the market. Do these differ substantially from the change in the FTI?

If you were to analyse the percentage changes in the prices of different shares compared with market index changes over a longer period, you would discover that some shares are more volatile than others.

The sensitivity of the price movements of a share compared with those of the market index reflects its *market risk*, and risk-averse investors will demand rates of return related to this risk.

In the section on diversification at the end of Chapter 5, you saw how risk can be considerably reduced by combining investments into portfolios. But even if all the shares on the stock market were combined into one portfolio, risk would not be entirely eliminated. The unavoidable element is the *market risk* or 'systematic' risk which afflicts all stocks and shares on the market.

The diversifiable or 'unsystematic' risk relates to the operating characteristics of each individual share, and because it can be virtually eliminated by diversification, it does not feature in the price investors are prepared to pay for the security (see figure 19).

There is a direct link between the price of a share and the shareholders' required rate of return. The CAPM approach suggests that the latter is only related to market risk. If, therefore, we compare the annual returns of a share over a period, with those of the market portfolio, represented say by the FTI, we should be able to ascertain whether the share is more or less risky than the market portfolio, and ascribe a higher or lower risk premium to it accordingly. Annual returns can be calculated by adding the dividend paid to the growth in the value of the share and relating the total to the market value of the share at the start of the year.

For example, a share purchased for £1 at the beginning of a year, which increases in value by the end of the year to £1.20, and which has paid a dividend of 10 pence during the year, has yielded an annual return of:

$$\frac{(£1.20-1.00)+.10}{£1.00}=30\%$$

Given that a number of years' returns for a share and for the market portfolio are calculated, they can be plotted on a graph to determine their relationship. Before this is done, however, the risk-free rate is deducted from the returns of the individual share and the market portfolio as it is included in both. Remember that it is only the market-related risk that we are trying to isolate.

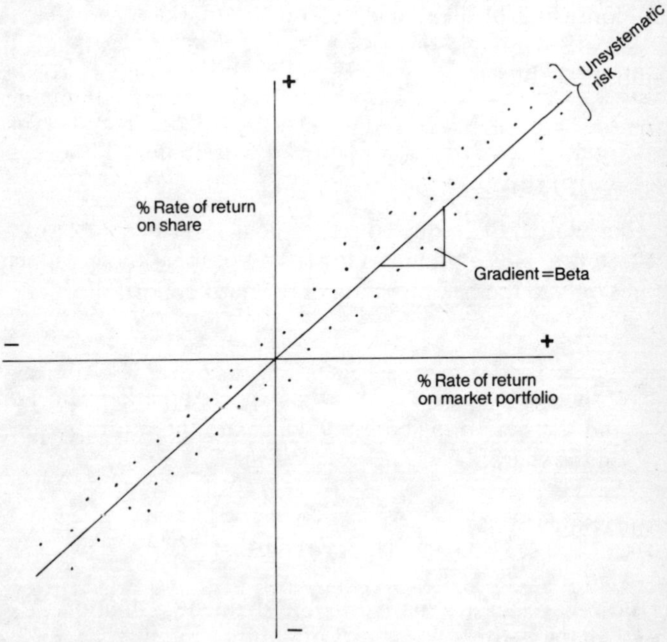

Figure 19. Excess returns of a share related to those on the market portfolio

Each coordinate on figure 19 represents the return on the share (vertical axis), at the time when the market return was that read off the horizontal axis. The characteristic line drawn through the coordinates is the 'line of best fit', and its gradient measures the sensitivity of the returns on the share against those of the market. If the gradient is 1 (i.e. 45°), the share's returns vary proportionately with those of the market, it has the same risk quality as the market portfolio, and it has a coefficient, known as its beta, of 1.

If the gradient is steeper at, say 1.5, the share has greater risk than the market and its beta is also 1.5. As shown in Chapter 5 this implies that, if the return on the market portfolio changes, the return on the share will change more than proportionately.

Assuming we know the average return required on a portfolio consisting of all the shares on the market, and that the Treasury Bill rate is the risk-free rate, we can estimate the required rate of return on any share:

$$\text{Required rate of return} = \text{risk-free rate (i)} + \left(\text{return on market portfolio} - \text{risk-free rate (i)}\right) \text{beta of the share}$$

or $RS = i + (RM - i)B$.

In other words, the required return on a security comprises the risk-free rate plus a premium for risk. Note that the beta factor applies only to the risk premium of the market portfolio.

Activity

If the risk-free rate is 6%, the expected market rate 12%, and the beta of a share 0.9, calculate the return required on the share.

$RS = i + (RM - i)B$
$= .06 + (.12 - .06).9 = .06 + .054 = .114 = 11.4\%$.

We now have an alternative to the dividend valuation model with which to estimate the cost of equity capital. As explained in Chapter 5 this is the capital asset pricing model (CAPM), and whilst it is based upon simplifying assumptions about the efficiency of capital markets, continuing research appears to substantially support its risk/return, market-based approach. Theoretically the dividend model and the CAPM, both being market based, should give the same result; but they both suffer similar difficulties in forecasting. Future growth has to be forecast for the dividend model; whilst for the CAPM overall market conditions, betas and the risk-free rate have all got to be forecast for the period to which the cost of capital relates.

One advantage of the CAPM to companies who engage in different activities with different risks is that an appropriate rate of return for each activity can be approximated by applying the return of a company in a similar risk activity. You will recall that this method of dealing with risk was also discussed in Chapter 5 under 'the risk/return relationship'.

Weighting the costs of capital

In estimating a company's required investment rate of return it is important to recognise that:

- past costs of capital are irrelevant; the costs must be those applicable to the future investment period;
- a *weighted average* of the costs of the different capital to be used must be calculated; for if the cost of the next tranche of capital obtained was applied, the required rate of return would change according to the type of capital used. This would lead to the acceptance of projects with lower returns when loan capital was obtained, and the rejection of projects not able to meet the cost of equity capital when that was obtained.

The desired capital structure of a company cannot be constantly maintained. Profit generated by operations will be continuously available for investment, thus adding to equity capital; and loan capital is more likely to be obtained at infrequent intervals in large amounts. It is desirable for a company to use the *target* structure that it considers optimal in calculating its weighted average cost of capital, to stabilise investment decisions.

Self-check

The capital structure of a company shown in its balance sheet is as follows:

	£
200,000 £1 ordinary shares	200,000
Retained profit	100,000
Shareholders' capital	300,000
10% debentures (repayable 2003)	150,000
	£ 450,000

The current market price of its ordinary share is £2.50, and a dividend of 10 pence has just been paid. A constant growth rate of 8% is expected during the next ten years. The debentures (nominal value £100) are quoted on the market at £90.

Assuming that the company believes that its present balance sheet capital structure is optimal, and will be maintained during the next ten years, calculate the company's weighted average cost of capital. Corporation tax can be taken as 50%.

Cost of ordinary shares: $\frac{D}{V_0} + g = \frac{.10\,(1.08)}{2.50} + .08 = .043 + .08 = .123$ or 12.3%

Cost of debentures: $\frac{I(1-t)}{V_o} = \frac{10(1-.5)}{90} 5.5\%$.

Weighted average cost:

	Proportion	*Cost %*	*Weighted cost %*
Ordinary shares	⅔	12.3	8.2
Debentures	⅓	5.5	1.8
			10

Review

The present capital structure of Newton Computers plc is as follows:

	£000s
Called-up ordinary share capital (£1 shares)	800
Retained earnings	400
	1,200
10% loan	600
	£1,800

The current market price of the ordinary share is £2.20, and a dividend of 10 pence per share has just been paid. Newton considers that its present growth rate of 10% per annum will continue into the foreseeable future, that its gearing is optimal and will be maintained in future in proportion to the *current market values* of its share and loan capital. The loan stock has a market price of £88 per £100 stock unit, including half-yearly interest due immediately, and is repayable in five years at £100. Assume a corporation tax rate of 50%.

Required:

1 Calculate the weighted average cost of capital of the company (use the dividend valuation model for this purpose).

2 If the interest rate on Treasury Bills is 8%, the average rate of return on all market shares 11% and the beta of Newton 1.2, calculate its cost of equity capital using the CAPM.

3 What is the purpose of the weighted average cost of capital?

4 Is a company's weighted average cost of capital necessarily applicable to each of its investment projects?

1 *Cost of loan capital:*

$$\frac{I(1-t)+\frac{1}{n}(V_n-V_o)}{\frac{1}{2}(V_n+V_o)}$$

$$=\frac{10(1-.50)+\frac{1}{5}(100-83^*)}{\frac{1}{2}(100+83)}$$

(*current price less accumulated interest)

$$=\frac{5+3.4}{91.5}=9\% \text{ (approx).}$$

Cost of equity capital

$$r=\frac{D_1}{V_o}+g$$

$$=\frac{10(1+.10)}{220}+.10$$

$$=15\%.$$

Weighted average cost:

	Market value	*Proportion*	*Cost %*	*Weighted Cost %*
Ordinary shares	£1,760,000	.78	15	11.7
Loan stock	498,000	.22	9	1.98
				13.68
			approx.	14%

2 RS=RF+(RM−RF)B=8+(11−8)1.2=11.6%.

3 The weighted average cost of capital is used in investment appraisal as the minimum required rate of return. A project with a positive NPV, or yielding a return in excess of this rate is deemed to be acceptable. Application of the weighted average cost ensures that both shareholders' and lenders' costs of capital are satisfied.

4 If all the activities of a business are subject to similar risk, then the weighted average cost of capital is appropriate. However, if a company carries on a diversity of operations, with significantly differing risks, as in the case of a conglomerate, then it should apply differential rates of return according to the risks of each activity.

The capital asset pricing model shows us that the return on any asset comprises the risk-free rate plus a premium for risk. The appropriate rate of return to apply to each activity can therefore be approximated by using the return of a company in a similar risk activity.

Part 6
Working capital management

16 Financing working capital

What is working capital?

Invested capital includes fixed and current assets. It is the latter less suppliers' and other short-term credit, which is referred to as *net current assets* or *working capital*.

The terms *fixed* and *current* assets are used to differentiate between those resources that will not completely revert to cash within a year and those that will, respectively.

The planning and control of current assets warrant the same skill and care as lavished on fixed assets, the twin objectives of current asset management being:

- to *minimise* the time between the initial input of materials and other resources into the operating process, and the eventual payment by customers for goods or services supplied; this is known as the *cash operating cycle*, and success in this aim will reduce investment in stocks, debtors and liquid assets to a minimum;
- to finance those assets as efficiently as possible; with the overall objective of optimising the return on total capital employed.

Working capital investment – A risk/return trade-off

Most people with bank current accounts maintain cash balances sufficient to meet their daily needs and for emergencies. Any money held in excess of these needs is wasted, as it could be better invested elsewhere to earn interest.

Anyone who finances needs by running an ever-increasing overdraft which is not backed by easily realisable assets runs the risk of bankruptcy. Somewhere between these extremes, a balance between risk and return must be struck; this applies not only to individuals but also to businesses.

Activity

The data given below relates to Apex and Base, two similar-sized companies in the same line of business. Before completing the following assignment, which involves the calculation of ratios, it might be helpful for you to refer back to Chapter 2 on ratio analysis, and in particular the section entitled 'Can the business pay its way?'

Now calculate the following ratios relating to the accounts of Apex and Base:

- **a** Current ratio.
- **b** Acid test ratio.
- **c** Number of days' sales outstanding.
- **d** Number of days' stock held.
- **e** Number of days' creditors outstanding.
- **f** Cash as a percentage of current assets.
- **g** Sales to capital employed.

Balance sheets of Apex and Base

	Apex	£000s	Base
Sources of funds:			
Share capital – Ordinary £1	500		500
Retained profit	1,100		500
	1,600		1,000

Uses of funds				
Fixed assets (net)		800		800
Current assets:				
Stock	400		200	
Debtors	400		200	
Cash	200		50	
	1,000		450	
Current liabilties:				
Trade creditors	150		200	
Taxation	50		50	
	200		250	
		800		200
Net assets:		1,600		1,000
Sales	1,500		1,500	
Profit after tax	105		105	
Profit % of net assets		6½	10½	

	Apex	*Base*
a Current ratio	5:1	1.8:1
b Acid test	3:1	1:1
c Debtors' days outstanding	97	49
d Stock days outstanding	97	49
e Creditors' days outstanding	36	49
f Cash as a % of current assets	20%	11%
g Sales to capital employed	.9:1	1.5:1

Activity

1 What is the overall reason for the difference in profit % between Apex and Base?
2 What are the factors contributing to this difference?
3 In which company would you invest? Why?

1 A lower capital employed by Base has earned the same profit as Apex, resulting in a higher return per £100 capital invested by Base.
2 Apex has at least double the investment in each of the current assets, and also a lower amount owing to creditors.
3 Given the higher return on capital invested, I would prefer

Base's shares to those of Apex. The comparative statistics show Base to be better financially managed than Apex, the latter company carrying too high a level of current assets to support its turnover.

The Apex Company is a classic case of *overcapitalisation* (or *undertrading*), with resultant lower profit return. Conversely, too *aggressive* a working capital policy, with current assets 'cut to the bone', might result in lost orders, either because minimal stocks cannot cope with the volume of orders or because customers are deterred by tight credit policies.

Financing working capital

Investment plans of a business need finance to cover:

- a *permanent* and growing layer of fixed and net current assets;
- *fluctuating* current asset requirements arising mainly from seasonal and customer demand factors.

The business must decide upon an acceptable ratio of debt to equity capital (or gearing); the debt proportion being financed by a judicious mixture of long-, medium- and short-term instruments with the object of minimising the cost of capital, at an acceptable level of risk.

Figure 20 shows alternative net working capital financing strategies, ranging from the most (D) to the least (A) risky. It is assumed:

- that fixed assets are largely financed by long- or medium-term capital;
- that the *servicing* of borrowed capital in the form of interest and capital repayments is met out of current net earnings, or alternatively, in the case of capital repayment, out of a renegotiated loan.

Strategy A uses *long-term finance* only, fully covering the risk of running out of cash due to fluctuating cash flows (the wavy line). The safety built into the permanence of this arrangement, however, has its costs. These are:

- higher cost of long- against short-term capital;

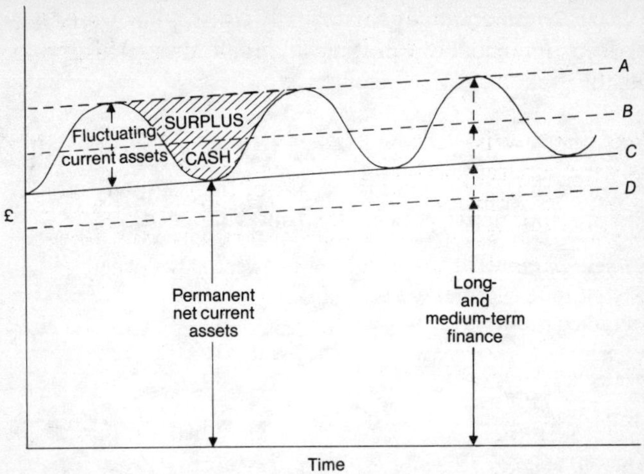

Figure 20. Financing working capital – balancing risk with cost (note: permanent net current assets are after deducting normal trade credit, accruals and other continuing current liabilities)

- risk of being shut in by a high interest rate, if interest rates fall;
- the need to pay interest in the troughs between fluctuations when the capital is not required – lessened to some extent by short-term investment interest on the surplus.

Strategy B leaves some fluctuating needs to be covered by short-term finance. It is more risky, therefore, than *A* because liquidity problems could arise if repayment of the short-term capital was due at a time when alternative financing might be difficult to arrange. In addition, short-term interest rates are more volatile than long-term, which makes cash flows less certain.

Strategy C covers all cyclical fluctuations by *cheaper* short-term borrowing, at the same time providing *flexibility* to repay the finance when it is not required. This is a lower cost arrangement than either *A* or *B*, but with a higher level of the risks specified in *B*.

Strategy D permits short-term financing of a layer of permanent net current assets – an extremely risky policy, especially if the assets financed are not easily realisable. This policy presents the greatest risk of insolvency.

Self-check

Assume that, two years later, Base, the company cited in the previous activity shows the following position:

Sources of funds:		£000s
Share capital – ordinary £1		500
Retained profit		1,100
		£1,600
Uses of funds:		
Fixed assets (net)		1,600
Current assets:		
Stock	400	
Debtors	400	
Cash	—	
	800	
Current liabilities:		
Trade creditors	300	
Taxation	100	
Overdraft	400	
	800	—
		£1,600
Sales		£3,000
Profit after tax		180
Profit % of net assets		11¼%

Required
Using the above information, **a** calculate the same ratios as those produced in the previous activity, **b** comment on the company's financial position.

a Current ratio 1:1.
Acid test.5:1.
Debtors' days outstanding 49.
Stock days outstanding 49.
Creditors' days outstanding 36.
Cash as a % of current assets nil.
Sales to capital employed 1.9:1.

b The *trading* results of Base appear to be very satisfactory. Turnover has doubled over the two years, and the return on capital employed has increased from 10½% to 11¼%, largely as a result of a more effective use of capital evidenced by an improved sales to capital employed ratio. Stock, debtors and creditors appear to be well managed. Unfortunately, this success has been bought at the risk of insolvency, as the current and acid test ratios testify.

All current assets are financed by short-term capital and if the overdraft cannot be renewed, permanent current – and perhaps fixed – assets may have to be sold to repay the debt. The company could be *technically insolvent* if unable to meet current obligations. Base is *undercapitalised* (i.e. overtrading) because it is financing long-term assets with short-term finance.

Sources of short-term finance

In Chapter 8 we summarised the main sources of short term finance to include: trade credit, bank overdrafts, bank loans, bills of exchange, factoring debts and invoice discounting, taxation and dividends unpaid.

Trade credit Most suppliers would cease trading if they did not grant customers time to pay. Trade credit and accrued expenses are a spontaneous and constant source of finance, therefore, upon which all businesses, but especially small ones, depend for many short-term needs.

Sometimes, cash discounts are offered by suppliers to encourage early payment of outstanding accounts. Ignoring this discount can be expensive. For example, a supplier offering 2½% if invoices are paid within 10 days might otherwise expect payment within 30 days. The cost of ignoring the prompt payment discount and paying at the end of 30 days would amount to an annual rate of interest of $(2.5 \div 97.5) \times (365 \div 20) = 47\%$ (approx.). Note that the extended period of credit is 20 days, i.e. 30 less 10, and that the amount of *additional* finance is not £100 but £97.5.

Activity

What would the annual interest rate be in the above example if the buyer takes extended credit of 60 days from the date of the invoice?

$(2.5 \div 97.5) \times (365 \div 50) = 18.7\%$.

The cost of taking extended credit from suppliers decreases dramatically with time, but of course the risks that supplies will be stopped, and credit-rating besmirched, act as brakes.

Bank overdrafts This is a much used facility for businesses to draw cheques up to an agreed credit limit and is largely arranged to cover seasonal cash shortages, and as *bridging* finance for the purchase of property and machinery. Subject to the credit standing of customers, overdrafts are generally renewable and are used as 'permanent' finance by some businesses although they can be called in at short notice by the bank.

Interest is charged on the outstanding balance each day, at bank base rate plus an additional lending premium related to the credit standing of the customer.

The advantages of an overdraft are:

- it is the cheapest form of short-term finance;
- it is easily and quickly negotiated, and easily renewed;
- security may not be required, although about 50% of all overdrafts are secured on assets or by personal guarantee;
- it offers the flexibility of sums being repayable or drawn without notice.

The major drawbacks are that overdrafts are generally repayable on demand, though banks normally allow notice of up to 6 to 12 months; and that short-term interest rates may be increased whereas long-term rates are fixed.

When considering an application for an overdraft, a bank will require information on current and past trading and financial performance of the applicant, together with cash and sales forecasts. The current and acid test ratios will be of particular interest to the bank.

Bank loans Short-term loans negotiated with banks and other financial institutions differ from overdrafts as they are arranged for a specific amount, for a specific period and are subject to specific repayment terms. The only flexibility may be in the interest rate, which may be fixed or variable. Security is normally required for a loan, and assessment of the applicant's credit status is more exacting than for an overdraft.

Bill financing As stated in Chapter 8, a bill of exchange is similar to a postdated cheque in that the person signing (accepting) it agrees to pay it some 60 to 180 days later. Meanwhile the person receiving it can sell it to a bank or discount house at a discount, thus providing needed funds. The discount rate is quite low because of the integrity of the acceptor – usually about 1% above bank base rate which may be lower than the cost of an overdraft to some businesses.

When used in connection with purchase and sale of goods they are known as *trade bills*, and provide a facility for a vendor to receive immediate payment for goods sold, and for the purchaser time to sell the goods before the acceptance is due for payment.

A *bank bill* is used to provide short-term finance for any purpose. It is drawn by the person requiring the finance, accepted by a bank or an acceptance house (which charges an acceptance fee) and discounted by the drawer at a bank or discount house. The drawer thus acquires low-cost short-term finance for the period stated in the bill, at the end of which he will have to reimburse the acceptance house, which will already have paid the bill when it was presented for payment by the discount house or bank.

The main advantages of bill finance are that it is as cheap as, if not cheaper than, overdrafts, and extends the volume of short-term finance available.

Factoring involves the sale of book debts to a factoring company on a continuing basis, the factor administering the sales ledger of the client and providing credit control and an optional insurance against non-payment of debts. It is, therefore, a management and financing service with financing being optional. Agreements are normally drawn up for an initial period of 12 months, continuing thereafter indefinitely until notice (of about 6 months) is given.

The cost of factoring includes:

- a *factoring fee* based upon the work involved in servicing the client's sales ledger; this is usually between 1 and 2% of *turnover*, depending upon the size and rate of turnover, and the average value of invoices;
- a *financing charge* on the amount drawn by the client on a day-to-day basis, at between 1½ and 2% over base rate;
- *collection charges* such as legal fees incurred in collecting older debts.

It is thus more expensive than bank borrowing, but provides additional management services that more than compensate for the difference in cost, especially in the case of growing small and medium-sized companies who lack credit control expertise.

The mechanics of factoring are that the client sends his invoices to the factor at, say, weekly interval, from which the factoring fee is deducted and the balance placed to the client's account. The factor sends the invoices to the client's customer, requiring payment to be made to the factor.

Meanwhile, the client may draw upon up to 80% of the balance on his account, according to need, and will receive the balance of each invoice when it is paid by his customer to the factor.

The main advantages of factoring are:

- capital is released immediately from accounts receivable, thus providing additional finance for business expansion and lessening the risk of overtrading;
- cash flows are more predictable, and credit insurance lowers the cost of bad debts;
- savings in accounts receivable administration and credit control;
- the provision of an expert, specialised credit control service;

- better terms can be negotiated with suppliers, and cash discounts on supplies taken advantage of.

Invoice discounting is solely a means of raising cash, by selling book debts to an invoice discounting company. The client company, however, continues to administer its own sales ledger in the normal way but, in addition, sends the discounting company copies of the invoices agreed under the arrangement.

The discounting company makes an initial payment of up to 75% to the client who, acting as agent for the discounting company, collects the debts from customers in the normal way and pays all monies so received direct to the discounting company's collection account. The discounting company finally accounts to the client for the balance of the invoiced amount due. It is a financing method more suited to the large, well-established, competently administered company.

The costs of invoice discounting include a *financing charge* of up to 2% above bank base rate, plus a service charge of between ¼% and 1% of each invoiced amount.

Unpaid taxation and dividends Delays in payment of taxation of up to 20 months can provide a valuable line of credit, as can dividends which can be delayed for up to 6 months.

Self-check

1 What might be the result of taking extended credit from suppliers when cash discount is not normally allowed?

2 A bank that 'accepts' a bill on behalf of a client is doing so in connection with **a** the bill of costs connected with factoring, **b** an invoice sent by a supplier, **c** a bank overdraft, **d** a bill of exchange, **e** a short-term loan. Indicate which is the most appropriate of the alternatives **a** to **e**.

3 In connection with factoring, which of the following is incorrect?

a Customers are not allowed cash discount if the supplier has factored his debts.

b The factor services the customer's sales ledger.

c A factoring arrangement always includes the provision of finance.

4 Simon Poacher's Pie and Pâté Company is experiencing a rapid expansion in sales, and requires approximately £50,000 additional working capital. Although the company has not yet reached its bank overdraft limit, it wishes to retain this facility to cover any cash flow emergencies. The two immediate financing alternatives are:

a to extend the credit received from suppliers by foregoing cash discounts; payment terms are currently 2% if accounts are paid within 10 days, net in 40 days; and purchases are running at £52,500 per month;

b to sell accounts receivable of £70,000 per month to a factor, who will charge a service fee of 2% on accounts purchased. The factor will make available to Simon 75% of the receivables, after deduction of a service fee of 12% per annum on total turnover. It is estimated that Simon will save £840 per month on sales ledger administration and bad debts if he chooses factoring.

Required:

a Calculate the cost per cent of each alternative.

b Which method of financing would you choose?

1 Customers who do not pay their accounts as agreed, risk damaging their credit rating. Supplies may be cut off, and business brought to an end.

2 d A bill of exchange.

3 a Factoring debts does not affect cash discount allowed to customers who pay their debts promptly.

4 a

Cost of taking extended credit: $\frac{2}{98} \times \frac{365}{30} = 24.8\%$ per annum.

The amount made available under this option is .98×£52,500=£51,450.

Cost of factoring:

Amount made available: amount sold . . .	£70,000	
less Fee 2%	1,400	
75%×	68,600	=£51,450
Costs: service fee 2%×£70,000 =	1,400	
Interest 1% per month (12% p.a.) ×£51,450 =	514	
	1,914	
less Administrative savings, etc.	840	
	£1,074	

$$\text{Finance cost} = \frac{1{,}074}{51{,}450} \times 12 \qquad = 25\% \text{ per annum}$$

b The costs of obtaining the same amount of finance are approximately equal, and both are equally flexible should the full amount not be required; the decision will therefore have to be made on qualitative grounds.

Taking extended credit might affect the company's credit rating if suppliers consider that it has liquidity problems. Using factoring provides finance immediately, and handing sales ledger management over to the factor leaves Simon free to concentrate on production and marketing. In addition, better terms may be negotiated with suppliers. Factoring would thus appear to be more attractive than extending credit in this case.

Review

At the end of last year the *cash operating cycle* of Briggs Engineering plc was 145 days, comprised of the current assets and liabilities shown below:

	Turnover period days	*Turnover factor*
Raw material Stock	80	Purchases
Finished goods stock	45	Cost of sales
Debtors	60	Sales
	185	
less Creditors	40	Purchases
	145	

The 'turnover period' is calculated by relating each working capital item to its 'turnover factor', and multiplying by 365. For example: (Stock of raw materials÷purchases)×365=80 days. Stock of raw materials at the beginning of last year was £20,000, purchases during the year were £130,031, and the gross profit for the year £78,469.

Required

1 Calculate the value of net current assets at the end of the year.

2 Given that Briggs's target 'turnover periods' for the year were 65, 35, 50 and 50 days respectively, for each of the working capital items, what should the investment in net current assets have been?

1

Working 1

Closing stock of raw materials=(80÷365)×130,031 = £28,500

Working 2		Opening stock raw materials	20,000
		add purchases	130,031
			150,031
		less Closing stock of raw materials	28,500
	Cost of sales		£121,531
Working 3		Gross profit	78,469
		add Cost of sales	121,531
	Sales		£200,000

Working 4 *Value of net current assets at the year end:*

	£
Stock of raw material (see working 1)	28,500
Stock of finished goods (45÷365)×121,531	14,983
Debtors (60÷365)×200,000	32,877
	76,360
less Creditors (40÷365)×130,031	14,250
	£ 62,110

2

Net current asset value should have been:

Stock of raw materials (65÷365)×130,031	23,156
Stock of finished goods (35÷365)×121,531	11,654
Debtors (50÷365)×200,000	27,397
	62,207
less Creditors (50÷365)×130,031	17,812
	£ 44,395

17 Controlling liquidity

What are liquid assets?

Liquid assets include cash in hand and in bank current accounts and assets easily and quickly convertible into cash. The latter covers bank and finance house deposits, and marketable securities of all kinds. Marketable securities usually have short maturity dates but equity shares, quoted on a Stock Exchange and therefore easily realisable, may be included in a portfolio of liquid assets.

Why do we need liquidity?

Activity

Why do any of us need an easily accessible reserve of cash?

First, you need it to pay for goods and services received and ordered. Even if your electricity board allows time to pay, you must eventually hand over cash for electricity consumed. Such payments are part of your normal day-by-day *transactions*.

Second, it is wise to maintain an emergency cash float in case something unexpected happens. Such a *precautionary* balance may be required for expenditure on wedding presents, or to pay an unexpected car repair bill.

Businesses also need liquidity to meet normal *transactions* expenditure on wages, materials, expenses and taxes; and as a *precaution* to deal with uncertainty of their cash flows. Any cash held in excess of *transaction* and *precautionary* requirements is wasteful unless it is held to meet some planned expenditure, such as plant replacement or taxation.

Efficient cash management – a prerequisite

Efficient cash management is a prerequisite for determining and maintaining optimum cash levels in business. Cash forecasting is of no avail if cash management systems are inefficient. Assuming that its control of debtors is efficient (see Chapter 19), and that customers pay their accounts within the time allowed, a business must ensure that customers' payments are speedily transmitted into its bank account.

Although this process appears straightforward, there are several ways in which it can be quickened:

- Ensure that cash/cheques are *banked daily*; the cost in interest lost because firms only make a weekly journey to the bank is surprisingly high.
- *Centralised banking*. Countrywide depots, shops and branches should be instructed to bank daily receipts for the *direct credit* of head office current account – ensuring that all cash is pooled and more efficiently deployed to benefit the whole business.
- Arrange to *direct debit* customers in respect of regular payments due; Automobile Association subscriptions are dealt with this way, and hire purchase instalments are largely directly debited.
- Arrange with the bank for *express clearance* of large value cheques; a fee is charged for this service but earlier access to cash should yield a benefit much greater than the fee.
- *Collect* large payments from customers *personally* to cut down postal delays; security companies or sales representatives may be useful here.
- The growing use of *electronic funds transfer* systems, allowing customers to pay their debts into suppliers' bank accounts by direct computer transfer.

Other ways to improve cash management include:

- Arrange insurance cover for cash in transit, and other balances held.
- Reduce the number of, and amounts held, in cash floats.
- Ensure a good relationship is maintained with the bank.
- Monitor internal check systems on cash frequently.

- Cover the risk of foreign currency fluctations by forward dealing.
- Prepare detailed short-term cash forecasts covering different time horizons.
- Ensure that excess cash is held in short-term investments to help earn its keep.

Self-check

Crane Auto Engineers plc maintained a centralised London bank deposit account, into which branches credited their net cash receipts at the end of each four-weekly period. The net cash flow for the Norwich branch was £100,000 per four-weekly period.

The recently appointed Norwich accountant realised that the delay in banking was losing the company interest, and he produced figures to illustrate the loss.

Assuming that the net receipts per four-weekly period are received in equal instalments at the end of each week, show how much additional interest could be earned by crediting the London account each week instead of every four weeks. The deposit interest rate is 13% per annum.

Currently interest is being lost on	£25,000 (¼×£100,000)	for 3 weeks
	£25,000	for 2 weeks
	£25,000	for 1 week
		6

Interest lost per 4 weekly period: £25,000 for 6 weeks @ .25%* per week=£375

Lost interest per annum . . . £375×13=£4,875

*Interest rate per week=13÷52=.25%.

What volume of liquid funds should be held?

If businesses knew future cash flows *with certainty*, cash forecasts would indicate precisely how much was needed at all times. In these circumstances strategy *C* in figure 20 would suit, with short-term funding arranged well in advance to cover known periods of cash shortage. Conversely, known cash surpluses could be invested to mature precisely when funds are required. With certainty, liquidity funding could be managed most efficiently and economically.

Uncertainty is the normal business condition, however, and strategies *A* or *B* in figure 20 may be more appropriate – providing permanent cash buffers to cover exceptional cash shortages. Holding cash has its opportunity cost, of course, and management must decide between covering the risk of running out of cash and reducing profitability. Policy will depend on the stage of business development, forecasts of future growth and short- and long-term cash forecasts.

In the early stages, a growing business, will tend to rely heavily on short-term borrowed capital because other sources of funds will be unavailable. The danger is that, if the business cycle turns down or government credit restrictions are introduced, the business can be most vulnerable. Worse, it could be heading for insolvency if overdrafts are restricted or are called in by the bank. This is a possibility, even if the current trading position of a business may be very healthy.

As a business grows and improves credit standing, it should be able to negotiate temporary borrowing to close a liquidity gap, but this will depend partly on what security it can offer for loans or overdrafts, and on general financial market conditions. If borrowing conditions become critical, and an issue of shares is not feasible, more drastic action may be needed if a business is to survive. The following could be carried out:

- *Rephase the repayment of existing debt capital* to increase current liquidity.
- *Time-related* actions such as delaying payment to suppliers, speeding up collection of debts and delaying capital expenditure.
- *Volume-related* actions, including cutting down on overtime, shift-work and part-time working, also temporary lay-offs.
- *Scale-related* actions, including reduced operating budgets, restrictions on capital expenditure, research and development, and marketing, reduction of inventory levels, reduced dividends.
- *Divestment* of subsidiary companies and loss-making divi-

sions and projects, selling undeveloped land and other surplus assets.

Self-check

1 Decisions about volume of liquid funds to hold are based on assessment of the return/risk trade-off. What does this mean?

2 Which of the following actions, taken to improve liqiuidity, are related to **a** time, **b** volume, **c** scale, **d** divestment of activity?

i Sale of surplus office block.
ii Reduction of overtime.
iii Delayed capital expenditure.
iv Reduction of inventory levels.

1 This implies that management have to assess the degree of insolvency risk they are prepared to tolerate, and balance this against lower profitability resulting from paying interest on cash held.

2 **a – iii; b – ii; c – iv; d – i.**

Cash forecasting

In Chapter 7 we discussed cash forecasting in the context of determining initial financing requirements. It is vital, however, that cash forecasting is a continuing exercise with forecasts covering different time horizons. Weekly forecasts for three months ahead; monthly forecasts for the coming 12 or 24 months; longer forecasts for up to five or ten years.

Cash forecasts help by pointing up any expected periods of cash shortage for which provision can be planned well in advance; or periods of cash surplus providing short-term investment funds.

The four most important features of preparing cash forecasts are:

- Account for *all* cash receipts and payments, including those of a capital nature; taxes; dividends; grants received; VAT; as well as all the normal operating cash flows.
- The expected *timing* of receipts and payments should be

reflected in the forecast, attention being paid to credit terms received from, and allowed to, suppliers and customers respectively. Note particularly the exact timing of large payments for assets or repayment of capital.

- The forecasts should be *updated* as frequently as uncertainty and change dictate; the use of microcomputers and financial models make this feasible for the smallest of businesses.
- *Deviations* in forecasts will inevitably occur, but, by producing a range of forecasts based on varying assumptions, they can be estimated. Alternatively, the *sensitivity* of forecasts to change can be examined by simulating the effect on net cash flows, of changes in single variables, or combinations of variables. These are areas in which the computer and financial models are increasingly applied.

Self-check

The estimated sales of Efco Cleaning Equipment plc for the next ten months October to July, are as shown below:

	£000s		£000s
October	120	March	200
November	160	April	240
December	280	May	320
January	160	June	360
February	160	July	320

Experience has shown that 75% of a month's sales are paid for in the month following, 20% two months following, and 5% three months following. Manufacturing materials are approximately 30% of sales value and are purchased and paid for one month before the month of sale. Wages and salaries represent approximately 40% of sales value, and are paid in the month of sale. Expenses representing 10% of sales value are paid one month later than the month of sale.

Capital expenditure costing £90,000 is due for payment in March; a dividend of £40,000 is payable in April; and £80,000 corporation tax is due for payment in August next. A government grant of £30,000 in respect of the equipment purchased is receivable in June. The balance of cash at the end of December is £30,000.

Required:

a Construct a cash forecast covering the months January to June.

b By using a computer financial model the accountant forecasts that:

i for the months January to March there is minimal risk of the cash balance falling below £20,000;

ii the distribution of possible net cash balances for May reveals a 30% probability of a cash deficit of £60,000.

What action might the accountant take as a result of this information?

a *Cash forecast January to June* £000

	Jan.	*Feb.*	*Mar.*	*Apr.*	*May.*	*June.*
Sales receipts:						
75% end of 1st month	210	120	120	150	180	240
20% end of 2nd month	32	56	32	32	40	48
5% end of 3rd month	6	8	14	8	8	10
Grant						30
	248	184	166	190	228	328
Materials	48	60	72	96	108	96
Labour	64	64	80	96	128	144
Expenses	28	16	16	20	24	32
Capital expenditure			90			
Dividend				40		
	140	140	258	252	260	272
Net cash flow	108	44	(92)	(62)	(32)	56
Balance brought forward	30	138	182	90	28	(4)
Balance carried forward	138	182	90	28	(4)	52

b i Short-term investments could be employed to 'soak up' the surplus cash of £118 at the end of January, and a further amount added through February. Some withdrawal from investments would occur in March, but a balance of short term investments could be held until mid-April.

ii If the capital payment of £90,000 could be deferred until later in the year, this would solve the expected liquidity problem in May; but failing that the accountant should ensure that an overdraft facility is arranged and available should the worst occur in May.

The range of short-term investments available

It is important to make maximum use of liquid assets with as little as possible being held as cash at any time, the remainder being placed in short-term investments. The investments most used for this purpose are:

- Overnight loans to banks and discount houses.
- Clearing bank deposit accounts; 7 days' notice of withdrawal required, but easily realisable in an emergency.
- Finance, discount house and merchant bank deposits; have a higher interest rate than clearing banks, but longer notice of withdrawal is required.
- Foreign and other bank deposit accounts; higher interest, but possibly greater risk.
- Treasury bills; maximum 3 months maturity; £50,000 minimum investment.
- Bills of exchange; maturing in 3 to 6 months' time.
- Certificates of deposit issued by banks and commercial and industrial companies; evidencing loans for fixed amounts, fixed periods and fixed rates of interest.
- Certificates of tax deposits issued by the Inland Revenue.
- Local authority deposits and loans for periods ranging from weekly to two-yearly.
- Government bonds with short maturities; no capital gains tax if held for more than one year.

These various homes offer a choice of maturities and returns to tailor a portfolio that will satisfy the six characteristics of short-term investment. These are: easy realisability, short maturities, low default risk, low arrangement expense, fair rate of return, and tax efficiency.

Keeping the cash balance to a minimum

Activity

What do you think are the main objectives of managing short-term investments?

- To maximise the return on the investments.
- To arrange for the maturities and cash requirements to coincide.
- To maintain an easily accessible bank deposit balance or overdraft facility, as a hedge against the uncertainty of cash flows.

Mathematical models have been used successfully to optimise transfers into and out of short-term investments. These models recognise that there are costs associated with *holding* cash (i.e. interest foregone), and cost of *withdrawing* cash from investments (i.e. administration and brokerage).

The *Baumol* model assumes a cash deposit into short-term securities at the start of a period, followed by smooth, predictable withdrawals to meet transaction requirements. The objective is to find the optimal level of cash withdrawal which minimises the total costs of holding and withdrawing cash.

Activity

Using the following symbols and assuming the conditions outlined in the previous paragraph, construct two separate models to show:

a the total cost of holding cash;
b the total cost of withdrawals.

T=total amount deposited at the commencement of a period
C=optimal cash withdrawal
i=interest rate on short term securities
b=fixed costs of each withdrawal.

The total cost of holding cash is $i(C \div 2)$. The total cost of withdrawals is $b(T \div C)$. As C grows larger, total withdrawal cost reduces, but holding cost increases. The optimal level of C will therefore be when withdrawal and holding costs are equal, i.e. when

$i(C \div 2) = b(T \div C)$
and $iC^2 = 2bT$
and $C^2 = (2bT) \div i$
therefore $C = \sqrt{((2bT) \div i)}$.

Activity

A company deposits its sales receipts of £50,000 into short-term investments at the beginning of a period. The investment interest is 8% and the fixed cost of withdrawing cash is £20 per withdrawal. Payments are predictable and even throughout the period. What is the optimal level of cash withdrawal?

$C = \sqrt{((2bT) \div i)} = \sqrt{((2 \times 20 \times 50{,}000) \div .08)} = \sqrt{(2{,}000{,}000 \div .08)}$
$= £5{,}000$.

Although this model captures the essential elements of the problem, it is rather unrealistic in assumptions regarding cash flows of the average company, which are frequently not predictable or smooth. Other, more sophisticated models have been developed to overcome the problems of uncertainty.

Review

1 There are many ways of speeding the process of transmitting the cash received from customers into suppliers' bank accounts.
  a Describe four such methods.
  b What is the benefit of speeding up the process?

2 In what essential respects does a cash forccast differ from a profit and loss account?

3 a What are the costs of holding cash?
  b If the maturities of short-term investments do not coincide with the need for cash, what costs will be incurred?

1 a Daily banking of receipts; centralised banking; direct debit to current accounts; express clearance of cheques; collect large payments from customers; electronic funds transfer.
  b There is an opportunity interest cost in delaying the banking of receipts.

2 a A cash forecast looks to the future; a profit and loss account reports on the past.
  b All cash received and paid in a period is included in a cash forecast; a profit and loss account is prepared to measure *profit*, which embraces all revenue and expenditure rele-

vant to a period, regardless of whether cash has been received or paid.

c Non-cash items such as depreciation are included in a profit and loss account.

3 a Investment interest lost, as well as opportunities for capital gains on investments.

b The difference between the necessary cost of borrowing to cover the cash shortfall and the investment interest earned. Also a possible loss of credit rating.

18 Controlling stocks

The need for stock control

Successful management of working capital reflects the degree of control exercised over each of its components – stocks, debtors, and liquid assets.

This does not mean that the separate elements of working capital are independent of one another. A change in policy in one will probably affect the value of another. For example, a critical liquidity problem might be solved temporarily by reducing stock levels to release cash, but stock shortages can result in lost sales and therefore a reduction in liquidity. Again, if customers can be persuaded to order in large quantities in return for quantity discounts, this would probably reduce finished goods stocks but increase debtors. Thus stock policy may affect, and be affected by, debtors and liquidity.

Controlled investment in stock plays a critical role in achievement of business objectives. Too high a stock level relative to a given volume of sales will reduce return on investment; too low a level, whilst reducing investment, may also reduce sales and therefore profit proportionately more. This is another example of the need to consider the trade-off between return and risk when making business decisions.

What factors influence stock levels?

Activity

From each of the following hints see if you can deduce a factor that influences the level of *finished goods* stocks in different industries.

1 Number of customers.
2 Foodstuffs.
3 Fashion, style and technology.
4 Harvests, fireworks, Christmas crackers.
5 Keen competition.
6 Nationwide distribution.
7 Quantity discounts.
8 Unique specifications.
9 Lost customers.

1 Anticipated *demand* from customers.
2 The rate of *deterioration* (shelf-life) of the product.
3 The pace of *obsolescence*, changes in style and technological development will constrain stockholding.
4 *Seasonal* nature of the product. For example, harvested foods may be wholly processed immediately after being gathered, thus boosting stock level at that time; Christmas crackers, fireworks and ice-skates peak in different seasons, but will probably be made for stock throughout the year, to reap the economies of even production levels.
5 *Uncertainty* of demand will call for higher stocks.
6 The need to *decentralise* stockholding into a network of national distribution depots may increase total stock.
7 *Transfer stocks* to customers by persuading them to purchase in larger quantities.
8 Whether goods are *made to order* or for stock.
9 *Lost profit contribution* has to be balanced against the cost of holding higher stocks.

The nature of, and demand for, the product largely influences *finished goods* stock levels. Likewise, *raw material* stocks will be affected by the nature of the product, with perishability a prime determinant of how much material can be economically held.

Uncertainty of product demand may also affect holdings of raw materials and components but the major factors here will be rate of usage in production and the time taken to replace stocks from suppliers.

Work in progress stocks depend on production processing time. Partly finished confectionary stock will be low therefore, whilst that in a factory producing computers will be high. It should be noted that increased output does not necessarily increase raw material and work in progress stocks, if the additional output is completed in overtime or additional shifts worked.

Optimum stock levels

The ideal situation is to carry no stocks of raw materials and finished goods, and a bare minimum of work in progress, but this can only be achieved if:

- raw materials are immediately and continuously available from suppliers when required;
- raw material and component purchase prices are no different whether one buys for stock or for continuous delivery;
- sales are stable and can be accurately forecast;
- production always proceeds on schedule;
- production facilities are easily adapted to changes in customer demand.

Although several of these conditions might be encountered in industry, it is doubtful whether all can be found together in a single manufacturer. Risks, opportunities and the circumstances discussed in the previous section dictate that 'buffer' stocks be maintained by the majority of firms.

From the *production manager's* viewpoint, uncertainties of raw material supply must be provided for. In addition, fluctuating or seasonal finished product demand will encourage him to:

- ensure there are adequate levels of raw materials and components to take the strain of a sudden increase in product demand; and
- produce for stock to realise lower costs per unit resulting from longer production runs.

The *sales manager* will be concerned primarily that adequate levels of finished goods are available to meet his customers' demands. Hold-ups in production and fluctuating demand can be insured against by holding larger finished goods stocks.

On the other hand, the *financial manager* has to reconcile the vested interest in flexibility and safety of managerial colleagues with the financial constraint of minimising total capital invested in stocks. To achieve this compromise, his three aims will be to:

- reduce to a minimum the total cost of holding and acquiring stocks;
- decide the stock reorder level for each item held, to ensure that demand can be met;
- add a safety stock to each item that is subject to uncertain demand or supply.

Minimising the stock control effort

It is well recognised in various value areas, comprising a number of items, that a comparatively low proportion of the items represents a high proportion of total value. Conversely, a high proportion of items represent a relatively low proportion of the total value. This is so in the case of debtors and stocks in most firms. The pattern might be:

Turnover value of stock items	*Over £50*	*£10–£50*	*Under £10*
% of total annual value	65	25	10
Number of items	10	20	70

In the case of stock the word 'value' refers not so much to value of individual items as to value in usage – which relates more to turnover. For example, a £10 stock item 'turned over' 50 times in a year represents £500 usage value, whereas a £50 item turned over 4 times has a £200 usage value.

Note particularly that the above table shows that 90% of the value represents only 30% of the items.

Close control of the high value items, perhaps by using the kind of mathematical approach discussed in the next section, will pay off handsomely; whereas the much larger effort needed to control the majority of items in stock will pay relatively poor rewards and can probably be dealt with by using less costly rule-of-thumb methods.

How much to order?

We stated earlier that one of the financial manager's prime aims is to reduce to a minimum the *total* cost of holding and acquiring stocks. Assuming that demand for an item is known, this minimum can be directly related to the frequency and size of orders.

> *Activity*
>
> If Percy Bend, a plumber, uses 10,000 of a certain pipe fitting fairly evenly throughout the year, and places only one order per year with his supplier, what would be his maximum and average stock levels?

Given that Percy just runs out of stock when the order is delivered, his maximum stock will be 10,000, and his average stock 10,000÷2=5,000. That is, half the time his stock will be greater than 5,000, and during the other half of the year less than 5,000.

Obviously the costs of *holding* such a large stock would be high, and would include building-related costs such as rates, heating, maintenance; insurance of both buildings and stocks; interest on the capital invested in stock; and deterioration and obsolescence.

Against that, *ordering* costs such as clerical salaries, costs of receiving and handling deliveries, would be relatively low – restricted in Percy's case to one order and one delivery. If two orders are placed, ordering costs will increase, but holding costs will diminish considerably as the average stock will drop to 5,000÷2=2,500.

We see that ordering cost grows as more orders are placed but stock holding costs diminish, until a point is reached at which ordering and holding costs are equal and their total is at a minimum. This point will indicate the most *economic order quantity* (EOQ), and can be represented by the following model:

$$\left(\frac{Q}{2}\times H\right)+\left(\frac{A}{Q}\times C\right)$$

where Q=quantity ordered
H=holding cost per unit
C=cost of placing an order

Self-check

Assuming that Percy Bend's annual holding cost per fitting is 8 pence, and the cost of placing an order £4, draw up a schedule showing the total cost of holding and ordering the fitting if the number of orders placed are 1, 2, 4, 5, 8, 10, 25, 50. What is the economic order quantity?

Number of orders placed	1	2	4	5	8	10	25	50
Quantity ordered	10,000	5,000	2,500	2,000	1,250	1,000	400	200
Average stock	5,000	2,500	1,250	1,000	625	500	200	100
	£	£	£	£	£	£	£	£
Annual holding cost @ 8 pence per fitting	400	200	100	80	50	40	16	8
Annual order cost @ £4 per order	4	8	16	20	32	40	100	200
Total annual cost	404	208	116	100	82	80	116	208

The economic order quantity (EOQ) is 1,000 fittings, because at this level total holding and ordering cost is minimal.

You will observe that holding and ordering costs are equal at the EOQ point. Thus $(Q \div 2) \times H = (A \div Q) \times C$, and after cross-multiplying, $Q^2 H = 2AC$, and $Q^2 = (2AC) \div H$ and finally $Q = \sqrt{((2AC) \div H)}$, which is the well-known EOQ model.

Self-check

Now check the answer in the previous self-check question by applying the EOQ model.

$Q = \sqrt{((2 \times 10{,}000 \times 4) \div .08)} = \sqrt{(80{,}000 \div .08)} = \sqrt{1{,}000{,}000} =$ 1,000.

The EOQ model is widely applied in industry but may need modification when the following limitations and circumstances apply:

- Where it is possible to substitute materials, switch to production of another item easily or defer sales without loss, lower stock levels are possible.

- Seasonal or climatic conditions may impose a peak inventory requirement on firms.
- Quantity discounts are not catered for in the simplest formula. Where the savings from such discount exceeds the extra cost of stockholding, a revised order quantity should be calculated to take this into account.
- Anticipated price movements and changes in fashion or technology influence the building up or running down of stocks, to the extent that demand cannot be easily estimated or is volatile.
- In order to accommodate a supplier and obtain keenest prices, it might be more advantageous to accept a delivery schedule imposed by the supplier. This applies particularly to long-term fixed-price contracts.

When to order

In the Percy Bend example, demand for the fitting is approximately 200 per week, with orders being placed every 5 weeks. If the supplier takes five weeks to deliver an order, then patently Percy will have to place a further order immediately upon receiving each delivery, i.e. when the stock level is 1,000, otherwise he will run out of stock.

However, supposing the supplier can meet each order in two weeks, at what stock level should Percy place each order to avoid running out of stock? The answer is, delivery time × average usage per week, i.e. $2 \times 200 = 400$ fittings, as depicted in figure 21.

When delivery times are slower and demand higher, safety stocks may have to be carried to avoid production disruption and possible loss of customer orders. The optimal safety stock will be that at which the total of the cost of holding safety stock and the profit from lost customers is minimised. If too much safety stock is carried, to the extent that no customers are lost, the cost of stockholding could well exceed the total of holding lower stocks and losing a few orders.

The most obvious way to provide safety stock is to set a reorder level higher than indicated by average demand and the supplier's normal delivery time; that is, to order sooner than

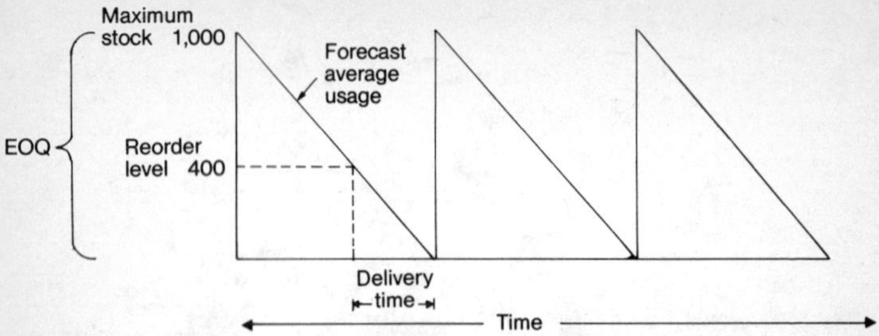

Figure 21. Reorder level when demand and delivery time are known

average usage requires. How much higher will be related to the probability of demand being higher than normal, and the cost of lost customers at different levels of safety stock. Mathematical models can be used to calculate safety stock but, owing to the subjective nature of some variables involved, particularly the value of lost custom, managerial judgement based on experience must play a large part in its determination.

Self-check

The holding and 'out-of-stock' costs associated with safety stocks of 50, 100, 150 and 200 units are respectively £20, £40, £60, £90; and £80, £50, £20, £10.

a What is the optimal level of safety stock?
b If this level of safety stock related to the Percy Bend pipe fitting, what would be the reorder level?

a 150 units, i.e. when holding and out-of-stock costs are at a minimum of £80 (£60+£20).
b 550 units, i.e. reorder level of 400 calculated in the previous activity, plus 150 safety stock (see **a** above).

Review

1 Which of the following will **a** restrict or **b** increase stockholding? Explain.
i A doubling of sales.
ii A product subject to rapid deterioration.
iii Uncertainty of demand.
iv Offer of quantity discounts to customers.
v A high volume of 'made to order' products.

2 New Plastics plc supply a container that is in regular and steady demand. Total annual sales are 80,000, and the annual cost of holding a container in stock is one penny. The cost of placing an order on the supplier is £3. Calculate:
a The economic order quantity (use the EOQ model).
b The total cost of holding and ordering stock.
c Whether a quantity discount of .1 penny per container is worth placing orders in 15,000 batches.

1 i b Stocks tend to follow the trend of sales.
ii a Too high a stock of low-shelf life products would lead to wastage.
iii b Additional safety stock will be needed to meet the uncertainty.
iv a Such a policy effectively transfers stock to customers.
v a 'Tailor-made' products are not carried in stock as finished goods.

2 a $Q=\sqrt{(2AC \div H)}=\sqrt{(2\times 80{,}000\times 3\div .01)}=\sqrt{48{,}000{,}000}=6{,}928.$

b $$\left(\frac{Q}{2}\times H\right)+\left(\frac{AC}{Q}\right)=\left(\frac{6{,}928\times .01}{2}\right)+\left(\frac{80{,}000\times 3}{6{,}928}\right)$$
$$=34.64+34.64=£69.28.$$

c Total quantity discount−(additional holding cost−reduction in ordering cost).

Total quantity discount=	$80{,}000 \times £.001 =$	80.00
Additional holding cost=	$\dfrac{15{,}000-6{,}928}{2} \times .01 = 40.36$	
less		
Reduction in ordering cost=	$34.64 - \left(\dfrac{80{,}000}{15{,}000} \times 3\right) = \underline{18.64}$	$\underline{21.72}$
Net saving from taking quantity discount:		£58.28.

19 Controlling debtors

Justifying investment in debtors

Investment in debtors must be worthwhile. In the simplest case, a business that is considering a change of policy from cash on delivery to granting credit would only do so if it estimates that additional profit earned on increased sales will yield a return greater than the opportunity cost of capital. Further changes in policy on credit must always meet the same criterion of profitability.

The consequential effects on stock levels and cash flow of changing credit policy must also be taken into account. For example, an extension of credit terms to encourage sales will increase debtors but may also push up stock levels required to support this higher level of sales. Cash flow will also be affected by delayed payment by debtors.

Investment in debtors can be released by factoring or invoice discounting but this can be fairly expensive unless, in the case of factoring, it is outweighed by considerable improvement in debt collection by the factor.

Self-check

The sales director of a company argued that if a change in credit policy increased *total* sales, then such a change was desirable. Do you agree with him?

An increase in sales caused by changing credit policy does not automatically add to profit. Such a change is justified only if the increased profit is greater than the consequent increased costs of carrying higher levels of debtors and stocks.

What factors govern investment in debtors?

Pike Electronics plc had experienced a rapid growth in sales thanks to dynamic marketing and production policies in this expanding and highly competitive area of the economy. The level of debtors had risen along with sales as the company offered normal credit terms to its customers both at home and overseas. As the investment in accounts receivable was now alarmingly high, and bad debts were rising, the managing director called for a review by his finance director of the company policies and practices concerning debtors.

> *Activity*
>
> Using the above information plus your own knowledge and experience, specify briefly the aspects upon which the level of debtors depends and upon which the Pike review will report.

Although practice will vary from industry to industry, certain factors are common to all businesses:

- The volume of *credit* sales will be a prime determinant, this in turn depending upon the general state of the economy, but particularly upon that of the industry concerned. Seasonality of sales and the incidence of customers' orders may also cause debtors to fluctuate.
- The credit policies followed, including:
  i the efficacy of *investigations* into potential customers' credit standing;
  ii the establishment of realistic *credit terms* covering maximum value, credit period and cash discounts. Credit terms in most industries are customary, but competition tends to induce firms to modify these when it is considered desirable;
  iii the level of customer *riskiness* accepted by the firm; extending credit to risky customers will increase sales and debtors, but will also increase bad debts, investment cost and administrative expense;
  iv any special terms offered to *export* customers.

- The paying practices of credit customers do not always accord with agreed terms. Some flexibility may have to be allowed, particularly in respect of large and valued customers.
- The effectiveness of *debt collection* organisation and procedures. Control costs should not exceed the value of debts prevented from going bad.

Self-check

Upon which of the following circumstances will the level of investment in debtors in a business primarily depend?

a The type of item bought by the customer.
b The level of customer riskiness.
c Special terms offered to export customers.
d The distance of the customer from supplies.
e The paying practices of customers.
f The effectiveness of debt collection.
g The total number of employees.
h The efficacy of credit status investigation.
i Realistic credit terms.
j Dividend paid to shareholders.
k The volume of credit sales.

b, c, e, f, h, i, k.

Assessing the credit status of customers

As a result of the Pike debtors' review, a qualified credit controller was appointed to head the accounts receivable section. One of his first tasks was to examine the various methods used by the company to obtain information upon which to base credit decisions:

- *Credit agency ratings* published by Dun & Bradstreet on most businesses. The company had a regular subscription arrangement with this agency. Information used to compile these ratings tends to be limited to that already obtainable from published accounts.
- *Financial statements* obtained directly from customers,

whether published or not, revealing liquidity, gearing, trading and other relevant information.

- Sales representatives and company officers are used for direct enquiry purposes.
- *Trade associations* who have organised credit reference departments provide information regarding 'blacklisted' businesses who have defaulted on their debts, e.g. the Building Trades' and Motor Traders' associations.
- *Bankers' references*, usually made through the company's bank on the potential customer's bank. This is not a very penetrating investigation, normally being limited to an acknowledgement that an account is kept and has been maintained satisfactorily.
- *Trade references* provided by the potential customer. Recommendations from existing trading connections of the customer are obviously more satisfactory than bank references, although they could be chosen by the customer to paint the most favourable picture.

Because of the danger of losing sales through delayed credit enquiries, the Pike company tended to rely almost wholly upon agency credit ratings and sales representatives' reports in assessment of potential customers. Unfortunately, this 'broad brush' approach had proved less than rigorous, leading to increased bad debts. Moderate agency ratings were sometimes not reinforced by calling for special agency reports, and, in the case of potentially large customers, no special action was taken.

The credit controller therefore recommended the following additional guidelines:

- non-existent or poor agency ratings should always be followed up by trade and bank references in the case of potentially low value customers;
- as regards large order customers, a special agency report, and usually a direct personal approach for further financial information where this was not already available.

Self-check

'Credit agency ratings can be relied upon wholly to decide the credit status of a potential customer.' True or false? Explain.

False. Such information is restricted to that already obtainable from published accounts. Further reassurance might be necessary in the form of special agency reports, direct enquiries to the customer, and bank and trade references.

Establishing credit terms

Credit terms cover the maximum value allowed to each customer, the maximum time allowed for payment and frequently the offer of cash discounts for early payment of debts. Normally, if a customer is granted credit, he is subject to the suppliers' *standard* time and cash discount conditions but may be restricted as regards credit value. The plastic credit card system (e.g. Access) is a good example. Payment conditions, and interest on outstanding balances, are standard terms but the maximum credit value allowed varies with the customer's credit rating.

Maximum credit allowance A business may use *discriminant analysis* to rate the credit standing of its customers. This statistical technique weights the various factors covered by credit investigation such as liquidity, profitability, gearing, debt payment record, and ascribes a credit value (a rating) to each customer. The higher the rating, the more credit will be allowed; whereas lower rated customers may be requested to pay in advance or on delivery of goods.

The credit allowance may be further restricted so that the firm does not over-rely upon the payment practices of a few large customers. The supplier may calculate this amount as a conservative proportion of a customer's net asset value or of its own estimated *total* debtors.

Credit period The *minimum* credit period will be that customary in the particular industry but, as customers' cash flow conditions vary (e.g. they may be seasonal), some flexibility will have to be introduced in allowing time to pay. Typical terms are payment within 30 days of date of invoice (i.e. net 30 days), and payment by the end of the month following the date of invoice.

Cash discount This might be offered to shorten the average payment period and thus reduce investment in debtors. For example, if the terms of payment are currently net 30 days, and all customers pay their accounts on time, the value of debtors outstanding should be equivalent to 30 days' sales. If terms are changed to 2½% discount for payment within 10 days of invoice date otherwise net 30 days (i.e. 2½/10, N/30), and all debtors take advantage of the discount, investment in debtors will amount to 10 days' sales.

The value of cash discount to debtors is considerable. Using the data in the previous paragraph for example, on sales of £100 per month the effective rate of return on £100 paid 20 days earlier would be:

$$\left(\frac{2\frac{1}{2}}{97\frac{1}{2}} \times \frac{365}{20}\right) \times 100 = 46.8\% \text{ per annum.}$$

Note that only £97½ is received promptly after deduction of 2½% cash discount, but that this repeats itself approximately 18 times (365÷20) each year.

From the supplier's viewpoint the discount is an additional cost, but may be worth incurring if sales are increased or alternatively not lost to competitors (see the following section).

Self-check

1 What are the determinants of **a** the maximum credit value allowed to a customer, **b** the credit period?

2 What is the effective % annual cost to a customer who does not take advantage of a 2% cash discount for payment within 7 days, net 30 days?

1 a The customer's credit rating and the potential value of each customer's debts.

b Custom in the industry, competition, customer's cash flow conditions.

2 $\left(\frac{2}{98}\times\frac{365}{23}\right)\times100=32\%.$

Changing credit terms

Caution should be exercised in changing credit policy for not only must *customers'* reactions be anticipated but also those of competitors. The overall principle is that the benefits should always be worth more than the costs.

Extending credit terms to increase sales

The total annual sales of Unique Ltd are currently £2.4 million. The selling price of its product is £8 and its variable cost £6. The company is considering extending its average debt collection period from one to two months, and estimates that this change will increase sales to £3 million.

Existing customers are expected to take full advantage of the new terms, and the firm has sufficient existing capacity to increase production to the anticipated new level. The company's marginal cost of capital is 25%.

> *Activity*
>
> If the new policy succeeds, how much additional profit will be realised by the company?

Increase in sales £3–2.4 million= £600,000.

% Contribution per product $\frac{£8-6}{8}\times100=$ 25%.

Increased contribution 25%×£600,000=

£150,000.

Against this benefit of £150,000 has to be set the opportunity investment cost of the higher level of debtors, resulting from the delay in payment of an additional month.

In this respect, however, there is a difference between the increased investment in *existing customers'* debts, and those of *new customers*. The *sales* value of existing debtors, i.e. *including profit*, is deferred for payment by one further month, whereas additional investment in new debtors comprises *variable cost* of sales only.

Activity

a Calculate total debtors on existing sales under the old credit policy of one month.
b Calculate the value of debtors relating to *existing* customers under the new policy.
c Show the increase in debtors relating to existing customers.
d Calculate the value of investment in debtors relating to *new* sales (reminder: variable cost only).

a Present level of debtors: £2.4 million÷12 = £200,000.
b New level of debtors – existing customers: £2.4 million÷6 =£400,000.
c Additional investment – existing customers (**b**−**a**) = £200,000.
d Variable cost of debtors relating to new sales: (£600,000× .75)÷6 = £ 75,000.

Activity

a Given the company's 25% cost of capital, what is the cost of carrying additional debtors?
b Should the new policy be implemented?

a Total additional investment in debtors: £200,000+75,000= £275,000. Opportunity cost of additional investment: 25% of £275,000=£68,750.
b As the increased contribution from new sales, £150,000, is greater than the opportunity cost of carrying additional debtors, £68,750, the policy should be implemented.

Impact of bad debts and other costs

If customers are allowed to delay payment of their debts, some will default. Further, the longer the credit period allowed, the higher the incidence of bad debts as credit is allowed to lower quality (higher risk) customers. Costs of vetting new customers and collecting debts will probably increase.

Activity

Assume that Unique's existing bad debts are 0.5% of sales, but that this will increase to 10% in respect of the additional sales. Additional annual cost of vetting new customers and collecting debts will be £12,000. Should the new credit policy be implemented in the light of these extra costs?

			£
Increased contribution from new sales (see previous activity)			150,000
less Additional cost of bad debts 10% of £600,000	=	60,000	
Additional administration costs	=	12,000	
Additional debtors opportunity cost (see previous activity)	=	68,750	140,750
Net increased profit			£ 9,250

The marginal increase in profit is now so small that risks of introducing the new policy will have to be carefully assessed. Sensitivity analysis may help here. An additional point to note is that if productive capacity is not currently available to cope with additional demand, the costs of providing it will obviously nullify the proposal.

Offering or changing cash discount

Introducing or changing cash discount may embrace all the costs and benefits discussed above, as well as adding the cost of discount. Offering discount may attract additional sales and, therefore, increase debtors, if demand for the product is highly sensitive to price changes (i.e. is elastic). At the same time, earlier payment of debts will reduce investment in accounts receivable.

Pike Electronics' new credit controller had recommended that the company's credit terms should be changed to 2%

discount to customers who pay within 10 days of date of invoice, otherwise net 30 days. He considered that this policy would result in:

- the company's annual sales increasing from £3 million to £3.1 million, and that existing capacity could cope with this increase;
- bad debts would decrease from 2% to 1% of all sales;
- the average collection period would reduce from its present 50 days to 20 days;
- 80% of all customers would take advantage of the cash discount;
- administrative costs would reduce by £2000 per annum.

Activity

Produce the calculations submitted by the credit controller to justify his proposals, assuming that the company's cost of capital is 15%, and its contribution to sales ratio is 20%.

Costs:		£
Cash discount .02×.80×£3.1 million		= 49,600
Benefits:		
Reduction in bad debts – existing 2%×£3 million	= 60,000	
– new 1%×£3.1 million	= 31,000	= 29,000
Additional contribution 20% of £100,000		= 20,000
Reduction in administrative costs		= 2,000
Reduction in opportunity cost of debtors:		
Existing level of debtors 50/365×£3 million	=410,959	
New level of debtors 20/365×£3.1 million	=169,863	
15% of	=241,096	= 36,164
		87,164
Net benefit of offering discounts		37,564

It is possible of course that alternative changes in credit policy may be more advantageous than those considered above. For example, a 3% cash discount would increase costs even more, but produce considerably higher sales and low bad debt, investment and administrative costs. In examining such alternatives, the *optimal* point is that at which the *marginal benefits* are just equal to the *marginal costs*.

Self-check

1 If a company extends its credit period total debtors can be expected to be higher. Why will the new level of *existing* customers' debts be valued on a basis different to that applied to new customers?
2 What determines the rate of opportunity cost applied to investment in debtors consequent upon a change in credit policy?
3 Why should the rate of bad debts increase when the credit period is extended?
4 As regards each of the following state which may **A** increase or **B** decrease if cash discounts are offered for prompt payment of debts?
a Total debtors.
b Debt collection costs.
c Sales.
d Investment opportunity cost.
e Contribution from sales.
f Average debt collection period.

1 Because payment of *existing* customers' debts is extended by one month, the whole invoiced value, i.e. including profit, is counted as increased investment, whereas the investment in new debtors takes account only of *variable cost*, i.e. the incremental outlay.
2 The cost of the next best alternative use of the additional capital invested in debtors. This would normally be the company's marginal cost of capital, unless the additional debtors are to be permanently financed by bank overdraft or loan, when the cost of bank finance would apply.
3 Extension of the credit period delays the payment of debts, and the longer this delay the higher the bad debts. In addition, sales will be made to new, riskier, customers, a higher percentage of whom will probably default on their debts.
4 **a – B, b – B, c – A, d – B, e – A, f – B.**

Debt collection

The cost of each additional day's sales remaining unpaid can be high. For example, with a turnover of £3.5 million, approximately £10,000 of capital would be tied up in debtors for each day's sales outstanding. If the average collection period for debtors is, say, 5 days more than planned, then £50,000 is over invested in debtors, and, at an opportunity cost of 20%, this reduces profit by £10,000 per annum. Additional bad debts and administrative costs arising from the excess debtors would further diminish profit.

The need to inject adequate resources into the collection of debts is therefore equally as important as optimising credit terms.

This point was not lost on Colin, managing director of Pike Electronics, and he asked his new credit controller to outline a procedure that would deal with the company's debt collection most effectively at lowest cost.

The following were the major points submitted to Colin:

- Invoices and monthly statements of account should be forwarded to customers promptly.
- Prompt and courteous attention should be given to all customers' complaints whether concerned with the goods supplied or with invoices, and allowances made by sending credit notes when justified.
- *A progression of applications* for payment should be made, first by statement, then by either telephone or post. A telephone request is more personal, and can very often obtain better results than standard letters requesting payment. Progressively harsher and more personal letters should follow until the only course is to place the debt with agents or solicitors for collection.
- *Action through reputable debt collection agencies*, which act on commission, is normally effective in dealing with all but the hard cases, with follow-up solicitors' letters as final requests for payment.
- *Action through the courts* would be resorted to only after solicitors' direct action had failed. Court action should be deferred for as long as possible, for it is expensive and often

yields less than a direct compromise arrangement with the debtor.

- *In dealing with individual debts:*
  - if a debtor appears able to pay, rigorous collection procedures are in order;
  - if the account is small it will probably be less costly to proceed no further than a collection agency;
  - if the debtor is a valued customer but is in temporary financial difficulties, a compromise deferment of payment may be in order;
  - revise or withdraw credit facilities in the case of particularly bad payers.
- *Arrange credit insurance* for above normal credit risks, i.e. for exceptionally large amounts or extended credit periods. This relates particularly to export sales, when the government's Export Credits Guarantee Department should be approached.
- *Produce regularly updated statistics* of debtors including:
  - monthly analyses into types of customers, amounts outstanding, ages of debts and progress made in the collection of older debts;
  - graphs showing monthly trend figures of debtors against a moving annual sales figure;
  - the days sales outstanding ratio.

The Pike credit controller also produced an analysis of estimated staff and other costs required to support the proposed procedure most effectively. In his opinion, any increase in this level of cost would not be justified by the consequent savings in bad debts and investment in debtors; conversely, less expenditure would result in *marginally* higher bad debts and increased debtors.

Self-check

The annual sales of Unique Ltd are £2 million. Its current cost of debt collection is £30,000 per annum, with bad debts of 1% of sales, and the average debt collection period 45 days.

Would it be worth increasing its debt collection expenditure by £15,000 if bad debts fell to 0.5% of sales, and the average debt collection period to 35 days? The company's marginal cost of capital is 20%.

		£
Reduction in bad debts (1%−0.5%)×£2 million		10,000
Reduction in opportunity cost of debtors:		
Investment now (45÷356)×£2 million	=246,575	
Reduced investment (35÷365)×£2 million	=191,781	
20% of	54,794=	10,959
		20,959
less Marginal cost of debt collection		15,000
Net benefit from increasing collection cost		£ 5,959

Therefore the additional expenditure is justified, and more especially so if future turnover is expected to increase.

Review

Approximately a third of a company's sales relates to two categories of customers, *X* and *Y*, whose credit is limited in value. The current bad debt experience on each of them is 1% and 2% of sales respectively, but it is estimated that these credit restrictions are losing sales valued at £200,000 and £100,000 respectively.

If the company were to grant these customers unlimited credit and thus to recapture the lost sales, the bad debts are likely to increase to 5% and 10% respectively on the *increased turnover*, and the average collection period on the new sales would be two months. Assuming a contribution to sales ratio of 10%, and an opportunity investment rate of 12%, calculate whether the company should extend these credit terms.

			£
Increased contribution	10% × £300,000		= 30,000
less			
Increased bad debts *X*	5% × £200,000	= 10,000	
Y	10% × £100,000	= 10,000	20,000
Investment opportunity cost	$\frac{£300,000 \times .12}{6}$		= 6,000
Increased costs			26,000
Increased profit			£ 4,000

The surplus of £4,000 indicates that the new policy would be a viable proposition, but sensitivity analysis should first be applied to assess the risk of the proposal.

Part 7
Additional sources of finance

20 Government and institutional financial assistance

Introduction

Many additional finance and incentive schemes have been created by the government, EEC and private financial institutions to assist businesses that cannot find finance elsewhere. These facilities have emerged largely in response to pressure to:

- create new, and encourage existing, *small* businesses;
- encourage research, development and innovation;
- encourage investment and boost employment;
- assist in areas of high unemployment and industrial decline;
- help large companies and whole industries whose immediate collapse would cause disastrous economic and social consequences (e.g. British Leyland);
- encourage exports.

A high proportion of these additional funds are directed specifically at small and medium-sized firms, not only for the reasons discussed in the section on 'accessibility' of finance in Chapter 9, but also because the government places great importance upon development of new types of business activity to fill the vacuum caused by the decline of the older, traditional industries.

In this chapter we discuss some of the major sources of this additional finance, which is provided out of:

- public funds – for specific *regional* schemes;
- public funds – available nationally;
- private funds;
- European Economic Community funds.

The schemes discussed in this chapter were current in late 1983, but a continuing process of review, by government and other agencies, of the changing needs for financial support will inevitably lead to amendments to them.

Public funds available regionally

Assisted areas

Certain areas of the United Kingdom have experienced considerable industrial decline since the Second World War. A serious unemployment problem has therefore arisen. Consequently the government has designated them 'assisted areas' in three categories – 'special development areas', 'development areas' and 'intermediate areas', according to regional economic priorities.

Government assistance is in the form of *regional development grants* and *selective financial assistance.*

Regional development grants (RDGs) are made to manufacturers for approved capital investments in buildings, plant and equipment to be used in the special development areas (22% grant) and the development areas (15% grant). The grants are 'automatic' when expenditure has been incurred; they are not conditional upon job creation and do not reduce asset value for tax capital allowance purposes. They are administered by Regional Development Grant Offices.

Selective financial assistance is available on a discretionary basis, under section 7 of the Industry Act 1972, for new or developing projects undertaken anywhere in the assisted areas by businesses in the manufacturing, mining and construction industries. The assistance is in addition to RDGs. Service industry and office building projects, which are not entitled to RDGs, may qualify for selective assistance. In order to qualify for help the project must meet the following four criteria:

- it must be in the national economic interest, e.g. improve efficiency or increase exports;
- it will create or preserve jobs in the assisted areas;
- it must have a good chance of succeeding, and the bulk of the money required for the project must be available from private sources;
- it would not proceed if selective assistance was not available.

The assistance may take the form of interest relief grants, medium-term loans at concessionary interest rates or removal grants.

Rural areas

The Development Commission, through its agent the Council for Small Industries in Rural Areas (COSIRA), aims to regenerate employment in English rural areas by development of small manufacturing and service businesses of up to twenty employees. Horticulture and agriculture are excluded excepting for grants for the conversion of redundant farm buildings.

Medium– and long-term loans of between £250 and £7,500 are available, mainly to 'start-ups' or to young businesses in the designated 'rural development areas' and in the assisted areas. County advisers also offer consultancy services, and COSIRA has also cooperated with local authorities in the provision of small workshops and factories.

Scotland, Wales, and Northern Ireland

In addition to assistance available in assisted areas, and from EEC sources (see later), development agencies, including the Highland and Islands Development Board in Scotland, exist in these regions. They provide financial and other assistance to encourage industrial and commercial growth, particularly relating to small businesses, to improve the environment, attract overseas investment, train workers and encourage research and development.

Steel redundancy areas

A modernisation program by the British Steel Corporation and the reduction in capacity caused by industrial recession and foreign competition have resulted in extensive closures of steelworks with resultant employment loss. The closures are all within the assisted areas and, therefore, attract all the regional assistance for job creation previously discussed.

In addition, British Steel Corporation (Industry) Ltd was formed in 1975 by the British Steel Corporation to attract new industries to the steel redundancy areas. It offers financial assistance and advice for the setting up of new businesses, and assessment of investment projects. Although BSC (Industry) Ltd plans to cease operations in 1984, its functions will probably be continued by local enterprise organisations.

Businesses may also be eligible for assistance from the European Coal and Steel Community (see section on EEC).

Local authority assistance

General schemes Local authorities have *general* power under Local Government Acts, and in some cases *specific* power granted through private Acts of Parliament, to provide financial assistance to industry, if this is in the local interest. The assistance might include:

- the provision of premises for the benefit of industry, either by financing its purchase by loans secured on the property, or by letting it at favourable rents or short leases;
- loans or grants for plant or working capital;
- grants to firms incurring relocation expenses to their area;
- wages subsidies to small firms who recruit the unemployed;
- grants to encourage small firms (5 to 10 people) of up to £2,000, and loans of up to £10,000.

Derelict land Grants are available from the Department of the Environment, both to local authorities and private firms, for losses incurred in reclamation of derelict land.

Urban redevelopment programmes Additional powers have been granted under the Inner Urban Areas Act 1978 to local authorities with *severe inner area problems*, to assist commerce and industry in areas designated by the Secretary of State for the Environment, and to improve the living environment in those areas. Assistance may include loans relating to acquisition and site preparation of property; grants to assist with rent, or interest payable on loans to small firms; and loans or grants of up to £1,000 in each case towards the cost of establishing cooperative or common ownership enterprises. Funds are provided jointly by the local authorities and the Department of the Environment 'urban development programme'.

Enterprise zones As an experiment to encourage industrial and commercial activity, the government has set up 22 'enterprise zones' in UK cities and towns. Their sizes range from 140 to 1,100 acres. Benefits accruing to both new and existing enterprises in these areas include:

- exemption from rates on industrial and commercial property;
- exemption from development land tax;
- capital allowances on new buildings including hotels and offices;
- simplification of planning procedures, and a reduction in statistical returns to government.

This scheme is additional to the other regional provisions already discussed.

New town development corporations These offer special incentives for investment in their areas, including rent-free premises, and factories and workshops at special mortgage rates. These are in addition to other provisions for assisted areas.

Public funds available nationally

Small business loan guarantee scheme

Under this scheme the Department of Trade and Industry guarantees 80% of loans, up to £75,000, made to small businesses in most sectors of the economy. The finance is available through ICFC, the clearing banks and other designated financial institutions, to provide funds for potentially viable projects which would not be approved without the guarantee. A premium of 3% of the guaranteed amount outstanding is payable, in addition to the commercial interest rate charged by the lender.

British Technology Group (BTG)

This government-sponsored group was formed in 1981 by combining the National Enterprise Board (NEB) and the National Research and Development Corporation (NRDC). Its activities include providing funds for research and development of new technology, for small businesses with growth potential, and for companies within the assisted areas.

BTG is required to operate commercially, and therefore only supports *promising* projects that would not proceed without their backing. It expects to withdraw from schemes at the end of an agreed financing period, and arrangements by companies to buy back shares issued to BTG are included in financing agreements.

Support for innovation

The Department of Trade and Industry has recently streamlined its assistance for research and development (R&D), carried out by companies and research organisations. Support is for innovation in new or old technology areas that could improve the technological base of UK industry.

Support may take any of the following forms:

- grants towards the eligible costs of the project;
- shared cost contracts, usually in respect of longer R&D projects, where the department's 50% contribution is recovered

by a levy on sales of the resultant product;
- the purchase from designers by the department of pre-production equipment, with a view to encouraging its use by industry.

In addition, under the 'joint appraisal scheme', the department's technical appraisal of a project will be made available to help a project developer obtain funds from his bank.

The department is assisted in its assessment of R&D projects by five R&D requirements boards, each dealing with a broad sector of industry,chaired by a senior industrialist and containing strong industrial representation.

Enterprise agencies

These are local advisory organisations, usually funded by large companies with local authority support. Their task is to encourage growth of successful small businesses by providing useful local information and advice regarding new opportunities, and how resources such as premises and finance might be obtained.

Small engineering firms investment scheme

This was set up in March 1982 to assist small engineering firms to modernise their equipment. The scheme was reintroduced in March 1983, and £100 million in total is available in grants of up to 33⅓% of the net eligible cost of a project, which must not exceed £200,000. The types of machine eligible for assistance are specific, and include numerical or computer controlled tools and those including laser technology.

Other nationally available financial assistance

Many schemes exist to help different sectors of industry, such as agriculture (within the framework of the EEC common agricultural policy), shipbuilding, energy, forestry, hotels and tourism, transport; as well as the general field of employment and training administered by the Manpower Services Commission.

Taxation incentives

Capital allowances of 100% on plant and machinery (not cars), 75% on industrial buildings and 100% on small workshops may be allowed against the profit of the year of acquisition of the asset when calculating corporation tax. These allowances will disappear after 1985, however, and be replaced by writing down allowances over a longer period.

Corporation tax Small companies with annual profits of less than £100,000 can claim to be taxed at 30%. Marginal relief applies, so that the full 50% rate is not payable until profits exceed £500,000.

'Business expansion scheme' is intended to encourage outside investors to buy shares in unquoted trading companies. Up to £40,000 per annum (until 1987), can be subscribed for up to 30% of the equity capital of a company. Relief is given at the highest rates of income tax, so that up to 60% of the cost of the investment could be offset. Relief will be reduced if the shares are sold within five years of purchase.

'Venture capital scheme' If tax relief is not available under the business expansion scheme, under this arrangement an investor can set any loss on shares sold in a small business against his income rather than his capital gains. This relief also applies to investment companies investing in small businesses.

Purchase of own shares is now legalised, and allows owner-managers to regain control over their businesses through buying back shares sold to outsiders, after an agreed time.

Interest relief against tax is allowed to persons owning over 5% of a 'close' company, or managers of such companies, upon interest paid on money borrowed to buy shares in the company. Similar relief applies to investments in cooperatives and partnerships.

Private funds

Investors in Industry plc.

Investors in Industry owes its origin, in 1945, to the setting up of the Industrial and Commercial Finance Corporation (ICFC) and other finance corporations to help companies of all sizes who were unable to obtain capital from normal outside sources. These institutions were reorganised in 1973 under the umbrella of Finance for Industry, and again in 1983 as Investors in Industry plc. The latter is owned by the nine London and Scottish banks (85%) and the Bank of England (15%), and obtains its funds from domestic and international money markets.

Its business is now divided into three groups: its UK *investment divisions*, overseas *investment subsidiaries*, and *advisory subsidiaries*. Overall investment philosophy is to take a long-term view of investment opportunities and, normally, neither to seek control of aided firms nor to ask for board of directors' representation. There are five *investment divisions*:

- ICFC } serving small and medium-sized
- Ventures Division } companies.
- Head Office Division } serving large companies.
- Shipping and Energy Divison }
- Property division, providing premises for companies of all sizes.

ICFC is long established as the world's largest source of private risk capital for small and medium-sized businesses requiring amounts of between £5,000 and £2 million for long-term growth. Its investments in 1983 totalled £480 million in nearly 4,000 companies and because of its expertise in connection with smaller companies, it has access to all the EEC financial sources available to help British companies.

ICFC finance is tailored to individual company requirements. Loan repayment terms may be from 5 to 20 years, at fixed or variable rates of interest. Equity interests in aided firms are usually low.

Capital may be provided for business start-up or development purposes as shown in Chapter 9 (the financing decision).

ICFC has also helped managers purchase the whole or part of their employers' businesses – firms that might otherwise have been liquidated. These are called 'management buy-outs'. Finance is either jointly subscribed by ICFC and the managers or, in the case of large buy-outs, by ICFC arranging finance by a syndicate of institutions.

ICFC provides leasing and hire purchase facilities, and also assists companies who have passed through difficult trading phases, to reconstruct their capital foundations on firmer, forward-looking bases.

Venture Division specialises in supporting small, high-growth enterprises, particularly those in the field of technology. Financial and management support can be made available to businesses facing both technical and commercial risks, at a crucial stage in their development.

Head Office Division provides longer-term finance to larger companies by way of loans of up to £35 million and equity capital up to £5 million. The division had £300 million invested in 1983.

Shipping and Energy Division finances the acquisition of ships by medium- or long-term loans or leases (charters); and equity and loans for on-shore and off-shore oil exploration and production.

Property Division lends support to the other four financing divisions by providing premises. It also deals in sale and lease-back, and cooperates with local authorities to provide accommodation to help create jobs in inner city areas.

Investors in Industry Overseas

This includes subsidiaries in Boston, Dublin and Paris whose main activity is to assist UK companies to develop abroad.

The advisory subsidiaries

These include:

- Investors in Industry Consultants Ltd – providing management consultancy, particularly to smaller companies.
- Investors in Industry Corporate Finance Ltd – a member of the Issuing Houses Association, providing financial advice, sponsoring issues of shares and loans, and advising on mergers, acquisitions and reconstructions.
- Investors in Industry Portfolio Management Ltd manage pension funds, investment and unit trusts; and EDITH plc which purchases minority interests in unlisted companies to enable shareholders to raise sufficient cash to meet tax and other liabilities without having to lose control of their companies.

Equity Capital for Industry Ltd

This company was established in 1976 in response to criticism that the financial markets did not make sufficient provision for companies with growth potential that could not readily raise capital from traditional sources. ECI is owned by a consortium of institutional investors and has concentrated mainly upon helping manufacturing industry with amounts of capital ranging from £250,000 to £4 million. It normally requires a significant stake of at least 25% in the equity of each company it helps to finance.

Other private institutional organisations

Other private institutions providing mainly development finance include most *merchant banks*, who are particularly concerned to assist small businesses, and the following:

- Charterhouse Development Ltd – minimum amount provided £50,000, but not normally to new businesses.
- Gresham Trust Ltd – up to £250,000 to any one business including business start-ups.
- Norwich General Trust Ltd – help by way of medium-term mortgage loans between £6,000 and £500,000.

- Moracrest Investments Ltd – will invest from £200,000 to £500,000 including business start-ups.
- Small Business Capital Fund Ltd – formed by the Cooperative Insurance Society to provide development and start-up capital in amounts over £50,000.

European Economic Community assistance

Loans for investment projects principally located in the 'assisted areas', which create or safeguard jobs, are available from the European Investment Bank (EIB), and the European Coal and Steel Community (ECSC).

Loans from the EIB

The EIB was created under the EEC treaty to provide finance to alleviate regional economic problems in member states.

In the UK assisted areas and Northern Ireland, small businesses of less than 500 employees requiring loans of between £15,000 and £4.25 million can apply for assistance to the Department of Industry, or the Welsh or Scottish development agencies. Loans may be used to pay for up to 50% of the fixed capital costs of a project. They are usually repayable in up to 7 years, and a fixed interest rate of 1% or 2% below normal commercial rates is charged. The government gives a guarantee of repayment to the EIB.

Loans above £4.25 million can also be negotiated *direct* with the EIB, for periods of between 8 and 10 years, at current commercial fixed rates of interest. The projects should largely relate to the assisted areas, but manufacturing, service, tourism or infra-structure investments outside those areas will be considered if they benefit the whole community. A loan cannot exceed 50% of the fixed capital cost of a project, and a repayment guarantee is required from a bank or a parent company.

For an annual service charge of around 1%, the government will provide insurance cover for exchange rate fluctuations affecting the repayment of these loans, which are provided in foreign currencies.

Agreements have been made with the ICFC, Midland and

National Westminster banks, to assist in the provision of EIB loans for amounts up to £100,000 to small firms, both inside and outside the assisted areas. Currency exchange risk and repayment guarantees are provided by the banks at extra charges.

Loans from the ECSC

These serve two purposes:

- *To encourage the rational distribution of production and improve productivity in the coal and steel industries.* Loans at 3% below normal commercial rates are available by direct application to the ECSC.
- *To create new employment in the areas affected by the run-down of the coal and steel industries.* Loans of up to 50% of the fixed capital cost of each project are made for up to 8 years, at a fixed interest rate, subject to a rebate of up to 3% according to the number of jobs created.

The ICFC administers loans of between £5,000 and £1 million, though sums of up to £100,000 can be borrowed through regional development agencies and commercial banks. For loans above £1 million, application should be made direct to the ECSC. Exchange risk cover is available in all cases as for EIB loans.

EEC fixed-term loans of between £1,500 and £250,000 for up to 8 years have been available, through the ICFC to small businesses *wherever situated*, to finance fixed capital expenditure. Interest rates on these loans will be under current commercial rates and exchange risk cover is provided.

Appendix A: Present value of £1

n Year	5%	6%	7%	8%	9%	10%	11%	12%	13%
0	1.000	1.000	1.000	1.000	1.000	1.000	1.000	1.000	1.000
1	.952	.943	.935	.926	.917	.909	.901	.893	.885
2	.907	.890	.873	.857	.842	.826	.812	.797	.783
3	.864	.840	.816	.794	.772	.751	.731	.712	.693
4	.823	.792	.763	.735	.708	.683	.659	.636	.613
5	.784	.747	.713	.681	.650	.621	.593	.567	.543
6	.746	.705	.666	.630	.596	.564	.535	.507	.480
7	.711	.665	.623	.583	.547	.513	.482	.452	.425
8	.677	.627	.582	.540	.502	.467	.434	.404	.376
9	.645	.592	.544	.500	.460	.424	.391	.361	.333
10	.614	.558	.508	.463	.422	.386	.352	.322	.295
11	.585	.527	.475	.429	.388	.350	.317	.287	.261
12	.557	.497	.444	.397	.356	.319	.286	.257	.231
13	.530	.469	.415	.368	.326	.290	.258	.229	.204
14	.505	.442	.388	.340	.299	.263	.232	.205	.181
15	.481	.417	.362	.315	.275	.239	.209	.183	.160
16	.458	.394	.339	.292	.252	.218	.188	.163	.141
17	.436	.371	.317	.270	.231	.198	.170	.146	.125
18	.416	.350	.296	.250	.212	.180	.153	.130	.111
19	.396	.331	.277	.232	.194	.164	.138	.116	.098
20	.377	.312	.258	.215	.178	.149	.124	.104	.087
25	.295	.233	.184	.146	.116	.092	.074	.059	.047
30	.231	.174	.131	.099	.075	.057	.044	.033	.026
35	.181	.130	.094	.068	.049	.036	.026	.019	.014
40	.142	.097	.067	.046	.032	.022	.015	.011	.008
45	.111	.073	.048	.031	.021	.014	.009	.006	.004
50	.087	.054	.034	.021	.013	.009	.005	.003	.002

Note: the above present value factors are based on year-end interest calculations.

14%	15%	16%	17%	18%	19%	20%	21%	22%	23%
1.000	1.000	1.000	1.000	1.000	1.000	1.000	1.000	1.000	1.000
.877	.870	.862	.855	.847	.840	.833	.826	.820	.813
.769	.756	.743	.731	.718	.706	.694	.683	.672	.661
.675	.658	.641	.624	.609	.593	.579	.564	.551	.537
.592	.572	.552	.534	.516	.499	.482	.467	.451	.437
.519	.497	.476	.456	.437	.419	.402	.386	.370	.355
.456	.432	.410	.390	.370	.352	.335	.319	.303	.289
.400	.376	.354	.333	.314	.296	.279	.263	.249	.235
.351	.327	.305	.285	.266	.249	.233	.218	.204	.191
.308	.284	.263	.243	.225	.209	.194	.180	.167	.155
.270	.247	.227	.208	.191	.176	.162	.149	.137	.126
.237	.215	.195	.178	.162	.148	.135	.123	.112	.103
.208	.187	.168	.152	.137	.124	.112	.102	.092	.083
.182	.163	.145	.130	.116	.104	.093	.084	.075	.068
.160	.141	.125	.111	.099	.088	.078	.069	.062	.055
.140	.123	.108	.095	.084	.074	.065	.057	.051	.045
.123	.107	.093	.081	.071	.062	.054	.047	.042	.036
.108	.093	.080	.069	.060	.052	.045	.039	.034	.030
.095	.081	.069	.059	.051	.044	.038	.032	.028	.024
.083	.070	.060	.051	.043	.037	.031	.027	.023	.020
.073	.061	.051	.043	.037	.031	.026	.022	.019	.016
.038	.030	.025	.020	.016	.013	.011	.009	.007	.006
.020	.015	.012	.009	.007	.005	.004	.003	.003	.002
.010	.008	.006	.004	.003	.002	.002	.001	.001	.001
.005	.004	.003	.002	.001	.001	.001	.000	.000	.000
.003	.002	.001	.001	.001	.000	.000	.000	.000	.000
.001	.001	.001	.000	.000	.000	.000	.000	.000	.000

Note: the above present value factors are based on year-end interest calculations.

n Year	24%	25%	26%	27%	28%	29%	30%	35%	40%
0	1.000	1.000	1.000	1.000	1.000	1.000	1.000	1.000	1.000
1	.807	.800	.794	.787	.781	.775	.769	.741	.714
2	.650	.640	.630	.620	.610	.601	.592	.549	.510
3	.524	.512	.500	.488	.477	.466	.455	.406	.364
4	.423	.410	.397	.384	.373	.361	.350	.301	.260
5	.341	.328	.315	.303	.291	.280	.269	.223	.186
6	.275	.262	.250	.238	.227	.217	.207	.165	.133
7	.222	.210	.198	.188	.178	.168	.159	.122	.095
8	.179	.168	.157	.148	.139	.130	.123	.091	.068
9	.144	.134	.125	.116	.108	.101	.094	.067	.048
10	.116	.107	.099	.092	.085	.078	.073	.050	.035
11	.094	.086	.079	.072	.066	.061	.056	.037	.025
12	.076	.069	.062	.057	.052	.047	.043	.027	.018
13	.061	.055	.050	.045	.040	.037	.033	.020	.013
14	.049	.044	.039	.035	.032	.028	.025	.015	.009
15	.040	.035	.031	.028	.025	.022	.020	.011	.006
16	.032	.028	.025	.022	.019	.017	.015	.008	.005
17	.026	.023	.020	.017	.015	.013	.012	.006	.003
18	.021	.018	.016	.014	.012	.010	.009	.005	.002
19	.017	.014	.012	.011	.009	.008	.007	.003	.002
20	.014	.012	.010	.008	.007	.006	.005	.002	.001
25	.005	.004	.003	.003	.002	.002	.001	.001	.000
30	.002	.001	.001	.001	.001	.000	.000	.000	.000
35	.001	.000	.000	.000	.000	.000	.000	.000	.000
40	.000	.000	.000	.000	.000	.000	.000	.000	.000
45	.000	.000	.000	.000	.000	.000	.000	.000	.000
50	.000	.000	.000	.000	.000	.000	.000	.000	.000

Note: the above present value factors are based on year-end interest calculations.

Appendix B: Cumulative present value of £1 per annum

n Year	5%	6%	7%	8%	9%	10%	11%	12%	13%
1	.952	.943	.935	.926	.917	.909	.901	.893	.885
2	1.859	1.833	1.808	1.783	1.759	1.736	1.713	1.690	1.668
3	2.723	2.673	2.624	2.577	2.531	2.487	2.444	2.402	2.361
4	3.546	3.465	3.387	3.312	3.240	3.170	3.102	3.037	2.974
5	4.329	4.212	4.100	3.993	3.890	3.791	3.696	3.605	3.517
6	5.076	4.917	4.767	4.623	4.486	4.355	4.231	4.111	3.998
7	5.786	5.582	5.389	5.206	5.033	4.868	4.712	4.564	4.423
8	6.463	6.210	5.971	5.747	5.535	5.335	5.146	4.968	4.799
9	7.108	6.802	6.515	6.247	5.995	5.759	5.537	5.328	5.132
10	7.722	7.360	7.024	6.710	6.418	6.145	5.889	5.650	5.426
11	8.306	7.887	7.499	7.139	6.805	6.495	6.207	5.938	5.687
12	8.863	8.384	7.943	7.536	7.161	6.814	6.492	6.194	5.918
13	9.394	8.853	8.358	7.904	7.487	7.103	6.750	6.424	6.122
14	9.899	9.295	8.745	8.244	7.786	7.367	6.982	6.628	6.302
15	10.380	9.712	9.108	8.559	8.061	7.606	7.191	6.811	6.462
16	10.838	10.106	9.447	8.851	8.313	7.824	7.379	6.974	6.604
17	11.274	10.477	9.763	9.122	8.544	8.022	7.549	7.120	6.729
18	11.690	10.828	10.059	9.372	8.756	8.201	7.702	7.250	6.840
19	12.085	11.158	10.336	9.604	8.950	8.365	7.839	7.366	6.938
20	12.462	11.470	10.594	9.818	9.129	8.514	7.963	7.469	7.025
25	14.094	12.783	11.654	10.675	9.823	9.077	8.422	7.843	7.330
30	15.372	13.765	12.409	11.258	10.274	9.427	8.694	8.055	7.496
35	16.374	14.498	12.948	11.655	10.567	9.644	8.855	8.176	7.586
40	17.159	15.046	13.332	11.925	10.757	9.779	8.951	8.244	7.634
45	17.774	15.456	13.606	12.108	10.881	9.863	9.008	8.283	7.661
50	18.256	15.762	13.801	12.234	10.962	9.915	9.042	8.305	7.675

Note: the above present value factors are based on year-end interest calculations.

n Year	14%	15%	16%	17%	18%	19%	20%	21%	22%	23%
1	.877	.870	.862	.855	.847	.840	.833	.826	.820	.813
2	1.647	1.626	1.605	1.585	1.566	1.546	1.528	1.510	1.492	1.474
3	2.322	2.283	2.246	2.210	2.174	2.140	2.106	2.074	2.042	2.011
4	2.914	2.855	2.798	2.743	2.690	2.639	2.589	2.540	2.494	2.448
5	3.433	3.352	3.274	3.199	3.127	3.058	2.991	2.926	2.864	2.804
6	3.889	3.784	3.685	3.589	3.498	3.410	3.326	3.245	3.167	3.092
7	4.288	4.160	4.039	3.922	3.812	3.706	3.605	3.508	3.416	3.327
8	4.639	4.487	4.344	4.207	4.078	3.954	3.837	3.726	3.619	3.518
9	4.946	4.772	4.607	4.451	4.303	4.163	4.031	3.905	3.786	3.673
10	5.216	5.019	4.833	4.659	4.494	4.339	4.192	4.054	3.923	3.799
11	5.453	5.234	5.029	4.836	4.656	4.486	4.327	4.177	4.035	3.902
12	5.660	5.421	5.197	4.988	4.793	4.610	4.439	4.278	4.127	3.985
13	5.842	5.583	5.342	5.118	4.910	4.715	4.533	4.362	4.203	4.053
14	6.002	5.724	5.468	5.229	5.008	4.802	4.611	4.432	4.265	4.108
15	6.142	5.847	5.575	5.324	5.092	4.876	4.675	4.490	4.315	4.153
16	6.265	5.954	5.669	5.405	5.162	4.938	4.730	4.536	4.357	4.190
17	6.373	6.047	5.749	5.475	5.222	4.990	4.775	4.576	4.391	4.219
18	6.467	6.128	5.818	5.534	5.273	5.033	4.812	4.608	4.419	4.243
19	6.550	6.198	5.877	5.584	5.316	5.070	4.844	4.635	4.442	4 263
20	6.623	6.259	5.929	5.628	5.353	5.101	4.870	4.657	4.460	4.279
25	6.873	6.464	6.097	5.766	5.467	5.195	4.948	4.721	4.514	4.323
30	7.003	6.566	6.177	5.829	5.517	5.235	4.979	4.746	4.534	4.339
35	7.070	6.617	6.215	5.858	5.539	5.251	4.992	4.756	4.541	4.345
40	7.105	6.642	6.234	5.871	5.548	5.258	4.997	4.760	4.544	4.347
45	7.123	6.654	6.242	5.877	5.552	5.261	4.999	4.761	4.545	4.347
50	7.133	6.661	6.246	5.880	5.554	5.262	5.000	4.762	4.545	4.348

Note: the above present value factors are based on year-end interest calculations.

24%	25%	26%	27%	28%	29%	30%	35%	40%
.807	.800	.794	.787	.781	.775	.769	.741	.714
1.457	1.440	1.424	1.407	1.392	1.376	1.361	1.289	1.224
1.981	1.952	1.923	1.896	1.868	1.842	1.816	1.696	1.589
2.404	2.362	2.320	2.280	2.241	2.203	2.166	1.997	1.849
2.745	2.689	2.635	2.583	2.532	2.483	2.436	2.220	2.035
3.021	2.951	2.885	2.821	2.759	2.700	2.643	2.385	2.168
3.242	3.161	3.083	3.009	2.937	2.868	2.802	2.508	2.263
3.421	3.329	3.241	3.156	3.076	2.999	2.925	2.598	2.331
3.566	3.463	3.366	3.273	3.184	3.100	3.019	2.665	2.379
3.682	3.571	3.465	3.366	3.269	3.178	3.092	2.715	2.414
3.776	3.656	3.544	3.437	3.335	3.239	3.147	2.752	2.438
3.851	3.725	3.606	3.493	3.387	3.286	3.190	2.779	2.456
3.912	3.780	3.656	3.538	3.427	3.322	3.223	2.799	2.469
3.962	3.824	3.695	3.573	3.459	3.351	3.249	2.814	2.478
4.001	3.859	3.726	3.601	3.483	3.373	3.268	2.825	2.484
4.033	3.887	3.751	3.623	3.503	3.390	3.283	2.834	2.489
4.059	3.910	3.771	3.640	3.518	3.403	3.295	2.840	2.492
4.080	3.928	3.786	3.654	3.529	3.413	3.304	2.844	2.494
4.097	3.942	3.799	3.666	3.539	3.421	3.311	2.848	2.496
4.110	3.954	3.808	3.673	3.546	3.427	3.316	2.850	2.497
4.147	3.985	3.834	3.694	3.564	3.442	3.329	2.856	2.499
4.160	3.995	3.842	3.701	3.569	3.447	3.332	2.857	2.500
4.164	3.998	3.845	3.703	3.571	3.448	3.333	2.857	2.500
4.166	3.999	3.846	3.703	3.571	3.448	3.333	2.857	2.500
4.166	4.000	3.846	3.704	3.571	3.448	3.333	2.857	2.500
4.167	4.000	3.846	3.704	3.571	3.448	3.333	2.857	2.500

Note: the above present value factors are based on year-end interest calculations.

Index

Chris Brewster
Understanding Industrial Relations £2.95

Emphasizes the importance of management's role before explaining the involvement of unions and the state. The legal framework is shown in detail and later chapters examine industrial relations in practice, at the workplace and during negotiations. Ideal for use on Institute of Industrial Management, Institute of Personnel Management and NEBSS courses and for practising managers.

A Pan Breakthrough book, published in collaboration with the National Extension College.

Rita Harris
Understanding Office Practice £2.95

Explains and illustrates the structure and working methods of the modern office, covering all the traditional skills and devoting close attention to the impact of new technology. The book caters for many syllabuses and training courses: BEC General level World of Work, Office Machines and Equipment, Clerical Services; MSC Youth Training Schemes; SCOTBEC, RSA and LCCI Office Practice.

A Pan Breakthrough book, published in collaboration with the National Extension College.

Peter Clark

Using Statistics in Business 1 £2.95

Volume *1* shows how to acquire, judge and apply statistical information. Especially suitable for statistics courses at BEC National level in Numeracy and Accounting, RSA Stage II and LCCI Intermediate, it will also serve students of professional syllabuses: Institute of Chartered Accountants, Institute of Cost and Management Accountants, Institute of Chartered Secretaries, and Association of Certified Accountants.

A Pan Breakthrough book, published in collaboration with the National Extension College.

Using Statistics in Business 2 £2.95

Volume *2* shows how to present and draw conclusions from statistical information. It develops the ideas explained in volume *1*, and is especially suitable for statistics courses at BEC National level in Numeracy and Accounting, RSA Stage II and LCCI Intermediate. It will also serve students of professional syllabuses: Institute of Chartered Accountants, Institute of Cost and Management Accountants, Institute of Chartered Secretaries and Association of Certified Accountants.

A Pan Breakthrough book, published in collaboration with the National Extension College.

Management

☐	**Effective Leadership**	John Adair	£2.50p
☐	**Introducing Management**	Christopher, McDonald and Wills	£1.95p
☐	**The Effective Executive**	Peter Drucker	£1.95p
☐	**Management**	Peter Drucker	£3.50p
☐	**Under New Management**	Tony Eccles	£2.95p
☐	**Back from the Brink**	Michael Edwardes	£2.95p
☐	**How to Double Your Profits**	John Fenton	£2.50p
☐	**Inside Business Law**	David Field	£2.95p
☐	**Inside Employment Law**	David Field	£2.50p
☐	**How to Win Customers**	Heinz Goldmann	£2.95p
☐	**The Black Economy**	Arnold Heertje *et al.*	£1.95p
☐	**Managing People at Work**	John Hunt	£2.50p
☐	**Investment Appraisal for Managers**	Graham Mott	£1.95p
☐	**Managing With Computers**	Terry Rowan	£2.95p
☐	**Guide to Saving and Investment**	James Rowlatt	£2.50p
☐	**Reality of Management**	Rosemary Stewart	£1.95p
☐	**Reality of Organisations**	Rosemary Stewart	£1.95p
☐	**How to Manage**	Ray Wild	£2.50p
☐	**Bargaining for Results**	John Winkler	£1.95p
☐	**Dictionary of Economics and Commerce**		£1.50p
☐	**Multilingual Commercial Dictionary**		£3.95p

All these books are available at your local bookshop or newsagent, or can be ordered direct from the publisher. Indicate the number of copies required and fill in the form below 11

Name____
(Block letters please)

Address______________________________________

____

Send to CS Department, Pan Books Ltd, PO Box 40, Basingstoke, Hants
Please enclose remittance to the value of the cover price plus:
35p for the first book plus 15p per copy for each additional book ordered to a maximum charge of £1.25 to cover postage and packing
Applicable only in the UK

While every effort is made to keep prices low, it is sometimes necessary to increase prices at short notice. Pan Books reserve the right to show on covers and charge new retail prices which may differ from those advertised in the text or elsewhere

☐ An Int...
European Nove...
☐ An Introduction to Fifty
British Plays 1660–1900

All these books are available at your local bookshop or newsagent, or can be ordered direct from the publisher. Indicate the number of copies required and fill in the form below

....

Name____________________________________
(Block letters please)

Address__________________________________

____

Send to CS Department, Pan Books Ltd, PO Box 40, Basingstoke, Hants
Please enclose remittance to the value of the cover price plus:
35p for the first book plus 15p per copy for each additional book ordered to a maximum charge of £1.25 to cover postage and packing
Applicable only in the UK

While every effort is made to keep prices low, it is sometimes necessary to increase prices at short notice. Pan Books reserve the right to show on covers and charge new retail prices which may differ from those advertised in the text or elsewhere